Homing In

Bruce Bennett is Professor of English at the University of New South Wales at the Australian Defence Force Academy in Canberra. In 2005–06 he was Group of Eight Professor of Australian Studies at Georgetown University in Washington DC.

A Rhodes scholar from Western Australia, he is a graduate of the Universities of Western Australia, Oxford and London and is a Doctor of Letters of the University of New South Wales. He has held visiting appointments at universities in Asia, Europe and North America, served on the Australian National Commission for UNESCO and is a member of the Australia–India Council. His books include *An Australian Compass: Essays on Place and Direction in Australian Literature* (1991), *Spirit in Exile: Peter Porter and his Poetry* (1991), *The Oxford Literary History of Australia* (1998), with Jennifer Strauss, and *Australian Short Fiction: A History* (2002) and he is a chief investigator of Austlit: The Australian Literature Resource project at <www.austlit.edu.au>. He is a Fellow and Council member of the Australian Academy of the Humanities.

Homing In

Essays on Australian Literature and Selfhood

Bruce Bennett

*for Penny —
with love and best wishes
Bruce*

Australian Essay Series
NETWORK

University of Technology
Australia Research Institute

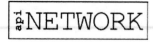
www.api-network.com

Published in 2006 by Network Books
The API Network
Australia Research Institute
Curtin University of Technology
GPO Box U1987
PERTH WA 6845

Australian Essay
General Editor: Richard Nile
Production Editor: Nina Divich
Cover Design: Phil Cloran

National Library of Australia
Cataloguing-in-Publication entry:

> Bennett, Bruce, 1941- .
> Homing in : Essays on Australian literature and selfhood.
> Includes index.
> ISBN 1 920845 26 7 (pbk).
> 1. Australian essays. 2. Australian literature.
> 3. Identity (Philosophical concept). I. Title.
> A824.4

Contents

For my brothers Jack and Glen

Acknowledgements

The essays in this volume have appeared previously in a variety of magazines or books in Australia and overseas. Their places of previous publication have been listed at the start of the Notes section for each essay. I wish to thank the editors and publishers of these publications in the first instance for their encouragement to test myself out in print and receive the kind of feedback that makes writing an act of communication. I thank them too for permission to reprint the essays, either wholly or in part, in this book. I also acknowledge the support and encouragement of Richard Nile at the Australia Research Institute, Curtin University, who asked me to consider a 'Selected Essays' volume to coincide with my time as Group of Eight Professor of Australian Studies at Georgetown University.

The volume is dedicated to my two brothers—Jack in Eugene, Oregon, and Glen in Perth, Western Australia—with both of whom the dialogue from our boyhood years continues. Family support and encouragement from Trish, Cathy and Michael continues to buoy me up through the hours of necessary seclusion of a scribbler.

I also wish to thank Susan Cowan for her assistance with some of the research for this volume and Nina Divich for her typesetting of the book.

Canberra, October 2005

No place is a place until things that have happened in it are remembered in history, ballads, yarns, legends or monuments.

Wallace Stegner

We are all exiles, who will not rest, but will dream and travel, seeking an alternative reality, a better future.

Ee Tiang Hong

Introduction

Re-reading the essays selected for this volume, I notice how many of them 'home in' on recurrent anxieties, interests and pleasures associated with notions of place, region, nation and a sense of belonging or displacement. As the author of these essays, I am forced to recognise that I still feel anxious, curious and uncertain about aspects of the Australia I inhabit and its place in the world, even as I enjoy its many pleasures. Perhaps that is why my reading shows me giving special attention to the observations, intuitions and ideas of a variety of Australian questers and mental travellers for whom 'home' remains an important but elusive and sometimes problematic concept.

With a population base of some 20 million people in the early years of the twenty-first century, Australia is widely recognised as 'punching above its weight' in the field of international literature in English. When questions of literary merit are raised, Patrick White's Nobel Prize for literature in 1973 is often cited, together with David Malouf's Impac award, Thomas Keneally's and Peter Carey's Booker prizes, Kate Grenville's Orange prize and the Queen's gold medal for poetry to Judith Wright, Les Murray and Peter Porter. Although some of these authors are discussed in the present book, readers will also encounter a variety of other Australian writers, living and dead, from colonial to post-colonial times, including Louis Becke, Jack Davis, Yasmine Gooneratne, Ee Tiang Hong, Dorothy Hewett, A D Hope, Clive James, Oodgeroo, John Boyle O'Reilly and Tim Winton. This heterogeneous group includes Indigenous Australians, immigrants, expatriates, long and short term residents and an Irish political prisoner. The main criterion for inclusion in these essays is not the canonical status of authors but their fruitful engagement with themes of alienation and belonging in a changing Australia.

In the international world we now inhabit, a sense of place is emphasised by many creative writers, sometimes as defence against deracination, sometimes as a celebration of childhood or another phase in the life-cycle. Yet finding a point of stability or belonging in some form of 'the local'—in a house, garden, suburb, sea or landscape, or nation or region, for instance—can be fraught with contradictions and difficulties as well as pleasures. Literary work can grow in these conditions, when the conflicting thoughts and feelings are filtered through imaginative and creative minds.

Individual and communal identities are forged in more shifting circumstances in contemporary multicultural Australia than they were in my parents' Anglo-Australian generation between the first and second world wars or during my own boyhood in Western Australia in the 1940s and 1950s. It was still possible in regional Australia, in the postwar years of reconstruction, to purvey a proud parochialism in a country of many (sometimes vast) parishes.

While strands or remnants of such allegiances with a state or region remain, they must now contend with other markers of national or global identity. The increased prevalence of television since the 1950s, jet air travel since the 1970s, and the internet and cellphone technologies of the late twentieth and early twenty-first century have combined to shrink what historian Geoffrey Blainey called 'the tyranny of distance' for Australians. The size of the vast Australian landmass has not changed, nor has the distance of our cities from others in the world. What has changed is the capacity of Australia's inhabitants to converse with each other and a wider world through the new technologies as well as through books, magazines and newspapers. But new empires have sprung up. The exchange of information and ideas is still restricted to a large extent by powerful publishing houses through which much public communication is filtered. In these circumstances, university teachers and researchers have an increasing responsibility to enter public discussion and debate through whatever publishing channels remain open to them, and to create new channels.

Australia's geo-political and cultural orientations have changed considerably since the 1960s, when a British colonial mindset was still prevalent. America's decision to enter the Pacific War after the Japanese bombing of Pearl Harbor in 1941 is widely perceived as saving Australia from invasion, and American popular culture prospered in Australia from this point, although British 'high culture' remained strong in Australian universities and other institutions through the 1960s. A 'new nationalism' in the 1970s, led by the Whitlam Labor government, re-oriented the cultural mindset towards Australian history and creativity. Since the 1970s,

Australians of different political and cultural outlooks have recognised that Australia's economic future and security depend heavily on improved relations with the countries of Asia. While literary and cultural links have been slower to develop with Asia than with the USA and Britain, our 'great and powerful friends', several essays in this book show that in literature, at least, the connections with Asia are growing.

The 22 essays in this book are revised versions of conference papers, journal articles or chapters from books published over the past decade or so. Through them, I hope that my engagement with the work of a number of interesting and challenging Australian authors will be conveyed. The genres in which I have chiefly published are literary history and biography. In both genres, I try to avoid simplistic determinism and to seek out 'the writer in the writing', in pursuit of the traditional humanistic goal of 'knowing ourselves and others'. In literary inquiry, this pursuit involves developing that curious intimacy between a reader and a writer in which the reader allows himself to enter the writer's ways of thinking and feeling and sees the world for a time through the other's eyes. This kind of empathy, or 'negative capability' as Keats called it, is an essential prerequisite to any deep appreciation of a writer's worth, and of humanistic inquiry more generally.

Thanks to university courses and associations for the study of Australia in Britain, Europe, the USA, and a number of countries in Asia and elsewhere, Australian literature, history and culture are being increasingly recognised internationally. But old habits die hard. In the era of British cultural domination of Australia into the post–second world war period, a typical response to Australian literature was: 'Is there any?'. More recently, when I was interviewed by a young member of the US Consulate for a visa to take up a professorship to teach Australian Studies in his country, he laughed incredulously at the prospect. I hope that readers of this book will recognise from my sampling that Australian literature comprises a substantial field of study with prospects of pleasurable engagement and that they will be stimulated to embark on their own voyages within it.

1

Living Spaces: Some Australian Houses of Childhood

In an age of increasing mobility, the house signifies stability. Its living spaces may seem a sanctuary, or a prison, or both at different times. Representing an achievement of men and women as makers, houses stand somewhere between the tent and the castle in the great chain of dwelling places, with aspirations generally expressed towards the latter. For at least a century, Australians have been majority suburban dwellers. Australian houses have generally been stand-alone structures, though this is changing, and the spaces within and between them are constituent elements in the identity of their inhabitants. There is an economics and a politics, but also a poetics of space which can be applied to housing.[1] Creative writers often negotiate the limits of the various spaces they have inhabited, especially when they attempt to re-forge the houses of their childhood.

In the history of Australian literature, the house signifies a rupture in the persistent British Victorian tradition whereby the fortunes of a family are forever stabilised and given palpable form in the family home. Henry Handel Richardson's trilogy *The Fortunes of Richard Mahony* graphically represents this rupture in colonial Australia, revealing the deep instability of the protagonist in his increasingly restless buying and selling of temporary dwelling places; in this respect he never leaves behind the tents of the goldfields. For some nationalist writers of the 1890s and later, the old bark hut

signifies a distinctive vernacular answer to the British aristocratic
tradition. By the mid-twentieth century, when Robin Boyd was
writing *The Australian Ugliness* (1952), Barry Humphries was
imbibing his source material for Moonee Ponds and Patrick White
was brewing his literary suburb called Sarsaparilla, Australian
suburbia was under attack. Post-war reconstruction was seen by
many Australian artists and intellectuals to be imposing a false
uniformity over Australians: elements of the middle-class had
turned on each other and themselves. Eric Rolls sums up a more
general view of houses at this time:

> Australian houses impose on the landscape. Suburban houses line
> up along the streets, lawns shaven, windows washed, roofs trim,
> doors closed, as though mustered by drill sergeants. 'Squad, atten-
> shun! From the right, number!' How many councillors would
> approve a house built back-to-front? They would fear it might fart
> at them.
>
> Country houses are collections of coloured boxes dropped in
> paddocks. They could never have grown up out of the soil.
> Dwellers in them are not so much protected as parcelled up.[2]

The metaphors here indicate the writer's sense of the unachieved
ideal of an organic relationship between house and land. Instead,
houses have become merely commercial products. More ludicrously,
they mimic the uniform attitudes of armed forces in a war which
has not been left entirely behind. A more ambiguous set of attitudes
is conveyed in Randolph Stow's novel *The Merry-Go-Round in the Sea*
(1965), in which Hugh Mackay's postwar assimilation into suburbia
is presented both as a working-class desire for comfort and security
and as a cop-out by his wartime mate Rick Maplestead, whose own
restlessness reflects that of many artists and intellectuals in the postwar years.

The suburbs and their houses had their strongest apologists in
the 1970s, including Hugh Stretton, Donald Horne and Craig
McGregor. One result of their persuasive revaluations has been a
more receptive audience for serious literary accounts of childhoods
in 'ordinary' suburbs and country towns. Above all, the Australian
house could be seen to play a legitimate part in the shaping of
individual lives. In this context, the destruction of a house may seem
a desecration of memory and identity. Hence one of the most
representatively shocking scenes in contemporary Australian writing

is the calculated burning-down of a house in Frank Moorhouse's discontinuous narrative, *The Electrical Experience*.[3] Moorhouse's protagonist, George McDowell, a figure based on the prototypical male of the author's father's generation, is named as an executor of an old friend's will in the New South Wales south coast country town where the narrative is set. He is given the task of burning down the house; it is a test of his will that he should carry through this commission from his dead friend in the face of opposition from the town. Moorhouse's graphic rendition of the event demonstrates his awareness of its significance not only for the individuals concerned but also as a symptomatic cultural event. McDowell's determined drenching with kerosene of furniture, books, paintings and even stamp albums is seen by him as a test of his own 'character' and determination. When the conflagration occurs, no trace is left of his former friend's family who had lived in the town since it had been incorporated as a municipality. The objects of memory, of a history, are obliterated. In the context of Moorhouse's later writings, the burning of the house has a deeply ambiguous set of significations: the writer's fascination with motels, pizzerias, rented cars and airports as vehicles of urban anonymity and mobility reinforce his sense of the passing of an age of the family house as repository of history in the postmodern age. However, Moorhouse's alter egos recurrently resist the erasure of memory and history and are snubbed by the Balmain bourgeoisie, among others, for doing so. Ejected from a fashionable commune in Balmain, a Moorhouse alter ego plaintively asks: 'Is there a commune for people who do not fit very well into communes?'.[4]

In spite of the pressures of post-modernity, the living spaces of houses remain a potent area of investigation for many Australian writers, especially in their exploration of identity formation in early childhood (an area into which Moorhouse has not yet ventured). A recurrent site of such investigations is the verandah or its later variant, the sleepout. Fiona Giles's collection of stories by nineteenth-century Australian women, *From the Verandah*, takes its title from Ethel Mills: 'She liked to see what was going on; and she said that in Australia most things happened on verandahs'.[5] In one of the jargon terms of today, the verandah is 'liminal space', a threshold to the outdoors world of men, the outback or adventure.

In late twentieth-century fiction and autobiography too, the outer reaches of the suburban house are often represented by the

verandah and sometimes the enclosed verandah as sleepout. David
Malouf's story *12 Edmonstone Street* is a small classic in its
exploration of identity through re-creation in memory of the child's
spatial relationship to the South Brisbane house in which he was
brought up.[6] His recreated memory of the verandah, where he and
his sister slept in home-made cots is recalled as being 'beyond our
parents' bedroom window, where we are in easy reach':

> The verandah is closed on that side by a fernery, or, as I see it,
> opens on that side into it. Diagonal slabs of unpainted timber gone
> grey with age are hung with stag horns, elk horns, orchids that
> sprout from fleshy knobs, and shaggy wire baskets of hare's foot
> and maidenhair. The ground is all sword-ferns round a pond with
> three opulent gold fish. Behind it is a kind of grotto made of
> pinkish-grey concrete, a dozen scaly branches of which, eaten raw
> in places, droop and tangle like the arms, half-petrified, half-rotting,
> of a stranded sea-monster.[7]

The underlying drama here is of separation from parents; its
keynote is fear. In retrospect, more calmly, the author sees
verandahs as 'no-man's-land, border zones that keep contact with
the house and its activities on one face but are open on the other to
the street, the night and all the vast, unknown areas beyond'.[8]
Malouf recreates the child as father of the man when he represents
his younger self rejecting the cot and refusing to stay there,
becoming 'a night wanderer, a rebel nomad trailing my blanket
through the house to my favourite camping places'.[9] In summary, he
sees a mixed pattern of inside-outside in these early, deeply-etched
memories: 'Perhaps it is this daily experience of being cast out and
then let in again that has made the house and all its rooms so
precious to me. Each morning I step across the threshold and there
it is, a world recovered, restored'.[10]

This reconstruction by David Malouf, in his early fifties, of his
pre-war childhood house is selective, as all such accounts are; it
explores the interiors and verandahs of the old Queenslander house
of his early childhood but chooses to exclude the brick house to
which his family with their upwardly mobile father from a Lebanese
family moved in 1947, when Malouf was thirteen. By contrast with
12 Edmonstone Street, the brick house seems 'stuffily and
pretentiously over-furnished and depressingly modern'.[11]

Another Brisbane-born writer, Peter Porter, has explored his childhood and youth in relation to a weatherboard house on stilts in Annerley, which he recalls as part of 'shabby genteel' Australia:

> We were on the Ipswich Road, an unlovely ribbon of shops, factories and hospitals winding out of Brisbane on the south side of the river ... Imagine a primitive interpretation of Le Corbusier's ideas, carried out in wood and painted in garish or depressing colours. Our house was only about five feet off the ground in front, but at least fifteen at the back, the ground sloped so steeply. It was mounted on wooden piles, each topped with a metal hat and coated in creosote to deter the white ants.[12]

This house has a schizophrenic history for Porter. Before his mother's sudden death when he was nine, the house opens out to a garden which offered Porter, in retrospect, a prospect of an Australian Eden, with his father gardening and his mother on the back landing shouting the names of horses she wanted to back to the woman next door who would then ring them through to the SP bookmaker.[13] After her death, Porter's self-image is of being cast out, retreating to the under-the-house region to solitary, joyless masturbation. Later, as an expatriate in London he lives in basement flats, seeing the city from below, critical of the moneyed elites, a world he transcends in the gods at the opera. In misery, and disappointment, especially, houses and flats share his gloom; gardens are where love and occasional hope are found. Houses of the mind go on and on.

One of the most common characteristics of Australian literary houses is their fragile insubstantiality. Perhaps this is the cue for memory to recuperate them. Like Malouf's and Porter's wooden houses in Brisbane, Dorothy Hewett's and Les Murray's childhood farmhouses in the country are of weatherboard and iron. Of these, Hewett's is presented as more poignantly idyllic because she has left it behind. At the end of her autobiography *Wild Card* she recounts a final return visit to the abandoned house in a denuded landscape near Wickepin in South-West Australia. The sense of loss is expressed in her vision of the trees:

> Two almonds, a few figs and one quince had survived. No she-oaks, no wattles, no tea-tree, no paperbarks, no bottlebrush, no salmon-

gums, no stables or sheds or post and rail sheep yards, only the concrete dip left like a scar in the home paddock, littered with iron and rusty machinery.[14]

There is no need for Hewett to return here again because the 'real' house of childhood remains in her memory and imagination. There is no need because, in Hewett's words, 'in the Dream Girl's Garden, in Golden Valley, in the districts of Jarrabin and Muckinupin, the first house lies secure in the hollow of the heart'.[15]

The task of recuperation is made both easier and more difficult for Les Murray by his return to live, with his family, adjacent to the 'weatherboard cathedral' of his childhood near Bunyah, in New South Wales. Romantic loss is thus tempered by realism. Yet childhood remains a recurrent source of inspiration. His poem 'The Sleepout' locates it precisely: 'Childhood sleeps in a verandah room in an iron bed close to the wall'.[16] Unlike Malouf's ambivalent inward–outward aspect in his sleepout in Brisbane, the defining characteristic of Murray's sleepout here is its predominant access to the outdoors, and to the broad freedoms of imagination:

> Inside the forest was lamplit
> along tracks to a starry creek bed
> and beyond lay the never-fenced country,
> its full billabongs all surrounded
>
> by animals and birds, in loud crustings,
> and something kept leaping up amongst them.
> And out there, to kindle whenever
> dark found it, hung the daylight moon.

The magic evoked by Murray is expressed as a quality of child-like vision but is stimulated by the architectonics of the common 'sleepout', where access to dreams is a mode of extroversion.

Real estate agents still try to sell buyers their notion of the 'dream house'. Tim Winton has distinguished between houses one can live in and those which can sustain dreams, though his dreams are not those evoked by most advertisements for property:

> Like most Australians I have spent much of my life in the suburbs.
> I was raised in the Perth suburb of Karrinyup. A quarter acre, a
> terracotta roof, a facade knocked out by some bored government

architect, a Hills Hoist in the backyard and picket fences between us and the neighbours. It was the sixties and the street was full of young families, State Housing applicants, migrants from Holland and Yugoslavia and the English north—foot soldiers of the great sprawl trying to make our way in the raw diagram of streets we slowly filled to make a new neighbourhood. I lived there happily for twelve years but I do not dream of that house.[17]

Instead, he dreams of the Christmas holiday shack at the mouth of the Greenough River, south of Geraldton. For Winton, the house offers a retreat from the heavy afternoon winds to reading spaces on bunk beds within, but its chief quality is its access to the outdoors, to the sea:

From the front windows you could see out beyond the eyelid of the verandah to the bright limestone road and the rivermouth. Out there, the sand was packed hard and cars could be driven across between river and sea. The surf hammered night and day, never calm, never quietly, blue all the way to Africa.[18]

An emergent 'Australian' pattern of childhood houses which offer access to a vivid natural world outdoors is reinforced in the autobiographical reminiscences of Aboriginal writers Jack Davis and Sally Morgan. Davis's childhood house in the 1920s is a 'tiny weatherboard and galvanized iron hut' near Yarloop in South-Western Australia, which his father enlarged to accommodate eleven children.[19] The boy's main living spaces are of necessity in the bush outside the hut, where he is at home with brothers, sisters and friends and a variety of pets including possums, magpies, wild piglets, ducks and bobtail goannas. Early childhood adventures in these spaces represent in Davis's narrative a happy prelude to his later tragic separation from family and home when he is sent to the prison-like Moore River Native Settlement.[20] In Sally Morgan's account of growing up in suburban Perth in the 1950s,[21] class differences and poverty as well as racial difference are evident. Her family's small, cramped State Housing Commission house is located in working-class Manning, which differs from neighbouring Como, Sally realises, when she compares her school lunches of jam and Vegemite sandwiches with the Como kids' salad lunches in plastic containers. While her alcoholic, war-injured father is alive, he commandeers the sleepout and back verandah and the house seems 'menacing' and 'surrounded by all kinds of eerie shadows'.[22] After his death, Sally finds comfort and security in the kitchen and the lounge-room where the open fire is stoked and rough beds are made up in. Thereafter, too, she and her sisters venture into the suburban bush-land and swamp, adding a variety of pets to the household but (a generation later than Davis and in the more ecologically trained suburbs) they return goannas, tadpoles, frogs, gilgies and other wildlife to the bush. The dynamics of such domestic movements and their human significance deserve closer attention, in autobiographies as in prose fiction.

It is clear that houses such as the above have become imaginatively alive to the writers who have inhabited them. Unlike the European aristocratic novel, these houses do not offer images of wealth or power. Nor do they offer the aesthetic qualities of 'charm'. Their association with childhood, however, makes them vehicles for the establishment of an aesthetic of innocence, where interior spaces are enlarged as signifiers of identity and the free spirit is drawn outwards to the natural world. With a different emphasis, the *politics* of houses and their inhabitants are explored in inner-urban environments by other writers such as Christina Stead and Helen Garner.[23] Frank Moorhouse explores with a country boy's fascination the possibilities of freedom and independence in inner-city spaces, ranging from private pads to communes.[24] But the representation of houses of innocence in childhood which open onto a natural world remains a powerful dream in Australian literature.

A major challenge evoked by the literary works I have discussed briefly here is to link their representations of living spaces with those of human sciences such as anthropology, architecture and human geography. Clifford Geertz's anthropological emphasis on localism and 'thick description' points in the direction of a deeper awareness of local (including domestic) living spaces.[25] A growing interest is evident among students of architecture in the *socio-cultural* factors in domestic space and their implications for design practice. For example, Londoners Julienne Hanson and Bill Hillier have used planning documents and literary texts to hypothesise that 'the order which exists in the interior of a dwelling and the way in which that interior is related to the exterior, are predominantly related to social relations'.[26] This analysis depends on British concepts of class and emphasises relationship to the street rather than to backyard, garden, beach or bush as in most of the Australian examples I have cited. Interdisciplinary research on urban renewal at the Australian National University has brought together architects, town planners, cultural geographers, heritage workers, public historians and others to question the value and significance of living spaces.[27] Much more serious attention should be given in cross-disciplinary studies to such investigations. If the spaces we construct and live in inform our value-systems and imaginings, as many Australian literary works indicate they do, these texts should form an important part of such cooperative investigation and research.

2

Australian Myths

Myth may be thought of as an invented story arising from a collective belief, which gives events and actions a particular meaning. If we want to restore this notion of the mythic tale to its former potency, we must resist, at least in the first instance, the current sceptical view that all myths are false and misleading. Among the many beliefs about myth is the one that 'truth' is an essential element in the mythic narrative. Another is that myths must have universal human significance. In this essay I envisage a more humble use of the concept, which does not rely on mystical universality or on some fixed notion of human truthfulness. Rather, I want to suggest that a modern nation's 'civilisation' can be gauged in part by the stories its citizens tell about each other and the world they inhabit; and that the myths they generate sometimes run in tandem with history, sometimes counter to its perceived tendencies as communities reformulate their sense of themselves.

Australia's twentieth century 'foundation myth' has been powerfully presented as the story of Anzac, or Gallipoli—a story that describes heroism achieved in defeat. The historical event from which the myth grew was a military landing at Anzac Cove, Gallipoli, Turkey, on 25 April 1915. From a non-Australian perspective, the story doesn't always seem as important as it does to Australians, and its ingredients vary. An American perspective in the *Encyclopedia Britannica*, for example, presents the place and its significance in these terms: 'Gallipoli was the scene of determined

Turkish resistance to the Allied forces during the Dardanelles Campaign of the first world war, in which most of the town was destroyed'.[1] Yet for Australians, the campaign was one in which eight thousand of their confrères were killed only fourteen years after the federation of the Australian colonies into a nation in 1901.

The timing of Anzac is significant. A story of ethical unity was required in order to give psychological force to the political reality of federation. Anzac provided the core of this story, although the New Zealand origins of the term have never received proper acknowledgement in Australia. As the inaugural Television Open Learning program in Australian Studies[2] emphasised, the myth crystallised many aspects of assumed Australianness such as courage, patriotism, bush values and the mateship of Australian men in adversity. This Anzac story remains a potent source of imagery for the advertising industry across the generations.

Many Australians would testify to the persistence of the Anzac myth in the second half of the twentieth and into the twenty-first century. In my own family, for example, my father used elements of this myth to present himself in a humorous light when he recounted stories of the action he did *not* see while in his terms 'pushing back the Japs' from the island of Morotai near Borneo in the latter phases of the second world war. Popular discourse such as the Anzac story has produced sometimes enters a single literary text and finds a memorable distillation there. Such was the case with Alan Seymour's play, *The One Day of the Year* (1962), which dramatised in unforgettable fashion the questioning of the Anzac legend by university students of the relatively innocent pre-Vietnam years. The play does not resolve the generational conflicts of attitudes and values it exposes, but it shows dramatically how a powerful myth can interpenetrate the activities of ordinary suburban living, causing responses ranging from confrontation to pacification.

The representation of the wife and mother figure in Seymour's play as a supportive homemaker—the 1950s 'mum' who continually makes cups of tea—is essential to that generation's definitions of 'home'. If this mother figure is on the outer circles of the Anzac myth she is at the centre of another: the myth of the primacy of family. As master narratives, both Anzac and the family have been questioned most vigorously by members of the 'baby boom' generation who were children in the 1940s and 1950s and have become writers, filmmakers or other contributors to mythmaking since the 1970s. The late twentieth and early twenty-first centuries have seen a resurgence of the Anzac myth as young Australians seek a foothold for their belief in Australia. The annual Anzac Day pilgrimage of Australian backpackers to Gallipoli reinforces this view.

Despite the proliferation of alternative stories, the Anzac complex remains a 'core' story of nationhood.[3] John Romeril's play, *The Floating World* (1974), for example, has a protagonist, Les Harding, who still trades off the 'Anzac' aspects of his second world war experience as Alf Cook does in *The One Day of the Year*, but in both cases a critique is implied. The essentially masculine orientation of most versions of the Anzac story and its tendency to exclude problems of ethnic or regional difference in the interests of a unifying story of mateship and national purpose have been questioned vigorously since the 1970s. Hence, for example, A A Phillips's assertively unifying title, *The Australian Tradition*, for his book of essays in 1958 was complicated and pluralised in Laurie Hergenhan's *Penguin New Literary History of Australia* (1988). One of the factors in this generational change was the professionalising of a literary culture in Australia, with the greater sophistication of inquiry that this brought. Another factor was the increasing political and social pressure exerted by minorities and perceived outsiders. In this context, the idea of a unitary Australian community was more difficult for politicians and visionaries to maintain. Regionalists, ethnicists and feminists all contributed to a multiplication of myths, all vying for authority within popular culture as well as in the burgeoning field of Australian studies.

Beyond Anzac, whose stories will circulate in contemporary Australia and be retold while others wither on the vine? Whose stories will be paramount? By focusing briefly on several perceived groups within the wider community, I will try to suggest how and why certain myths may be promoted or contradicted and the ways they reflect on myth-making. The groups I refer to are, first, the Aboriginal population and, second, immigrants, both European and Asian. The underlying question is whether a new pluralist conception of Australia, associated with a multiplication of myths, is leading to a breakdown of a sense of community or a reformulation of it.

The question of the primacy of Aboriginal culture for all Australians was raised by Bob Hodge and Vijay Mishra in their study

The Dark Side of the Dream.[4] Hodge and Mishra present two main arguments: that the historical suppression of Aboriginal culture requires its reinstatement, and, more controversially, that it represents the repressed 'dark side' of the Australian consciousness. Aboriginal culture has the necessary authenticity in this account to restore some sense of wholeness to the Australian psyche. According to Hodge and Mishra, Australia remains a 'neo-colonial' society. The tendency to binary categorisation (white/black, colonial/free, etc) gives Hodge and Mishra's book its fighting, revisionary quality, but it has been attacked by the 'postcolonial' camp in academic criticism for oversimplifying the alternatives and not recognising the necessary 'hybridity' of racial and historical origins in settler societies such as Australia's.[5] If the latter tactic seems to represent a spiking of Aboriginal guns by a neo-Europeanist culture of complexity, it also makes the valid point that any mythology of 'pure' origins does not stand up to close examination.

Other books that analyse literary texts by or about Aborigines, such as those by J J Healy, and especially Adam Shoemaker, provide more detailed and convincing sociohistorical contexts which satisfy the reader that culturally specific circumstances operate in the production and reception of Australian Aboriginal texts.[6] Shoemaker convincingly concludes his study with the statement that 'three major elements coalesce in Black Australian literature—cultural nationalism, literary talent, and Aboriginal pride'.[7] Any Australian-based critique of modern Aboriginal literature must thus take proper account of all three elements and not resort to oversimplified international parameters applied to the Australian case.

The production and transmission of Aboriginal stories has changed radically since the second world war. Whereas the principal mediators or translators of Aboriginal stories to a wider population in the 1940s and 1950s were European Australians—such as the anthropologists Strehlow, Elkin and Berndt—most Aboriginal stories since the 1980s that have caught the literary and popular imagination have been written, or told fairly directly, by Aboriginal Australians. Appropriation of Aboriginal material by whites has been more closely interrogated than ever before, but this did not prevent the careless or fraudulent misrepresentation of Aboriginal identity in a number of cases.[8]

The distinction between generations becomes evident in a consideration of Ronald Berndt's translation of the north-east Arnhem Land Aboriginal song-cycle, the Wonguri-Manjikai Moon-bone song, which in turn became the principal source for Les Murray's style and sentiments in 'The Buladelah-Taree holiday song cycle', a long poem celebrating this white Australian poet's own 'spirit country' of the Manning River area in northern New South Wales.[9] Berndt's translation was intended to replicate Aboriginal oral delivery but its phraseology, rhythms and repetitions are characteristic of the King James version of the Christian Bible:

'The evening song'
from *Song Cycle of the Moon-bone*

Up and up soars the Evening Star, hanging there in
    the sky
Men watch it, at the place of the Dugong and of the
    Clouds, and of the Evening Star.
A long way off, at the place of Mist, of Lilies and of
    the Dugong.
The Lotus, the Evening Star, hangs there on its long
    stalk, held by the Spirits.[10]

Ronald Berndt's Anglophone background is evident, as this song-cycle proceeds, in echoes of the Song of Solomon and the Book of Job from the King James Bible. These books are, of course, themselves translations. The myth, as reproduced in these images of the Evening Star, is of the sacredness of place and an order of things controlled by the Spirits; its version of the lived-in environment is both physical and spiritual. But its principal filter is the archetypal literary and spiritual text of Western civilisation. Clearly, the purity of vision that is implied emerges from very mixed sources.

A generation later than Berndt's collection of these songs, Black writer Mudrooroo Narogin (formerly Colin Johnson) writes his own versions of song-cycles in which the language more closely simulates the oral delivery of the Nyoongah people in the south-west of Western Australia with whom he associates himself and draws on a high-brow British literary inheritance. The notion of a 'pure' literary inheritance (Anglicised) thus gives way to the more eclectic intertextuality of a post-modern age.

In *The Song Circle of Jacky* and especially *Dalwurra: The Black Bittern*,[11] Mudrooroo's language combines traditional Aboriginal rhythms and repetitions with eclectic international influences including some myths of Asia. *Dalwurra* is the Aboriginal word for a black bird that used to inhabit the wetlands of Mudrooroo's native Avon Valley. Mudrooroo's allegorical protagonist is presented as a typically non-migratory bird that nevertheless migrates, travelling from Australia through Asia to Europe and back again. In this way, he partakes of the conditions of the traveller, one of the archetypal figures of Western literature; like Odysseus he comprehends not only his own fate but also that of many people in the contemporary world. Whereas Ronald Berndt's translation of a traditional Aboriginal song-cycle had evoked a quasi-religious 'music of the spheres', Mudrooroo Narogin evokes the dislocation and disorientation of a post-1960s generation which, in Australia as elsewhere, is culturally defined by its search for imaginary homelands.

The myth of home, of a place of belonging, is especially prevalent and poignant for Australia's Indigenous people because they have been so patently displaced. The poetry of Oodgeroo Noonuccal (formerly Kath Walker), the autobiographical prose work, *My Place*, by Sally Morgan and the plays and poems of Jack Davis and the work of many other Indigenous writers dramatise this central loss—of places known and loved, of homes lost and the strategies to regain them in memory and imagination. In some respects, this mythic story can claim to be the master narrative of contemporary Australia.[12]

Whereas a recurrent note in much contemporary Aboriginal myth-making is of deprivation and loss (although, by Davis and Morgan especially, it is often dramatised humorously) a more optimistic note is injected by Aboriginal politician and songwriter Ernie Bridge. Politicians are, of necessity, professional optimists. As Minister for Agriculture, Water Resources and the North-West in the Western Australian Labor Government in the late 1980s and early 1990s, Ernie Bridge combined his political role with that of a country and western folksinger and evoked a jaunty myth of progress through the harnessing of natural resources and industrial development.

In an appropriation of leading myths of the white settler society—recalling Henry Lawson, Ned Kelly, Anzac-style patriotism and bush mateship—Bridge and his family produced a recording called *The Great Australian Dream,*[13] in which he sang of a visionary project to build a pipeline, which would carry fresh water from the sparsely populated north-west to the more densely populated south-west of Western Australia—a distance of some three thousand kilometres. In a style reminiscent of the American folksinger Woody Guthrie, Bridge was true to his name in linking a unique brand of environmental populism with a hint of the Aboriginal legend of the life-bringing Waugyl or Rainbow Serpent, thus refurbishing a dominant Western myth of progress based on the growth of cities and industrial development.

The hope engendered by this version of a typically eclectic modern myth which draws on the discourses of mystique and vision to fulfil the technological dream of progress through the exploitation of natural resources, seems to have been illusory. The opposition of those increasingly powerful modern mythmakers, the economist 'rationalists', the discovery of alternative water supplies and a change of government combined to deflate increasing community fascination with the project, and it was shelved. (Surprisingly, in a later State government election in Western Australia in 2005, Liberal leader Colin Barnett attempted to revive this dream but failed to convince electors when he miscalculated the costs of a 'canal' from the North West to metropolitan Perth.)

What remains, however, is the song of a larger-than-life dream of an assimilated Aboriginal politician, combining pragmatic concerns and Dreamtime possibilities, which kept a dream alive in the popular mind, aided by press and television coverage. Of interest here is the mixed provenance of this dream and its almost mad clarity, which somehow floats beyond its material circumstances and enabled it to capture a community's imagination for a time. The conservative tendencies of this myth of hope are important—that it draws on local and national patriotism and established images and ideas in order to build faith in a 'new' vision. Also of importance is the overtly political motivation of Ernie Bridge's 'Great Australian Dream': the myths of contemporary Australia often have significant political contexts.

While Aborigines have contributed increasingly in recent decades to a wider understanding of the myths that might drive Australian civilisation, so too have immigrants from Europe and Asia. Some of their published work has been restricted to the minority language communities, but since the 1970s conscious policies and programs of multiculturalism have opened avenues towards a wider reading community. From an Aboriginal perspective, Mudrooroo Narogin called this process 'centring the fringe'.[14] From the perspective of Australian writers born in other countries, the title of Sneja Gunew and Kateryna O Longley's book of literary essays, *Striking Chords*,[15] indicates an aspiration (of the editors at least) towards engaging the attention of a wider community and thus contributing to national mythmaking.

The extent to which certain individuals or groups might inhabit a 'fringe' or contribute directly to national thinking is one of the vexing questions of contemporary cultural debate in Australia. The fringe, edge or margin has seemed a convenient metaphor to highlight the alleged position of regional, feminist, Aboriginal and immigrant writers and artists, and, to some extent, use of the metaphor has strengthened the political leverage of these groups in the cultural debate. Such groups represent the outsider's claim to a voice on the national stage, and 'natural justice' seems to require scope for mobility and stronger transmission of views. Of course, there are some who argue that there is no such thing as a national culture—that the notion itself implies a false 'centrist model'.[16] But to change the metaphor from the spatial relations of centre-margins to the play of light, as in 'mutual illuminations', as Gunew proposes,[17] may not strengthen the pluralist argument. There remain important differences among immigrants in terms of their view of the desirability as well as the achievability of integration into a community of prevailing Australian myths and values; some will continue to propose a separate cultural role in their adoptive country. These are important matters of emphasis in the debates about multiculturalism and nationality in Australia in the twenty-first century, and the ways of describing them need careful thought.

One of the post–second world war immigrant groups that received little attention in *Striking Chords* is the Hungarians, who have had a disproportionately large influence on Australian intellectual and cultural life. Like other political refugees from postwar communism in central and eastern Europe, the Hungarians settled in Australian cities and attempted to create new lives there. Usually well educated in their home country, they were often the

sons and daughters of the managerial or land-owning classes. I have
had the pleasure of knowing a number of the Hungarians who
came to Australia in the 1950s and will refer briefly to ways in which
several of them have contributed to the reinforcement or adaptation
of prevalent myths.

Consider the brothers Paul and Julius Kovesi, who had lived in a
town near Budapest until the Communist 'reforms' of the late 1940s
made conditions impossible for them. After the usual immigrant
hostels and menial jobs following their emigration to Australia in the
early 1950s, Paul and Julius studied for university degrees in
Australia and then England before being appointed to academic
positions, in English and Philosophy, respectively, at the University
of Western Australia. Paul recreated there his mythical golden age
from the imaginative literature of Augustan England. King's College
Chapel in Cambridge was his spiritual oasis, occasionally visited.
Paul's outlook was cosmopolitan—he became an inveterate reader
of the *New Yorker* and *Punch*—but London increasingly
disappointed him as it became less 'English'. In a pilgrimage with
him to Jane Austen's family home in Chawton, Hampshire, in the
early 1970s, I observed that this was the civilisation in which Paul
would have liked to have been at home. However, for all his
gallantry of manner, and *noblesse oblige*, one felt that the break with
Hungary in his early twenties had left him feeling forever adrift. It
was left to his wife, Julia, to play the alternative role of the integrated
immigrant. Although Julia, too, earned an Australian university
degree (in dentistry) she gained her sustenance from the physical
earth and a myth of the land, grafting her invented role of peasant
and homemaker on to notions of the Australian pioneer settler. She
developed a fruitful suburban garden and was fabled as one of
Perth's best cooks. While observing all this from an ironically
humorous distance, Paul retained the manner of a person whose
soul was elsewhere. Husband and wife together played out the
antinomic roles of European Australian mythology—those of exile
and settler.

The commonly persisting assumption of the 1950s and 1960s
that Australia could be an extension of Europe in the southern
hemisphere affected Paul Kovesi's brother, Julius, in somewhat
different ways in the ideological sphere. Busy and bustling, and a
witty worrier of ideas, Julius Kovesi developed philosophical skills
to dismantle what he knew with absolute certainty was the false

ideology of Marxism, from whose practices he had escaped. By the early 1960s he was countering the idea of a socialist Australia held by an increasing number of left-liberal Australian intellectuals. Julius Kovesi argued that the tendency to romanticise and generalise the notion of alienation from Hegel and the early writings of Marx was dangerous, for it extrapolated too readily from particular experience to the 'Big Animal', society at large.[18] 'Nature' posed a special problem for Kovesi; language, he argued, was 'slanted against human achievement in spite of the fact that all our human life is a human achievement', and he was particularly critical of appeals to 'nature' and 'natural law' by Marx and many others. 'Progress', he asserted, was not a bad ideal, especially in the face of a civilisation under attack by 'knockers and levellers'.[19] The myth of progress was well suited to the 'development at all costs' approach of the conservative political parties in Australia at this time. Another Hungarian emigre of this time, librarian and novelist Andrew Domahidy, expressed a view common among his confrères of Liberal Party Prime Minister R G Menzies as a hero:

> We applauded everything that Mr Menzies did and said. Menzies was strongly against the communists. At that time [the Cold War] we were so polarised that only black and white existed. That was the main reason we supported Menzies. And secondly, because he opened up many things. He did a lot for the universities, which again appealed to us. He was an inspiration to us and, I think, to the whole country.[20]

The idea of Menzies as hero, and his vision of an Anglo-Australia in the southern seas clearly appealed not just to Domahidy and his friends but also to many other European immigrants, who would object strenuously to the official policies of multiculturalism of the 1970s and later as reducing the chances of the children of immigrants to 'find their own identity as Australians'.[21]

As a novelist though, Domahidy's political concerns were overtaken by other interests, summed up in his alternating images of nature in his home country of Transylvania and his adoptive Western Australia. Domahidy's only novel translated into English, *Shadows and Women* (*Arnyak és asszonyok*), is dominated by the experience of expatriation. After his arrival in Western Australia, the novel's progagonist muses on his condition: 'You become an émigré in your own land; all of us have become émigrés on this earth. Some are local foreigners, others are foreign locals'.[22]

The site on which these transformations are inscribed in the novel is landscape—principally the loved and remembered landscapes of Transylvania and then the new landscapes of south-western Australia. The generic myth drawn on is that of the pastoral tradition in literature and painting. Domahidy's remembered country is the rural County Szatmar on the borders of pre-war Hungary and Romania. Like other mythic regionalists, such as Thomas Hardy, William Faulkner or Randolph Stow, Domahidy recreates his country of childhood and youth with loving attention to sensuous detail. The counterpart to this mythic world is the author's 'second love' registered in the landscapes of south-western Australia. Of this adaptation, Domahidy commented:

> The most difficult thing for me was to come to terms with the trees. They are so different. This pale, almost greyish green after the lush European greens was at first difficult. But somehow it happened, I came to love it and that is why I am still here.[23]

Inevitably, when one myth is overlaid on another and differences are observed they become a focus of attention. But the registering of detail tends to occur within conventional limits. For example, Domahidy's Hungarian *émigrés* see Australia as a potential extension of the European imagination and thus without a history of its own. Moreover, 'nature', which philosopher Julius Kovesi had analysed in a sceptical, anti-romantic light, is presented by Domahidy in a much more romantic way. South-western Australia, for example, is perceived by Domahidy in gendered terms that recall D H Lawrence and Molly Skinner's image of this country in *The Boy in the Bush* as 'so big, so soft, so ancient in its virginity'. By contrast, Domahidy's view of the north-west, like Xavier Herbert's, is clearly of a 'man's world'. The north-west landscape, in Domahidy's eyes (recalling, to some extent, Peter Cowan in this) is 'masculine': 'It is very cruel and beautiful in its cruelty. It has no femininity'.[24]

The myth of Australia as a cultural extension of Europe was countered most powerfully in the 1980s and 1990s by the view that 'we are part of Asia'. Whereas official versions of this view abounded, as part of an attempt to encourage economic and trading links in what is now called the 'Asia–Pacific region', cultural mythology has typically been slower to respond, both to economic changes and to the increasing Asian element in the Australian population.[25] Nevertheless, the early stages of a readjustment of perspectives occurred and was evident in some parts of literary culture. Former career diplomat Alison Broinowski's survey of Australian impressions of Asia, *The Yellow Lady*,[26] is also a critique of the 'tenaciously Eurocentric' outlook of Australians and itself contributed to the then officially prescribed encouragement of changed perspectives.

A psychological analysis of the ambivalence of Australians towards Asia was ventured by the cultural anthropologist Annette Hamilton in terms of fear and desire. Australian cultural representations of Aborigines and Asians, according to Hamilton, stem from their positions at the 'empty heart' and 'fragile boundaries', respectively, of the Australian consciousness.[27] Although Hamilton's assumption here of a 'national imaginary', deriving from Durkheim and Lacan, might not be sufficiently sensitive to regional or intercommunal differences, it provides a basis for reconsidering Australian myths of Asia. What is needed, in addition, is the kind of theorising that might facilitate a consideration of interactive mythologies within the still-open concept of the 'Asia–Pacific region'.

One place to begin is with the protagonist figures, the heroes and anti-heroes of myths. A series of papers in the book *Myths, Heroes and Anti-Heroes*[28] opens up this area, raising questions about the purpose, function and construction of myths of different societies in countries of the Asia–Pacific region. Myths range from the journalistic construction of Don Bradman as an Australian sporting hero to the uses of the *Mahabharata* in societies outside India, including Fiji. It is even suggested in one playfully intertextual chapter, by an Indian-born Australian from Fiji, that the *Mahabharata* provides the perfect mythic structure for international cricket.[29] There is no sense here of commonwealth countries still straining under the yoke of a British empire; rather, old cultural icons are being reinvented and reassimilated in new ways according to changing conditions.

Among the issues provoked by myths of heroism or anti-heroism are questions of authority. Thus, for example, Sharifah Omah shows how the myth of divine kingship in Malay history, with its lessons about the sanctity of the ruler, has been a useful political tool in recent times. Japanese scholar Orie Muta also reveals how the state manipulation of hero worship has operated in Japan, both in the literary culture and beyond, but she also points to the emergence of anti-heroism in tandem with literary modernism in that country. Filipino novelist F Sionil Jose tells of the writing of his novel *Po-On* in which he lays down his definition of the hero as a peasant revolutionary 'at a time when heroes in my country are movie stars and socialites turned politicians, soldiers who have betrayed the constitution, and even returning widows with three thousand pairs of shoes'.[30] Images such as these from the literary and social cultures of 'our region' provide important new contexts for Australian writers and readers against which to test their own myths of egalitarian democracy, mateship and the 'fair go' principle. At the same time, internal revisions are occurring, for example, in the increasing status and authority of women, both in the literary culture and beyond, and in the serious attention given to Aboriginal mythology.[31] Increasing attention to the rights of women and of native peoples is, of course, part of an international (partly United Nations–inspired) movement in the Asia–Pacific, as elsewhere.

Perhaps the most important convergence of myths among the people of Australia, New Zealand and countries of the Asia–Pacific occurs in their preoccupation with notions of home, belonging and exile. Myths of the land, and particular landscapes, occur as constellations within these stories. In another book arising from an international conference on literature of the Asia–Pacific region, *A Sense of Exile*,[32] Australian myths are explored and criticised alongside those from China, Fiji, India, Korea, Malaysia, New Zealand, Papua New Guinea, the Philippines, Singapore, Sri Lanka and Thailand. What emerges is a number of culturally specific but interestingly convergent stories about displacement and dispossession, caused by invasion and forced or voluntary migration. Certain primal oppositions recur, for example, in versions of 'paradise' and 'hell'; and, as the Indian literary historian Meenakshi Mukherjee points out, a state of 'exile of the mind' has had important linguistic and literary ramifications in India and throughout the region.[33]

The territorial impulse is not necessarily aggressive and can express itself in a variety of mythic formations. Singaporean critic Kirpal Singh has explored this aspect of the Malaysian-Australian poet Ee Tiang Hong's life and work. Ee left Malaysia for Australia in 1975 when he 'could no longer accept, intellectually or emotionally, the official and Malay definition of the Malaysian nation and culture'.[34] As a fifth-generation person of the Baba culture in Malacca, with its unique fusion of Chinese and Malay elements, Ee thought of Malacca as 'home'. In his collection *Tranquerah*[35] Ee was, as Kirpal Singh remarks, 'bodily in Perth but spiritually in Malaysia—more profoundly in Malacca'.[36] The stories he tells in verse, then, are principally of the lost, remembered home, the place of childhood and family history, of cultural continuity. Streets, shops, houses and the sea are its visible elements but memory, imagination and feeling are its real driving forces. Kirpal Singh remarks that: 'If the exile leaves home because of a sense of marginality within his community, the price of exile is yet a further marginalisation'.[37] However, this can be a fruitful writing position for some authors, and in a later poem 'Coming to', Ee Tiang Hong tells a personal story of migration, which strikes a chord with many contemporary Australians:

On terra firma, Australis

don't ask me how I got out, Eddy,
and, Bruce, this isn't a suicide note,
Heaven forbid! No sailing
to Byzantium, either. Indeed,
thankful just to have survived then—
around an edge of consciousness,
new faces, fellow Australian.[38]

I have argued elsewhere that the lost Australian is such a recurrent figure in Australian literature that it indicates a deep national anxiety, and that, in order to better understand this condition, more attention should be focused on constructions and deconstructions of place, region and community in the literary culture.[39] In an age of increasing human and material mobility, the psychology of homelessness and its consequences is in urgent need of re-examination, and the myths of writers and artists might be helpful. Similarly, myths of heroism and anti-heroism seen as culturally specific formations but with important comparative dimensions, could be examined for the light they throw on different societies' constructions of selfhood, status and authority.

But myths can be enjoyed in their own right, too, for the pleasure they give through linguistic, visual or musical play. These elements of play and pleasure in mythmaking are too often forgotten by critics and cultural commentators, yet they are the very elements that have the capacity to rebuild the common understandings of communities, to give them, within the context of a proliferating pluralism, the human basis for their continuance as communities.

Nostalgia for Community: Tim Winton's Essay and Stories

A pork chop lay limp and congealing on his plate among diced carrots and peas. He sipped a whisky. The crowd in the hall was buzzing with anticipation. At the top table the talk was of the West Coast, of kingfish, snapper and sharks. Of the westerly as a wild wind or a sea breeze. Of football and writing.

When Tim Winton rose to read from his extended essay *Land's Edge*[1] to a packed audience at University House in Canberra his bulky figure seemed not at all dwarfed by the lofty Leonard French mural or by the atmosphere of conservatism that this architectural icon of the Australian National University evokes. Winton's reading took us elsewhere—to the open spaces of Western Australia's coasts and to a childhood of perceptions untutored by manners or tradition. Paradoxically, the cloistered interior seemed to enhance his images and stories. With humour and irony, underpinned by a recurrent note of nostalgic romanticism, he created in the hall an atmosphere of community built on his sense of an Australian frontier openness. I was reminded of how *Land's Edge* grew from the dual experiences of separation and return:

> I lived in a city, finished school and endured university with the coast always close as it mercifully is in Perth. I wrote books, married, had children and travelled. In Europe I tried the landlocked existence. In Paris I experienced my first apartment and my first truly dispiriting body of water, the Seine. The city itself was a revelation, an astounding and beautiful place, but after six months I found myself crazy for the margin. At St Malo on a freezing,

windblasted day I stood on the dun beach at low tide with the choppy channel out there before me and felt enormous relief at the air and sudden space, but I couldn't say I suddenly had my bearings again. Even on the Galway coast, at the cliffs of Moher that reminded me so strongly of Albany, when I at last saw west, recognized the wildness of the weather coast, the familiar loneliness and romance of being at the last edge, I was still hesitant, unsure of myself, troubled. It just gave me a taste for the real thing.

For five years now I have lived in a redneck crayfishing town of six hundred people and seven hundred dogs. I am by turns sociable and reclusive. I have my own library and houseful of kids and I go to the sea every day I can. Those days I can't, I have the smell of rotting seagrass and the blast of the Fremantle Doctor to remind me I'm close. The summer air is white with blowing sand. We live morning and afternoon the way I did as a boy in Greenough. Thank God we don't outlive all of our childhood fancies.[2]

Land's Edge is a meditative essay, interlaced with mini-narratives, which questions why a boy's summer holidays by the Greenough shore should have taken hold of his imagination and transformed him as his suburban Karrinyup experience in the 1960s never did:

I often wonder about these two childhoods of mine, the one contained and clothed, between fences, the other rambling, windblown, half-naked between the flags. Is it just nostalgia? Have I idealized these summers and chased their myth all my adult life? Did the suburban boy simply imagine himself a coastal life?[3]

Winton's answer to his own question is no: he did indeed live both these lives, but he lived the coastal life 'harder, with more passion'. This is a reminder of the traditional distinction (in fiction as in life) between routine and intense experience. The duality of modes is necessary. For Tim Winton in his early thirties looking back to his early childhood, a single room in the beach shack offers access to intensity. This room is the 'library':

It was no bigger than a bedroom but it was four walls of books, a world unto itself. There were regiments of books, whole blocks and processions of uniform editions: Somerset Maugham, Dickens, George Eliot, Balzac, Melville, Twain, Mrs Gaskell, Virgil, Homer, Edmund Burke, Galsworthy, J B Priestley, Poe. There was a fruity, illustrated edition of *The Decameron* in two volumes, and an early edition of *Mein Kampf*, whose author sounded familiar. Leather spines, dust-jackets from the twenties, thirties and forties, pocket

editions, bookclub editions, rat-punctured art books, Gilbert and
Sullivan librettos, tomes on medicine and the human body. All this
finally told me that the tall people who slipped me the odd *Archie*
comic on our weekly bread and milk trip were not ordinary people.
Ordinary people had a Bible, a set of cheap encyclopaedias, stacks
of *As You Were* and *Reader's Digest*; a yarn by Ion Idriess, perhaps,
but not all this. This was outrageous, and it was probably just the
overflow they couldn't squeeze in at home.[4]

The life of intensity is made possible by these 'outrageous' riches
compared with the books of 'ordinary people'; yet one of Winton's
strengths as a writer is his democratic instinct which infuses
apparently ordinary people, places and events with extraordinary
imaginings and feelings, while suggesting that they are all part of a
distinctively Australian community.

An imagination which oscillates between routine and intense
experience, such as Winton's, is often driven by its owner's sense of
incompletion. One of the main impulses in Winton's writings is
indeed towards a quest for completion or wholeness. In an interview
in 1991,[5] Winton commented on the impact of his visit to Europe
in terms not of adventure, or even of split identity (as in Judith
Wright's 'double tree' of a joint European and Australian
inheritance), but of separation from the sources of personal
wholeness represented by his Australian 'home':

> When I got to Europe I knew the moment I set my foot down that
> I wasn't European. I'd been brought up all my life to think that I
> was a European. I'm not even faintly European. I looked at the
> glories of Europe from behind a smoky glass. It was like this huge
> gulf; I admired but it wasn't hugely connected with me. I felt torn,
> almost, like torn out of the soil from home. Then when I came
> back I knew what was going on. I knew if I stayed away too long
> I'd be adrift, and I felt like I was going to wither up and die. I knew
> this is where I belong. I know my continent, I know my country, I
> certainly know my landscape as to what it means to me. No-one's
> really going to be able to convince me that I don't belong here.
>
> I'm connected to the land and the landscape and the sea, and the
> colour of the light, and the smell of eucalypts, the whole thing. I
> wouldn't say it's a kind of new Aboriginality, I wouldn't even feel
> that I had to even chase after the term, but it's a feeling of
> belonging.[6]

Winton has remarked that he is not ashamed to live in Western Australia as a white Australian with a strong sense of place and belonging, but that the black man in his widely acclaimed and best-selling novel *Cloudstreet*[7] 'serves as the conscience of the people, a "guardian angel" who is rejected ... the guy is saying: Learn to belong, don't break community. Basically, he is saying, "It is a grave offence to break a place"'.[8] Winton here reveals his commitment to place, region and a community for all which combines everyday ordinariness and an almost mystical sense of *communitas*, a holy place where the spirits of all might rejoice together in a place of communal belonging.

This quest for completion or wholeness is recurrently evident in Winton's novels *An Open Swimmer* (1982), *Shallows* (1984), *That Eye the Sky* (1986), *In the Winter Dark* (1988), and, especially, *Cloudstreet* (1991), but the principal focus here will be on his less noticed books of short stories, *Scission* (1985) and *Minimum of Two* (1987).

The short story is one of the most popular and important forms in Australian literary history. However, because of its links with journalism (most stories are first published in magazines or newspapers and only a small proportion find their way into book form) the short story is neglected by critics and commentators. Tim Winton has been an inveterate short story writer. By the time he was nineteen he had written about fifty stories.[9] Earlier, since primary school, he had been writing poetry. Typically, the modern short story is a mix of the techniques of journalism and poetry.

The impulses of both are evident in Winton's first two collections of stories. Moreover, the short story, through its very slightness of form and its vulnerable status beside the 'big gun' forms of poetry and the novel, always seems to testify to incompleteness. Since incompleteness, and its counterpart, the quest for wholeness, are dominant themes in Winton's writings, they bear further examination in his short stories.

The title of Winton's first book of stories, *Scission*,[10] challenges the reader with its strangeness, but the publishers, wanting to intrigue readers just enough to sell the book, have defined the unfamiliar term on the back cover: *scission*: 1. the action of cutting or dividing as with a sharp instrument; 2. division, separation, schism. Both senses of the word are used in the book's long title story and in the shorter story 'My Father's Axe'. Winton's image of wholeness in 'My Father's Axe' is presented early in the story:

I used to watch him chop with it when we drove the old Morris and the trailer outside the town limits to gather wood. He would tie a thick, short bar of wood to the end of forty feet of rope and swing it about his head like a lasso and the sound it made was the whoop! of the headmaster's cane you heard when you walked past his office. My father sent the piece of wood high into the crown of a dead sheoak and when it snarled in the stark, grey limbs he would wrap the rope around his waist and then around his big freckled arms, and he would pass me his grey hat with bound hands and tell me to stand right back near the Morris with my mother who poured tea from a Thermos flask. And he pulled. I heard his body grunt and saw his red arms whiten, and the tree's crown quivered and rocked and he added to the motion, tugging, jerking, gasping until the whole bush cracked open and birds burst from all the trees around and the dead, grey crown of the sheoak teetered and toppled to the earth, chased by a shower of twigs and bark. My mother and I cheered and my father ambled over, arms glistening, to drink the tea that tasted faintly of coffee and the rubber seal of the Thermos. Rested, he would then dismember the brittle tree with graceful swings of his axe and later I would saw with him on the bowman saw and have my knees showered with white, pulpy dust.[11]

This finely detailed realistic writing presents a ritual event in the narrator's childhood. The magic moment when 'birds burst from all the trees around' reinforces the celebration of a moment when the family is fully together, and the father a hero. This is vivid nostalgia.

The narrator's transfixed gaze on his father is recalled also in surf at the beach: 'He taught me to brace myself side-on to the waves and find footholds on the reef and I hugged his leg and felt his immovable stance and moulded myself to him'.[12]

The narrator's perspective is from a later age, after his own marriage when he has relegated his parents to a 'Home' and moved into theirs. The story's crisis occurs when the son, plagued by guilt at the disappearance of his father's axe, dreams of himself chopping the wood when the axe-head shears off the handle and 'in a slow tumbling trajectory ... sails across the woodheap and unseats my father's head from his shoulders'. His father's eyes are 'transfixed at the moment of scission in a squint of disappointment'.[13] The story might be criticised for its overly neat paralleling of this dream of the son killing the father with a subsequent one in which the narrator is himself the object of scission, as well as for its placement of news of the father's actual death at the 'Home'. But the story shows

Winton experimenting early with short fiction which plays out the dramas of male identity formation through a disturbing and never wholly resolved symbolism. If the nightmares seem too buoyantly told and the notation of behaviour recurring across generations a little too neat at the end, the story nevertheless reveals an author ambitiously attempting to chart the difficult waters of contemporary fiction technique. Winton has remarked that 'My Father's Axe' found him a route between realism and the kinds of fabulism which were prevalent in the 1970s. He didn't want to write either: 'What passed for realism denied me a whole wedge of material—the numinous. Surrealism faked it in order to escape restraint ... I wanted to include both realms because I think this is true realism: the supernatural and the natural accepted as one thing, as inclusive'.[14] Anticipating *Cloudstreet*, Winton added that his world is one 'where pigs speak in tongues and angels come and go'.[15] There were to be more daring and flamboyant experiments than 'My Father's Axe'.

If the dominant problem explored in 'My Father's Axe' is that of authority, and of how a son might replace his father in the world, the title story 'Scission' explores a sexual jealousy which feeds on itself and leads to a man's murder of his wife. Some reviewers of the book were perturbed by its 'insistence on bizarre violence',[16] but what stands out in the title story is its development of an 'ordinary' suburban situation and the passions and secrets that lurk beneath its surfaces. In 'My Father's Axe', the realistic substratum of a masculine culture is reminiscent at times of Henry Lawson's or Gavin Casey's short stories. 'Scission', on the other hand, infuses an Australian suburban situation with some of the hyper-reality of Robert Coover's or Donald Barthelme's urban America. The story is notable for its cinematic techniques, including erratic shifts of time and place and the recurrence of obsessive images. Winton's work is generally sympathetic to religious sensibilities but in 'Scission' he shows the hazards of cultish sects for certain individuals: the boorish, inarticulate protagonist of this story is described by his self-destructive father as 'a half-Jehov-wit-Latter-Day-Saturday-Cultist'. Unable to control his jealousy of his departed wife, who has become a photographic model, he summons up the hatred and self-righteousness of his adopted religion as ammunition against his hapless ex-wife. With its combination of documentary and hyper-realist techniques, 'Scission' shows Winton aiming for authenticity of a special kind.

The thirteen stories in 'Scission' are chiefly concerned with domestic conflicts in a variety of West Australian settings. The early stories, including 'My Father's Axe', explore crucial relationships between fathers and sons. In 'A Blow, A Kiss', a boy waits with a motorbike accident victim by the side of the road while his father drives off to seek help. 'Come on, Dad. Come on, Dad. Come on, Dad', he says to himself. The author observes that 'the boy often prayed to his father in his absence. God, he decided, was just like his Dad, only bigger. It was easier to pray to him and hope God got the message on relay'. This shrewdly humorous observation of the adolescent male sensibility is complemented by a sense of the mystery of an intimacy that can be so easily shattered. Scission, or at least separation, seems endemic to a relationship that is full of mysteries, secrets, uncertainties and, sometimes, betrayals. Although the diary-form story 'Wake' is ostensibly about a young man whose girlfriend has left him, it too focuses on the young man's relationship with his parents, especially his father. When father and son go jogging together at night, the moment of emotional truth is between them:

> His father is quiet in the darkness. Neither lets the other ahead. The sky thunders. They run in the gentle rain. As they turn for the return lap, his father asks him suddenly: 'Have you ever wept? Cried, I mean?'
>
> He does not reply. Nothing more is said. Rain hisses about their feet.[17]

One of the sources of this story's fictive power lies in its use of the diary form in which ritual details recur with slight but significant variations, such as the delivery of fish to his house by a friendly Italian fisherman, at the seaside town (perhaps Fremantle) where the young man lives and tries to write. The girl does not return, the cycle of the week is not completed and the tensions it exposes remain unresolved. Winton works on such patterns of irresolution in other stories too.

Another device with which Winton works in his first book of stories is the gap between sections of a narrative. In 'Scission' this method is made to work like cinematic cross-cutting to vary focus and tempo. In 'The Oppressed' the gaps are thematically related to the ethnic misunderstandings between Australians and Chinese Vietnamese. The narrative is presented in four numbered blocks, but these are themselves fragmented within by passages of italicised print in which the narrator's unspoken thoughts expose aspects of a recent past which lies behind present tensions and difficulties. The Chinese narrator's girlfriend Hoa brings with her a troubled past of violence on the refugee boats:

> She only ever told me once, late at night when most of the crew were resting and in Chinese in case they weren't. How the Thais dragged her across the deck by her legs and tied them apart with all the other people sobbing and looking away. How she had heard them beating the young men, tearing the instruments from the boat, smashing, urinating, threatening, leering as she waited mutely, too frightened to speak until she saw things which made her cry out and she tasted the brass end of the rifle butt in her mouth, the oily, bloody taste, and the fragments and singing nerves she could not spit out. I could not know it as she did, but I had things of my own.[18]

Images of violence are juxtaposed ironically against images of Australian institutions. The technology of a new Parliament House, for example, seems curiously inadequate beside the difficulties and divisions of such lives. Through a series of tentative personal interactions, Winton nevertheless indicates that in spite of the gaps between—of racism, ignorance, violence—the attraction towards difference of a younger, educated generation holds out some hope for a disparate though cohesive Australian community.

In Winton's first collection of stories, *Scission*, we can see an understated but generally powerful use of Christian insights and values. The title story, 'Scission', as indicated, provides an example of the perilous abuse of religion as violent perversion. The story 'Lantern Stalk', on the other hand, tells of a young man 'playing soldiers' at an army cadets' training exercise. The imagery of warfare recurs; the young man, we learn, represents a battleground for his estranged parents. He is confused, uncertain. His dreams reveal a state of high anxiety. Preoccupied with himself and his parents, Egg tries to achieve the objective of the mock military exercise—to reach a light on a distant sand dune without being discovered. Instead, the boy gets lost and stumbles upon a farmhouse where the local farmers and their families are holding a revivalist baptism service for a child in their midst. A nostalgia for the warmth of communal acceptance is answered, as if miraculously, in a service where bread and wine are offered and accepted. An air of super-reality pervades the scene as the boy looks into the baptised child's eyes which seem 'the colour of the night sky' and he is pronounced the child's godfather:

> The dog whined outside. Someone fiddled with an accordion. The night seemed so real. He could do nothing but stand and watch and listen and feel the panic of wonder ... He was more than himself. He felt deeper and wider. He felt as though he was more.[19]

In this story the war games are transfigured. The boy has a revelation of some essential truth, an epiphany, as, caught between the states of dreaming and waking, he stuffs the gift of rainbow cake in his pocket and makes for the lantern on the hill.

'Lantern Stalk' is one of a number of Winton's stories which attempt to go beyond the submerged epiphanies of James Joyce's fiction towards a more buoyant acceptance of angels, voices and communion in everyday life. Thus in the story 'Wilderness', for example, an ex-schoolteacher who has suffered a nervous breakdown accepts the biblical admonition to 'go into the wilderness and wait'. A bizarre comedy ensues during which the man believes himself saved by two angels, who are revealed to the reader as nature-loving bushwalkers. Salvation, it seems, has many faces.

If fracture constitutes the unifying motif of Tim Winton's first collection of stories,[20] his second collection, *Minimum of Two*,[21] seems to search more intensely for that 'obscure grace' which might hold individuals and communities together.

Flannery O'Connor, the American Southern fiction writer, much admired by Winton, remarked that 'Fiction can transcend its limitations, only by staying within them'.[22] As in O'Connor's stories, Winton finds mystery and transcendental qualities in the apparently ordinary lives of unremarkable 'local' people. He has observed that people are 'trying to rediscover the lost language of their souls'[23] but does not impose this on readers by presenting his characters as figures in obviously prefabricated allegories.

The *Minimum of Two* volume derives in part from the story of that name, in which the first-person narrator discovers that his wife's rapist is coming to the end of his 'minimum of two' years' prison

sentence, and is driven to seek revenge. The story doesn't greatly
exceed the scope of a journalistic narrative of a rape and its
consequences. However, the title's significance ramifies in the
collection as a whole to indicate the constraints and possibilities of
human interaction. The epigraph to the volume is a playground
chant: 'One and one make one/and one/and one and one make
one'. In spite of this playground insistence on unchangeable
singleness, certain stories in the book are a reminder of the biblical
injunction towards community: 'When two or three are gathered
together ...'. Although many pressures drive individuals to solitary,
anti-social fates, the obverse has a more powerful impetus in
Winton's fiction. His short stories, especially, reveal a desire for
community in defiance of what he perceives as its general
breakdown in modern society. This is one of the most powerful
motives for regional identity in Winton's writings. The
incompleteness of the solitary individual indicates a pervasive desire
for completion in the lives of others; and places on the margins of
'civilised' Australia may provide the best hope for a revival of
community.

The primary basis of community in Winton's fiction is the family,
where 'blood and water' express and sanctify the bodily needs of
individuals seeking an extension of themselves. Here, Tim Winton's
links are more obviously with the contemporary dilemmas explored
in Frank Moorhouse's 'discontinuous narratives' and Robert
Drewe's stories than with Lawson or Casey. Unlike Moorhouse's
ironic chronicles of modern urban tribes in Sydney in the 1970s,
however, the central figure in Winton's stories typically rejects
intellectual sophistication and turns to 'flesh and blood'. Thus in the
story 'Gravity', for instance, Winton's alter ego, Jerra Nilsam, rejects
the pretentious 'Deep and Meaningfuls' of partygoers and sinks into
melancholy as he grapples with the recent death of his father. The
searing loss of the father leaves no room for irony as the young
man, now a father himself, reflects on a backyard shed, which his
father built for him before he was overtaken by cancer. The son
accepts the gift as his 'Ark'. The shed is the father's practical,
physical legacy, for it is the haven, the refuge where the son may
carry on his vocation of writing. No gift from the father is given
such un-ironic endorsement in the stories of Moorhouse or Drewe.
The Christian parable is carried by the convincing rendition of the
young man's state of mind and the physical details of his suburban

existence. With the assurance of father-love, the son can turn from the concerns of alienated intellectuals to his flesh and blood family where a primary love reveals itself. The sanctification of daily living, as in the story 'Gravity', is a dangerous topic for a writer of short fiction, for it may tempt him towards idealisation, sentimentality and oversimplification. Winton's instinct for what the community of readers can accept generally enables him to avoid these reefs. Moreover, he is aware that writing from a Christian perspective in Australia since the 1970s is 'very much writing against the current' (imagery of the sea is never far from his mind), with the result that readers 'can't decide whether you're a radical or a conservative':

> Not only is it a kind of post-Christian age, technically speaking, it's an anti-Christian culture. I think that's one reason why I'm read. I'm an oddity, I think.[24]

In this context, Winton's stories in *Minimum of Two* about travels and returns serve to show the need for an anchor, a sense of belonging, in defiance of the widespread alienation and restlessness which have dominated much twentieth-century poetry and fiction. In 'Nilsam's Friend', for example, the protagonist's boyhood friend returns to the Perth suburbs after a holiday in Greece, wearing tiger-striped calico pants and a black T-shirt with the inscription SURFERS AGAINST NUCLEAR DESTRUCTION. The friend has turned thirty and can't make up his mind where he belongs. After talk of Greece and the pull of Europe, Jerra thinks of his commitments to wife and son but catches himself wondering 'what it was like to see the same creamy light, the same blue eye of the ocean, the same sky-colours somewhere else'.[25] The too-easy antithesis of civilisation (in Europe) versus nature (in Australia) is only marginally complicated in this story, but in another, related narrative, 'Distant Lands', the attractions of vicarious experience are exposed when a girl working in a bookstore is fascinated with the lunchtime visits to the shop of a man who comes not to browse but to read a book called *Distant Lands*. The moment of crisis and the girl's response are more important than other aspects of her life; they reveal what the short story most poignantly offers, the necessary incompleteness of an individual. It would be mistaken to suggest, in view of Winton's recognition of the need for community, that he idealises the concept out of existence. Human communities can be mean-minded, parochial and exclusivist. In the story 'Laps', for example, Queenie and Clive Cookson (whom readers will recognise from the novel *Shallows*) express anger at the 'development' of Scarborough beachfront:

> The little men with big money were tearing up the beachfront to build hotels for the Americans and neither of them could stand the sight of the cranes and steel skeletons and hardhats and the awful wound in the ground where the burger joints and pinball parlours had been.[26]

This is the authentic voice of localism. Winton is sympathetic to it but humorously reveals that it also harbours a romantic's desire for an impossible state of permanence and continuity:

> 'They're tearing up the fount of my youth,' Clive would say and wave his arms like a Shakespearean actor.[27]

When the couple return to the south coastal town of Angelus (Albany), in a kind of postscript to *Shallows*, Queenie is keen to confirm her past as having passed, thus enabling the new life commenced in Perth to have its own validity. When they visit the house on the hill where Queenie was brought up and where husband and wife have lived before the birth of their daughter, Clive remarks: 'Houses don't matter'. The force of nostalgia insists otherwise, investing house and surroundings with the power to give individuals an identity. Yet this is a place from which Queenie has been excluded because of her vigorous protests against the killing of whales. Returning to the killing jetties they find a museum. Attuned to the complexity of possible reactions to a place, Winton shows Queenie's sadness for a place she has campaigned so bitterly to destroy. Wanting to confirm her ancestral origins by revisiting the grave of her father, Queenie is ordered off the land. In spite of such rejections, she insists to her daughter that Angelus remains a 'special place'. Clive responds that it is 'just a place'. The daughter's wish is to go home. In this antiphony of contrasting responses to 'place' and 'home', Winton reveals the emotive power of the territorial imperative, but also deftly shows how it can differ from individual to individual. Recalling that her father is buried in the hill and requires only 'his own six feet', Queenie realises that her own element is not the land but the sea.

In Winton's story 'Bay of Angels', the Swan River is presented as both a gathering place and a place of cleansing and restoration:

We waded out. The cool water was stained from its path through the hills but it was clean. We breast-stroked out toward the line of moored boats. I dived to the bottom and came up laughing.

'Middle of a city and it's clean water!'

My friend cut the water beside me.

From there it seemed as though the city block was resting on water. King's Park sat green above it. The sky was the colour of sleep. I rolled on my back and saw the old university, pretty and fatuous in its nest of foliage. At night the shores here would germinate with the light of lamps and the sound of people laughing and wading with nets and calling after children. There would be fires and the smell of cooking prawns, the hiss of beer-cans, faint music and the commotion of somebody stung by a cobbler. There would be cars revving. There would be the dark way of the water.[28]

Water places can be destructive too, but here the scene is idyllic, recalling some of Robert Drewe's re-creations of this same foreshore.[29] Nature predominates and the culture that Winton prefers is clearly the popular culture of the prawning parties to that of the 'pretty and fatuous' university. The scene is a prefiguring of the picnic by 'the beautiful, the beautiful, the river' in the concluding stages of Winton's novel *Cloudstreet*,[30] in which old divisions are swept away and the Lambs and Pickleses begin to dance to an accordion in a scene which suggests both a folk festival and a Negro spiritual. In 'Bay of Angels', a short prose piece without the capacity to evoke the breadth of community of *Cloudstreet*, Winton ends instead with an epiphanic moment in and out of time, a transfiguration of place:

We sat there a long time, and as I waited for it all to come out I saw a host of white-sailed yachts sweeping down in the wind. Bay of Angels. The sails were like the wings of angels. My heart fattened with joy.

My friend began to weep.

I sat there with my mouth open.[31]

The keynote of this story is an experience of visionary wonder which sweeps irony and self-conscious cleverness out of the picture.

In his essay *Land's Edge* and the books of short stories *Scission* and *Minimum of Two*, then, Tim Winton shows that nostalgia has its valid human uses and that it may even be an analogue to the common spiritual longing for a prelapsarian, Edenic state of existence. Moreover, the longing and desire for home, family and friends, and aspects of the past in most of Winton's central characters reveal important sources of emotional identity and need. But the short stories, especially, reveal by their deliberate and often intriguing sense of incompleteness that divided individuals need also a wider sense of community. From the hints and clues provided by Winton's essay, fiction and interviews, his imaginary community is a heterogeneous, broad church of people who don't fit into any institution.[32] His characters, usually situated at a land's edge, are seldom active politically. Written in the 1970s and 1980s, these stories of 'little' people evoke a totally different west coast community from the WA Inc. mythology of those times. Nor are these characters 'religious' in any usual sense. Living on the margins of civilisation, Winton's characters are intent on getting by rather than getting on. In this process, as his short fiction especially shows, they have their occasional epiphanies, moments of insight which reveal them to be part of a wider human family. Winton's essay and stories are important literary productions in their own right as well as pointers to the powerful need, more fully expressed in *Cloudstreet*, for a rediscovery of the sources of community in Australia.

I left the top table at University House and walked down among the buzzing crowd who had heard Tim Winton speak. 'Wonderful', one of them said to me, 'so unpretentious, funny and sad'. 'Made me feel good to be alive', said another. Perhaps, after all, Winton's community does extend from land's edge to within the walls of the 'pretty and fatuous' universities.

4

Expatriate Voices

Some have sung with siren voices luring us towards other lands. Others have boomed like bullfrogs from the swamps of doom. Many have remained silent to us, however, these alter egos, voices of ourselves transported, in exile.

While the tourist or traveller may seem a figure of fun, a point of parody as in Murray Bail's novel *Homesickness* (1980), the expatriate seems to threaten something deeper in a fragile national psyche. He or she seems to raise the hard questions: Where do I belong? What is my place on the earth?

Debate about the eligibility of certain novels for the Miles Franklin Award indicates the problematic status of location as a criterion of value in Australian literature in the late twentieth century. The exclusion of Elizabeth Jolley's novel *The Georges' Wife*, Frank Moorhouse's *Grand Days* and Maurilia Meehan's *Fury* was evidently based on the judging committee's attempted fidelity to Miles Franklin's will, which states that the prize should be awarded for a published novel or play 'which is of the highest literary merit and which must present Australian life in any of its phases'. (Franklin died in 1954.) By contrast with the 1950s, a psychobiography of 'the Australian life-cycle' might describe this country in a 'coming out' phase in the 1990s—a phase of which Miles Franklin, in one of her many oscillations of mood, temperament and opinion, might have approved.

As one of Australia's best known nationalists, Franklin remains one of our country's least known expatriates, remembered chiefly for the prize she bequeathed. Neither Colin Roderick's biography[1] nor Jill Roe's collection of letters[2] satisfactorily exhumes the buried life of Franklin's 27 years from 1906 to 1933 as an expatriate Australian in Chicago, London and the Balkans. What seems clear in the story of her life, however, is an emotional and imaginative struggle with the contending forces of her masculine and feminine selves (a motif also in Moorhouse's and Jolley's work) as she contends continually with the possible meanings of 'home'. Marjorie Barnard presents a romantic image of Franklin's patriotic feelings:

> Miles loved Australia. In all the years she spent overseas its beauty haunted her and its ghostly rivers sang in her memory. Her love was focused on the bush and within the bush on the mountainous, well watered country where she was born, the Monaro.[3]

A love of the land in Franklin's writings does seem to derive from images of childhood in this way, but what the formulation omits is the pain of separation, of which the pleasurable images were arguably a sublimation.

In Franklin's exploratory years when she was away from Australia, experimenting with pseudonyms and alternative selves, her anxieties and uncertainties of identity were further exposed in her attacks on a more famous literary expatriate, Henry Handel Richardson. Franklin's criticisms of Richardson reveal the fragility of her assertive view of the superiority of home-nurtured talent. Marjorie Barnard observed that Franklin was 'exceedingly bitter' about Richardson, whose sin was that she had left Australia and become 'a permanent expatriate'.[4] Yet Franklin herself was a long-term expatriate and impermanency, the major theme of Richardson's trilogy, *The Fortunes of Richard Mahony*, is a state Franklin's letters suggest she understood. In spite of this, Franklin asserted strongly that a writer could not 'depict Australia faithfully without being years [here], right in the life',[5] and her various literary manifestos reinforce this contention. Behind the practical point about a writer's necessary knowledge of the places (especially landscapes) she writes about, lies a more emotional, possessive identification of self with the land of one's birth. The dynamics of Franklin's outlook in different phases of her life-cycle remain to be explored fully. They may be more interesting and complicated than the point at which she arrived as a public patron of the arts, a nationalist and a patriot.

Miles Franklin's vehement criticism of Richardson's decision to stay in another country has its latter-day counterparts in critical reactions to Australian artists who left their native country for foreign fields, or, more usually, cities. Nellie Melba advised Ray Lindsay: 'Get out of this country. It's no good for any artist!'.[6] The advice was taken by many. Geoffrey Serle's list of expatriate Australian writers in the interwar years includes: Barbara Baynton, Henry Handel Richardson, Spenser Brodney, Frederic Manning, Helen Simpson, W J Turner, Chester Cobb, Godfrey Blunden, Bertram Higgins, Miles Franklin, Christina Stead, Catherine Duncan, Mary Fullerton, Dorothy Cottrell, Velia Ercole, Jack and Philip Lindsay, Martin Boyd, Eric Partridge, Alwyn Lee, Graham and Colin McInnes, Alan Moorehead and James Aldridge.[7] Not all of these were 'permanent' expatriates but their departure caused A A Phillips to comment that Australian writing had been 'robbed of a leaven of venturesome minds'[8]—a remark that failed to take account of the fruitful development of talent, in at least some of these writers, through changes of environment.

Since the second world war, and especially in the late twentieth and early twenty-first centuries, the concept of expatriation has changed in response to rapid developments in air travel and communication technologies. The notion of permanency in any kind of life situation has become almost untenable. Nevertheless the *Macquarie Dictionary* has noted three senses of the verb 'to expatriate': (1) to banish (a person) from his native country; (2) to withdraw (oneself) from residence in one's country; and (3) to withdraw (oneself) from allegiance to one's country. Australian expatriate writers have usually conformed to the second category though some have felt banished by personal or social circumstances. The third use of the verb applies in significantly different ways to different expatriates, some having cut off all former affiliations and loyalties while others retain accent, customs and allegiances to the native country through many years.

Patrick White is in some ways an emblematic expatriate. White's absence from Australia from the ages of 17 to 36 was 'corrected', according to one version of this moral tale, when he returned to Australia 'permanently' in 1948. White's expatriate years have generally been of less interest to commentators and critics than his Australian years, though his years in Britain and Europe are explored in David Marr's *Patrick White: A Life* (1991). Elizabeth Jolley is an

English expatriate and, therefore, in Australian parlance not an expatriate at all but a 'migrant'. Born in Birmingham in 1923, Jolley moved to Western Australia in 1959 and has lived there since. Understandably, the Australian content of her novels has been of special interest to Australian readers and critics since she started publishing books of fiction in Australia in the late 1970s. Perhaps sensing this, as well as needing to feel psychologically ready, Jolley waited until her persona and reputation were established in the minds of Australian (and overseas) readers before embarking on her 'English' trilogy, *My Father's Moon* (1989), *Cabin Fever* (1991) and *The Georges' Wife* (1993). For White and Jolley, significant shifts in their places of residence preceded their major work.

Whereas White and Jolley are both considered major Australian writers, the status and authority of those who left Australia's shores and became 'permanent' expatriates are more questionable. Barry Humphries, Clive James, Robert Hughes and Germaine Greer, for example, have received mixed criticism in their native country. Others, including Peter Porter, have received far less attention than the range and quality of their work deserve. The chief avenues of fame for expatriate writers such as these have been international newspapers and magazines. Increasingly though (especially for James and Humphries) television has been the medium that has brought them fame.

Expatriate writers can bring distance and a sense of perspective when they return to their native country. Great tides of world history are evoked in the expulsion of Alexander Solzhenitsyn from Russia and his return there, 20 years later. The returns of Australian expatriates to the country of their birth could scarcely match the intensity of occasion excited by Solzhenitsyn's return to Russia. Yet it was one of Australia's voluntary exiles, Robert Hughes, whose book *The Fatal Shore* (1986) convincingly compared Australia's convict origins with the Russian gulags of the twentieth century. More typically, Australian expatriate writers in recent years have served the function of questioning or redefining the meanings of 'home' for Australians in comic or satiric, rather than tragic, terms.

The glossy, coloured program which reintroduced Clive James to Australian audiences in 1994 for a series of 'one night stands' showed him in the company of international celebrities including Tony Curtis, Jane Fonda, Kiri Te Kanawa, Ronald Reagan, Elle Macpherson and Kylie Minogue. The image of 'home' which

James's brochure evoked was of a retreat from the business of international fame. His light verse poem 'Go Back to the Opal Sunset' catches the appropriate note:

> Go back to the opal sunset, where the wine
> Costs peanuts, and the avocado mousse
> Is thick and strong as cream from a jade cow.
> Before the passionfruit shrinks on the vine
> Go back to where the heat turns your limbs loose,
> You've worked your heart out and need no excuse.
> Knock out your too-tall tent-pegs and go now.[9]

The poem shows James's verbal dexterity and his canny awareness of the power of advertising imagery in the evocation of nostalgia. This is one side of James's public persona. He can also be a thoughtful and sophisticated literary commentator and critic.[10] In his popular one-night stands, however, the temptation of glibness was difficult to resist: his ridicule of Australia 'standing tall in the Pacific basin' (the rhetoric is ridiculous but the idea isn't) and an over-ready acceptance of the monarchy indicate that he had lost touch with the aspirations of many contemporary Australians (and obviously gained touch with others).

The return to Australia of Barry Humphries in his 60th year, in 1994, was remarkable for the sustained vivacity of his one-man performance. Readers of his vivid autobiography *More Please*[11] might have been excused for wondering how the alcoholic wreck of that book could rise again. Yet there was Les Patterson, full of chardonnay and cheerful vulgarity, doing what Humphries has described as 'stating the obvious at length, which is particularly Australian'.[12] Through the 1970s and 1980s, Humphries says he had commuted between England and his 'homeland', without ever being quite sure where he really belonged[13]—a sentiment that becomes almost a refrain in the autobiographical writings of many Australian expatriates in their middle years. As in Clive James's show, contemporary satire was less effective than the more deeply embedded images of the 1950s and 1960s. Cleverness and close observation were evident in Humphries' satiric character of Daryl Dalkeith, a Christopher Skase look-alike with WA Inc. characteristics, but he lacked the depth of accumulated feeling in Humphries' *tour de force* with Sandy Stone. Sandy, who first appeared in a revue at the New Theatre in Flinders Street, Melbourne, in

1959,[14] was resurrected in 1994 with superb theatricality and feeling. What began as a satire on the vapid lives of Australian suburbanites in the 1950s returned as a wondrously detailed and expanded piece of sharp-eyed nostalgia for a lost age.

Less theatrical imaginative returns to Australia than those of Clive James and Barry Humphries can afford a darker, more disillusioned edge. The most chilling and heartfelt moments in Germaine Greer's autobiographical search for her father, *Daddy We Hardly Knew You*,[15] reflect her sense of placelessness:

> I was suddenly chilled by the sense of not belonging, of never having belonged anywhere. Perhaps I had everything wrong, who I was, who my people were, what my language meant.[16]

At the end of her autobiographical odyssey Greer still does not know whether the elusive father ever did love his daughter: 'In finding him I lost him', she concludes. 'Sleepless nights are long.' In a later article for the *Guardian Weekly*, Greer expanded didactically on her view that 'Home is an illusion':

> Home is not only a fiction, it is a pernicious fiction. If you believe there is a place where you belong you'll break your heart looking for it.[17]

The happiest day of her life, Greer asserted, was the day she ran away from home. 'Australia was, and ever shall be someone else's country'. Living in England and Italy herself, she remarked in the same article:

> the migrant's adopted home is never home but the migrant is too changed to be welcome in her old country ... Exile being the human condition, no government subsidy can provide the chariot that will carry us home.[18]

Greer's bleak outlook has its parallels in aspects of Peter Porter's poetry, but we find there a more comprehensive, witty and resilient persona interested in exploring the many faces of expatriate experience.[19] When Porter was invited to take part in Adelaide Writers' Week in March 1994, and travel more widely in Australia, it was a neat parallel with the occasion of his earlier return to the same city for Writers' Week in 1974. That earlier occasion had been

Porter's first return to Australia since 1954. The time gaps are significant for the intensity of experience. For Porter, 1974 was a crucible of change: the year of a love affair in Australia and his wife's suicide in England. His visit to Australia then seemed an 'annunciation' to which, for a variety of family reasons, he did not ultimately respond. His return, at age 65, following a number of visits in the intervening years, made him feel 'at home' but in a less wide-eyed and excited way than in 1974.

Denunciations by Australians of the deserters who left their country for other shores recur less frequently now than when those shores sang with the siren voices. In this new situation, dialogue may improve. In spite of some continuing postcolonial attempts to ridicule or vilify the British for the condition Australians find themselves in, and the unsettling effects of the republican debate, Peter Porter expressed a belief that the two countries (Britain and Australia) were not quarrelling with each other at a significant level. To a large degree, their world-views were complementary and culturally compatible. By contrast with Clive James, Porter approved of Australian republican aspirations:

> Why have a sovereign who lives abroad? Many Australians are still proud that they are descended from British stock but they don't see themselves as part of a British identity. Therefore why stick around with the head of that identity.[20]

Porter's story, like that of other Australian expatriates (in an increasing range of countries), deserves to be part of the wider Australian story of quests, border crossings, dreams, desires and accidents. I was reminded of why this is so at the Fourth Annual Regional Poetry Festival held in Canberra at the National Library of Australia in June 1994. The topic was 'A Sense of Place'. Philip Hodgins had been reading from his poems set in country Victoria when he paused and quoted from Porter's poem 'On First Looking into Chapman's Hesiod':

> Some of us feel at home nowhere,
> Others in one generation fuse with the land.

Whereas Porter presented a sense of himself in the first of these lines, Hodgins's sense of self was expressed in the second. The moment was a poignant reminder of the intersecting realities that contribute to personal and poetic identity. Similarly, Porter's brilliant

'Essay on Patriotism', with whose sceptical conclusions I disagree, opens avenues of thought and feeling on a topic which has inspired far too much pious generalising. What is patrotism? Why does is still matter? These remain important questions for Australians as the pressures for global awareness grow alongside new pressures for 'homeland security'.

These brief observations on the views and experience of Australian expatriates may lead to no conclusions for Miles Franklin Award judges, except that the definition of 'Australian literature' should be as inclusive as possible. In attacking the judges for excluding certain novels, Rosemary Sorenson asserted that their views were 'stodgy' and tied to 'a precious literality'.[21] In her view, place or setting should be put aside and 'provenance' (place of origin or record of ownership, according to the *Macquarie Dictionary*) should take over as the principal criterion: 'If someone has moved in and out of Australia, if someone is building a fiction around that sensibility ... then that someone is fulfilling Miles Franklin's wishes for a book that portrays a "phase of Australian life".'[22] Peter Craven also considers there may be room for some 'creative interpretation of Miles Franklin's bequest'.[23]

The counter-argument to these views might take a stronger view of the importance of representations of place in Australian literature. Liam Davison has observed a prevalent tendency to criticise some writers' obsession with Australian landscape for its allegedly 'debilitating effect on the development of a national literature, as if we should somehow have grown out of it by now'.[24] Davison remarks that this 'obsession' is not peculiar to Australia, nor is it something Australian writers should be 'striving to shrug off like the remnants of adolescence'. The same might be said about Australian history. However tangled were the feelings that led to Miles Franklin's antipathy to the 'permanent' expatriate, Henry Handel Richardson, it is likely that she would approve most strongly of writings which emphasise Australian landscapes and people in what Liam Davison describes as 'a communal remembering that invests a landscape with meaning'.[25]

Whatever the outcome of any legal interrogation of Franklin's bequest, the Miles Franklin Award, reflecting the outlook of that writer, should not be allowed to carry the mantle of all that is important in contemporary Australian writing. Other major awards (including the Australian Literature Society's Gold Medal) can and will emphasise other qualities within the broad confines of 'literary merit'. There is no reason why every award in Australia should be completely 'open' in its assessment. But a closer attention to Australia's expatriate voices should ensure that we listen more sympathetically to the increasingly problematic relationship between 'home' and 'away' and think flexibly about Australia as a part of the international community.

Ee Tiang Hong's *Nearing a Horizon*

Ee Tiang Hong, one of the finest English-language poets in the Asia–Pacific region, died at his second home in Guildford, Western Australia on 27 April 1990. Born in Malacca in 1933, he was educated in Malacca and Singapore and migrated to Perth with his family in 1975, becoming an Australian citizen in 1979.

In addition to his important early work in Malaysia (see Essay 2), Ee's contribution to Australian education and letters was considerable. While a lecturer in Education at the Western Australian College of Advanced Education (now Edith Cowan University), he completed a PhD in Education at the University of Western Australia. He was an academic as well as a poet and published significant scholarly work in the field of Education, both in Malaysia and Australia, including the monographs *Education in Malaysia* (1971), *Reading and Thinking* (1971; 1975), *Education in Southeast Asia* (1979) and *Curriculum Theory and Development* (1979).

It is as a poet, however, that the name of Ee Tiang Hong will be chiefly remembered in the Asia–Pacific region as Australians, Malaysians and Singaporeans increasingly recognise the value of inter-cultural exchanges, and lives like Ee Tiang Hong's are 'shared' between countries. Before the publication in 1994 of *Nearing a Horizon*,[1] which was written chiefly in Western Australia, Ee Tiang Hong had published four volumes of poems, *I of the Many Faces* (1960), *Lines Written in Hawaii* (1973), *Myths for a Wilderness* (1977) and *Tranquerah* (1985). Each of Ee's volumes of poems shows poetic qualities and illuminates aspects of the 'I' of 'many faces' which this complicated, cosmopolitan and humane writer has chosen to reveal to his readers.

I first discovered Ee Tiang Hong as a poet in 1971 when I was editing a special 'Singapore and Malaysia' issue of the quarterly literary magazine *Westerly*. This was the first of a number of issues of the magazine which focused on aspects of contemporary literature in the Asia–Pacific. Once having 'discovered' such a talented poet, *Westerly* invited him to publish occasional poems there in the future. I met Ee Tiang Hong the person in Singapore and also, from time to time, after he arrived in Perth to live in 1975. I always warmed to his quiet, hesitant conversation spiced with sharp observation, wit and understated humour. When I was invited to the University of Singapore as a Leverhulme Fellow in 1976, and visited Malaysia, I was able to read Ee's work in its Southeast Asian context. In doing so, I rediscovered the poetry at a deeper level of appreciation. Writing of his poetry after this for the Australian literary magazine *Meanjin*, I thought I discerned in him a characteristic quality of leading English-language poets of Malaysia and Singapore, which I described as the 'subdued ego'.[2] I saw this in a positive light. Instead of exhibiting the poet's ego for display, his verse, like that of Edwin Thumboo, Wong Phui Nam, Lee Tzu Pheng and others, more quietly asserted the complexity of social forces and politics in their societies. Deep feeling was expressed in the interstices of observation and experience rather than trumpeted from the confessional.

At its best, Ee Tiang Hong's poetry demonstrates T S Eliot's notion of successful verse, with 'every phrase/And sentence that is right (where every word is at home),/Taking its place to support the others,/The word neither diffident nor ostentatious,/An easy commerce of the old and the new'. Typically, though, Ee's oceanic mind had also assimilated the late Romanticism of Yeats with its search for true moments beyond the mobility of masks. The more Ee Tiang Hong stripped his verse down to essentials, the more it seemed he was conveying both irony and feeling in the spaces. Later, in the 1980s, I began reading the work of an Australian-born poet living in London, Peter Porter, who also managed (though often in very different ways) this unusual combination of intelligence, irony and feeling. What Porter and Ee had in common was their sense of exile, a powerful and pervading sense of finding themselves excluded and powerless. Paradoxically, this is the position from which the subdued ego may write itself back into contention. From the sidelines, an identity can be reconstructed from such ruins. In doing this, Ee's poetry speaks of losses and gains, the mixed economies of living for displaced people everywhere.

The late years of the twentieth and early years of the twenty-first century provide pre-eminent conditions for the experience of exile. We live in an unparalleled age of migration among haunted and hopeful refugees. In the peculiar conditions created by postcolonialism, in its many variations, the most dramatic form of exile occurs when one is forced to leave one's native region and country and to settle elsewhere. Less dramatic but similarly traumatic for some is the experience of mental exile in one's native country, which may precede emigration. Ee Tiang Hong's mental and emotional life, as he transposed it in his verse, comprehends both forms. Ee saw himself as a political *émigré* from Malaysia, where the anti-Chinese race riots of 13 May 1969 had led to humiliating reductions in freedom and authority for Chinese Malaysians including himself. As a seventh generation, Straits-born Chinese whose family had assimilated many aspects of Malay and Western cultures while retaining their own, Ee had a powerful sense of the town of Malacca and its surroundings as 'home'. Not surprisingly, in his last book, he returns in memory to this milieu, where he has given the names of streets and houses a mythological significance, taking pleasure in the multi-racial, multi-cultural influences—Portuguese, Dutch, Malay, British, Chinese. His departure from Malaysia was impelled by his sense of a monocultural direction in Malaysia which then seemed impossible to negotiate effectively or to change.

The Australia to which Ee Tiang Hong moved in 1975 was a country in a ferment of change. As one of its first moves, in 1973 the Whitlam Labor Government formally abandoned the White Australia Policy, which had restricted non-European migration. Increasingly, the Asia–Pacific was seen as a legitimate trading-ground for Australia. As in Canada, multiculturalism became official policy and a new outlook for Asian Australians became possible. But little is known yet about the mental and emotional lives of the new Asian Australians, their burden of the past, their hopes for the future.

Ee Tiang Hong's poetry plays a pioneering role in this new phase of Australian cultural history. In his epilogue to *Myths for a Wilderness*, he pictures himself in his hometown of Malacca 'at the crossroads of the great civilisations'.[3] A decade and a half later, in *Nearing a Horizon*, we hear the voice of the *arrivant* in his poem 'Coming To', which registers Australia as a place of near drowning, regaining consciousness, finding land, 'new faces, fellow Australian'. In 'Comment', he recognises that Australia is not one of the imperial powers and that his voice from there will not carry the power or resonance it might carry from elsewhere. In 'Done', he recalls the traumatic choice that was made: 'We chose Australia—stable government,/salubrious climate,/Wide open spaces/and nearness to Asia'. Australia is 'Canaan and cornucopia', 'a refuge/where we may pause to think, to make/a future for another age'. While this pause is necessary, the poet wants more, searching in 'Perth' for some kind of correlative symbolism for the resonant Malacca of his personal cultural history. Knowing his own centre he searches for the centre of Western Australia's capital city but cannot find it: 'The city has no centre, focal landmark,/no Place de la Concorde, Padang Merdeka, Tien An Men,/no particular square, terrace, public park'. If the compulsion of a common purpose is not to be found in this city's expression of Australian culture, where will it be found?

Like other writers from Western Australia, Ee Tiang Hong finds his central symbol in the river Swan which meanders through the capital city and past the house where he and his family chose to live, upstream near Guildford. Through the poems in this book, Ee Tiang Hong has made these stretches of the Swan River imaginatively his own. For Aboriginal writer Jack Davis, the Swan River is the spirit place of the life-giving Rainbow Serpent or Warrgul (in his play *Kullark/Home*).[4] To Tim Winton, in his novel *Cloudstreet*,[5] the river is a place for fishing, for family picnics on the banks, and of drownings—a place where life is given and lost. Ee Tiang Hong's view of the river is more sombre; its observer presents himself as a solitary, ruminating figure, an exile, charting the course of life which he observes with a wry irony.

To say that *Nearing a Horizon* is a book written in the shadow of death is not to diminish its importance. On the contrary, the author's knowledge of his cancer and imminent death concentrated mind and heart to a remarkable pitch of thought and feeling in this volume. The poems have a honed-down bareness and a recurrent quality of parable, as if the freedom to generalise (but not too wildly) had been given. In 'Plain View' he presents his persona 'Sprawled on a patch of grass, in the/navel of a valley' in his new country, surrealistically hailing these Australians through his paper microphone in the voice of his ancestors. Few are paying attention. In time, more Australians will be listening to these voices. The poem's concluding lines are gnomic: 'Ever our face is a mask, every utterance a/stylization. Silence is the purest language'. The lines distil the paradox of speech and silence, recalling Randolph Stow's presentation of his poems as a 'counterfeit silence'.[6] Ee Tiang Hong's words evoke a plangent recognition of the fragility of words and communication.

A younger self of this poet wrote himself a romantic epitaph in his second book of poems, *Lines Written in Hawaii*: 'If I should die,/Return me/To the sand and mud/Where winds and tides ago/I sang a childhood'. The Swan River in Western Australia is a long way from the Straits of Malacca and that childhood. Nevertheless, this last book of a pioneer Asian Australian should help to bring thinking people of these two places closer together.

6

Dorothy Hewett's Garden and City

As readers and students of literature, we are sometimes led to believe that literary and geographical realities are wedged forever apart, the one as a wholly mental condition and the other as an objective physical actuality. Yet place, appropriately conceived, is a meeting ground of mental, emotional and physical states and as such is a suitable focus for the literary imagination. As cultural geographer J Nicholas Entrikin has remarked, place is always understood from a particular point of view. It is both 'a context for our actions and a source of our identity'.[1] The decentred viewpoint of the physical environment by the theoretical scientist, and of some theorists of the arts, should be questioned. Edward Relph has stressed the phenomenological basis of place:

> Geographical reality is first of all the place where someone is, and perhaps the places and landscapes which they remember—formal concepts of location, region or landforms are subsequent. It follows from this that geographical space is not uniform and homogeneous, but has its own name and is directly experienced as something substantial or comforting or perhaps menacing. It is the space of earth and rock, water and air, the built space of towns and villages, or landscapes expressing entire complexes of human intentions.[2]

Such geographers challenge students of literature to meet them somewhere in the delimited realms of space we designate as place. Eudora Welty's assertion of the centrality of place to her conception of literary activity does this when she claims place as 'the crossroads of circumstance, the proving ground of "What happened? Who's here? Who's coming?"—that is the heart's field'.[3] As in the American South, and to some extent the American West, one can discern a powerful habit of place-making among Western Australian authors ranging from Peter Cowan to Randolph Stow, Elizabeth Jolley, Jack Davis, Robert Drewe and Tim Winton, for all of whom this part of Australia has been a haunting presence demanding some form of fictional reconstruction.

For Dorothy Hewett, imagery of place and especially of the remembered places of childhood is a necessary prerequisite to the figuration of human behaviour and action. This almost obsessive affiliation with place as 'the crossroads of circumstance' and the heart's field' (to use Eudora Welty's phrases again) has its origins in Hewett's isolated childhood (until the age of twelve) on her parents' farm near Wickepin in the Great Southern region of Western Australia, which Margaret Williams accurately perceives as the chief source of Hewett's long poem 'Legend of the Green Country' and her 'pastoral' plays, *The Man from Mukinupin* (1979), *The Fields of Heaven* (1981) and *Golden Valley* (1985).[4] Williams has commented that all of these plays 'are concerned with imagination's power to heal the gulf between the human world and nature (including the rift in human beings' own divided nature) and with imagination as the only true means of resistance against the ravages of materialistic "progress"'.[5] Yet Hewett's imaginative engagement with other Western Australian authors who seem to share this outlook, especially Randolph Stow, Peter Cowan and Tim Winton, and British writers for whom 'organic' notions of local environments have counted, such as D H Lawrence, the Brontës and the Lake District poets, give her representations of place an intertextual richness and force.

Early influences on Hewett's poetry which represent the two sides in this perceived fracture of sensibility are Judith Wright and T S Eliot. Like Wright, Hewett is an intuitive responder to Romantic doctrines of the sanctity of nature. In Eliot's footsteps, the mystique of the city offers both appeal and revulsion. Behind both, and in spite of Hewett's professed atheism, lies the biblical duality of good and evil, Paradiso and Inferno, the traditional dialectics of literary representations of place.

In the personal mythology of Dorothy Hewett's life in art, wherein places shape the individual and are in turn transformed by her in memory and imagination, 'garden' and 'city' are crucial signifiers. Her seminal essay 'The Garden and the City'[6] sets the scene: 'There have been two places central to my imagination ... the state of Western Australia and the city of Sydney'. In both she was struck by 'an almost Utopian physical beauty' but underneath the skin of either society (the body metaphor is characteristic) 'the corruption ... is palpable'. In the case of Western Australia, the 'worm in the bud is secretive' whereas in Sydney 'the materialism is vulgar, articulate, unashamed'.[7]

Already one can see the biblical origins of an allegorical Eden ripe for spoiling in the West and the city of Mammon and Moloch in the East. But these polarities are not fixed: their imaginative dynamism derives from their changing roles in the life cycle of a person born into a family living on a wheat and sheep farm at Malyalling via Wickepin, who lived from her early seventies until she died in 2002 in a stone house with an iron-roof and verandah, reminiscent of an old farmhouse, at Faulconbridge in the lower reaches of the Blue Mountains near Sydney. If houses are palimpsests of the imagination, it is tempting to see a return to the earliest imprints of childhood here; or, to change the metaphor, a return towards beginnings in the life cycle. Empirical details blur the pattern, however: Sydney, symbolic city of this author's growing up was only an hour and a half away and Arcadia was rent apart by the racket of heavy traffic to and from Sydney on the Great Western Highway outside the front fence and by goods trains at the back. In imaginative and emotional terms, Sydney appears as the city Hewett had to have; and she seems unable to leave it entirely behind. This aspect of the personal mythology would be confirmed by Dorothy Hewett herself, reminding those who listened to, or read her, that her lifetime was in fact split into two parts—around forty years spent in Western Australia and a similar period in New South Wales, mainly Sydney.[8] But within these apparent contraries, certain ambiguities and contradictions occur. These arise from Hewett's cumulative sense of a plurality of Australian places and their imaginative possibilities.

In an interview, Dorothy Hewett commented:

I think I wear places out in my head. I'm a terrible user and I use places and perhaps people too, to a certain extent. I drain them, I get whatever I can from them and then I've got to go somewhere else.[9]

Along with this honest admission of the ruthless egotism of a writer, however, goes a strong sentimental attraction to certain places and people, especially when they are revisited in memory. One is reminded of Randolph Stow's poem 'Ishmael' when his poetic persona asks: 'strip me likewise of softness, strip me of love/leaving a calm regard, a remembering care'. Hewett had more trouble attaining this state than Stow, but the impulse remains.

In the classic Romantic mode, places are recalled for Hewett by their association with situations which produced powerful emotions. Thus, for example, just as the south-west coast of Western Australia, and Augusta in particular, reminded Peter Porter of the Brisbane bays of his boyhood in his poem 'The Ecstasy of Estuaries',[10] Hewett's images of south-coast New South Wales near Bermagui (not far north of Eden) remind her of childhood holidays near Albany on Western Australia's south coast. Such examples could be multiplied. Distance may do more than make the heart grow fonder; it may give perspective, test memory and clarify the emotions.

Dorothy Hewett's first garden, as her recuperative imagining presents it sixty years later in the autobiographical *Wild Card*, is the one attached to the farmhouse of her childhood, 'the sense of childhood become myth', which 'sits in the hollow of the heart':

The little gate opens into the garden with the pink Dorothy Perkins rose climbing on the wire fence, the Geraldton wax bush blooming. The house is ringed with almond and fig trees. In spring the almond blossom falls in white bruised drips on the couch-grass lawn. In summer the twenty-eight parrots crack nuts over our heads till our father goes for the shotgun. At Christmas time we sit on the verandah preparing the nuts for the cake with a silver nutcracker. The twenty-eight parrots flash green and black as they fly away, the nutcracker flashes silver in the sun. We carry the almonds into the kitchen, plunge them in boiling water and peel off the skins, till they curl like brown tissue paper and the almonds emerge smooth and creamy white.[11]

The metaphoric pressure here is towards inclusion. The speaker/author is neither above nor below, but imaginatively enters 'into' the space designated as 'garden'. The father is the central figure here; throughout Hewett's writings he is the one who counts, brought low though he ultimately is by separation from the land he has tamed and the censorious, suburban ways of his wife. This garden of childhood dreaming is a charmed place where the father maintains order with his gun; and it leads in two opposite directions, outwards to the paddocks and the far horizon and inwards to the kitchen, the source of sustenance. A balance and order are sustained despite (or because of) the absence of the mother.

Martin Leer points out that the garden in Australian writing is part of 'the conceptual apparatus Europeans brought with them to Australia'[12] but Hewett gives it her local habitation and name. For example, Hewett's grandparents' house on three-quarters of an acre in South Perth, named 'Cathay', is recalled as another, second magic garden. 'It became a kind of Garden of Eden for me,' Hewett reminisced, 'it was a beautiful garden with fruit trees, I suppose not unlike this place [at Faulconbridge] in a way, lots of trees and flowering shrubs and with a marvellous view of the river as well'.[13] (And without the Blue Mountains traffic, she might have added, with its reminders of Sydney.)

Superimposed on these images is the garden of the University of Western Australia campus where, in the autobiography *Wild Card* and the play *The Chapel Perilous*, and elsewhere, a serpent ('the snake of change, sex, adulthood, the joining outwards to the corrupt world')[14] has comprehensively entered the formerly safe enclosure and takes her unawares in groves of trees, on sports grounds or by the river. The garden's most allegorical rendering occurs in Hewett's fifth volume of poems, *Alice in Wormland* (1987), written in the author's early sixties in various places including eastern and Western Australia over the previous five years and often exuding a strong sense of the locality and circumstance of their composition. As the book's title suggests, the protagonist Alice has moved through the life cycle from the Wonderland of childhood to the contemplation of her mortality as part of Wormland. This recognition makes the garden a more focussed, intense place of desire and imagining. The chief contrast is between the haunting presence of Wormland and the earlier 'Dream Girl's Garden', where:

There were dolls & rocking horses
gilt hornets built clay houses on the verandah

> tom-tits swung dry grass nests in almond trees.
> This was Eden   perfect   circular
> the candid temples of her innocence
> the homestead in the clearing
> ringed with hills
> the paddocks pollened deep in dandelions
> the magic forest dark & beckoning.

The dark forest, beckoning, will of course attract the young adventuress, but inside, a certain primal innocence remains like a birthmark on the writer's literary conceptions of her self. Nim, the speaker's idealised companion/child/lover in *Alice in Wormland* might be thought of as the son of T S Eliot's Fisher King, but he also anticipates idealised figures of the lost 'other half' of Hewett's Romantic yearnings, including Billy Crowe in *The Toucher*—idealised males whose evil is never quite realised for what it is because she is rebelliously attracted to it. In *Alice in Wormland* this Nim waits:

> curled like a leaf
> in the womb of time
> his fisherhat folded
> his rods plaited
> his bait tin ready.

As a virtuoso of roles and styles throughout her writing career, Hewett experimented with different ways of representing her garden and city worlds. Don Anderson acutely observed of her second volume of poems, *Windmill Country* (1968), (the co-authored volume with Merv Lilley, *What About the People!* (1963) was her first), 'the long unrhymed narrative line' was reminiscent of Whitman in 'trying to contain the land'. Hewett was coping with 'the tyranny of distance', attempting

> to take things into herself by naming them, to understand her puritan ancestors who were so intimately a part of the land which shaped them, made them mean and avaricious.[15]

Her poetry in this volume furthermore was 'energetic and muscular, representing a sensibility arguing strongly with time and place, wrestling with atavism and tradition'.[16] A variety of moods and responses to place and time occur in other books and sequences of poems. For example, place and state of mind interact with almost symphonic effect in Hewett's series of poems first published in *Overland*, written at Mornington Peninsula on Port Phillip Bay in Victoria (*On the Peninsula* and *Return to the Peninsula*), in which keenly observed imagery of place musically counterpoints the writer's recovery from two serious operations.[17] Like Beethoven's String Quartet in A Minor, (opus 132), in which the slow movement includes allusions to the composer's illness, these poems are generally quiet, contemplative, echoing the rhythms of a re-emergence into life, but they occasionally erupt with the storms of Hewett's passionate engagements with people and places.

Cities offer different challenges to the literary imagination. However, it is interesting to note that Perth does not figure in any archetypal sense as 'the city' to Dorothy Hewett, though she lived there (chiefly in South Perth among what she termed 'the bourgeoisie' through her Communist days) from 1935 to 1949 (between the ages of twelve and twenty-six); and then again, after her nine years in inner-city Sydney (especially Redfern and Rockdale) from 1958 until 1974, when she finally severed herself from Perth as her principal place of residence. Hewett's main literary representations of Perth are as suburbia. To some extent, her Perth recalls Tom Stannage's memorable history, *The People of Perth*,[18] in which he characterises the central tendency of successive communities there as a particularly successful but ambivalent and in part self-destructive quest for 'internal peace'.[19] Dorothy Hewett's poem 'Sanctuary' in her third collection, *Rapunzel in Suburbia*,[20] presents Perth as a place of quiet suburban desperation where suicide seems the chief option for wild spirits:

> This nervous hollow city is built on sand,
> looped with wires, circled with shaven trees.
> The bleeding pigeons tumble outside the windows,
> the children wring their necks.

Such images recall the atmosphere of Randolph Stow's novel *The Suburbs of Hell* (1984), Peter Cowan's book of stories *The Empty Street* (1965) or, further back, Philip Masel's neglected novel *In a Glass Prison* (1937). Trapped in 'the backyards of the bourgeoisie' with Merv Lilley in her second phase of domesticity and children, Hewett records her sense of restriction in *Rapunzel in Suburbia*. South Perth enters the book symbolically as the place of the zoo.

However, another kind of wildness is desired, expressed in Cat Stevens's popular song of the period, 'O! Baby, Baby,/It's a Wild World', which provides the title of the book's central section. But the Romantic longing for freedom, danger and wildness in the years of her return to Perth is most typically expressed by Hewett in images of a lost, remembered world, in a Sydney of occasional escapes from the socialist realist routines of *Bobbin Up*, when she had lived dangerously as a go-between for Communist Party functionaries at rallies and clandestine meetings:

> O to live dangerously again,
> meeting clandestinely in Moore Park
> the underground funds tucked up between our bras,
> the baby's pram stuffed with illegal lit.

The place from which remembering occurs here is the imaginative tower to which, like Yeats, the poet has retreated to spin visions, and gain perspective. As Nicholas Hasluck and Fay Zwicky point out, 'the outer landscape is now internalised, it has become larger than life, the stuff of legend ...'.[21]

Hewett's images of Sydney as a city of dreams are fractured, kaleidoscopic, in a modernist mode in her poetry, representing half a lifetime in different precincts of this city in a variety of emotional states. The more solidly specific novel *Bobbin Up* has provided knowledge and insights for at least one social geographer of postwar Sydney, who finds the novel as valuable a source as Ruth Park's novels.[22] According to Hewett's own testimony, she found Sydney 'territorial'; certainly the topography, architecture and circumstances of the three suburbs she principally inhabited— Redfern in the 1950s, Woollahra in the 1970s and Darlinghurst in the 1980s—offered radically different perspectives on experience. The house in Jersey Road, Woollahra, for example, became the author/hostess's 'salon' for Sydney playwrights and poets[23] just as the house in South Perth had been for Western Australian writers. (Post-Redfern, all Hewett's Sydney houses were important meeting places for writers, artists and other drop-outs.) The house at 195 Bourke Street, Darlinghurst, however, eventually became a place of disenchantment. Just off Oxford Street, and a short walk down the hill from the neon-lit sleaze of 1980s King's Cross, the Bourke Street house was located next door to a brothel and across the road from a church; always alert to the symbolic resonances of her dwelling places, this house and its surroundings came to epitomise an end of urban romance. In Dorothy Hewett's hands, this was achieved in a distinctly theatrical way:

> The mafia play Johnny Cash
> at the barbecue
> the bikies drag their girls
> home by the hair
> down Wisdom Lane
> the molls argue
> *25 bucks to suck you off*
> *a French letter*
> *because of AIDS*
> & no kissing
> the paraplegics line up
> in their wheelchairs
> for a fuck.

If this scene smacks of 'over the top' melodrama, it is important to recall Hewett's own self-valuation that, although she had a strong memory, like Hal Porter, she lacked 'imagination'. Her first job was as a reporter for the *Daily News* and many places and incidents in her poetry, prose and drama emerge from remembered events in her own life. Visitors to the Darlinghurst house for example, have vouched for the details in her poem. It is also noticeable that in the prose and poetry which situate Hewett's alter ego in fictional versions of the Bourke Street house, she is placed not in the streets themselves, as in *Bobbin Up*, but above them, from the point of view of a watcher, looking down (again like Hal Porter, though not from a cast-iron balcony). Implicit in this positioning is not the perspective of Gothic romance, as in the towers of Rapunzel, but a distancing made possible by age. Esther expresses revulsion at a de-romanticised Sydney in *The Toucher*:

> Is the dawn streaking the horizon while I lie here in this dark, cluttered house mired in the city like a huge old warehouse of half-forgotten dreams, redolent with them, dusty and stinking like the city tip?[24]

The time had clearly come to be up and away where nature was closer, the air cleaner and the spirit could again expand. The Blue Mountains beyond Sydney offered Hewett her next, and last, writerly retreat.

In his review of Dorothy Hewett's last novel, *The Toucher*, David English[25] accurately observed that this is 'a water book' in which 'the estuary, the beaches and cliffs from childhood, deaths by drowning, tourists out surfing, the fishing, the last voyage' are predominant. There is no quiescence in this though. Albany and the south coast of Western Australia are not calm like Victoria's Mornington Peninsula and Port Phillip Bay in *Peninsula*. The Romanticism is Byron's rather than the Lake Poets' as, in David English's words, the novel's protagonist is 'swept by great waves of memory' expressed in 'a defiant poetic surrealism'. The Albany and surroundings of Hewett's childhood, which she revisited in 1987, were not a place to slip quietly towards a clichéd 'eventide'. Dylan Thomas's 'Do not go gentle into that good night' expresses more appositely Hewett's rebellious sense of the *in*appropriateness of a 'proper' attitude to conventions such as ageing gracefully. The secret of Hewett's power to embarrass by excess, to overflow the page, is evident when, in *The Toucher*, her protagonist Esther is spoken to by the garden: '"Be told", said the garden'. She refuses to be 'told', even as a crippled, wheelchair-bound septuagenarian. She will not accept the garden's order and quiescence. Like earlier Hewett protagonists, she is impelled by romantic desire and physical need to one more grand adventure. In *The Toucher*, Hewett's last novel, garden and city give way to the sea and the notion of a voyage 'past the islands into an unknown light and an ultimate darkness'. The immortality which Sally Banner's adolescent confidence had foreseen beyond the limitations of Western Australian suburbia in *The Chapel Perilous* is countered by the older writer's recognition of mortality in contemplation of Australia's southern seas. The garden has become too enclosing a symbol; the city no longer offers salvation by excitement and anonymity. The tower is no longer necessary. The sea draws her beyond old limits towards 'an unknown light and an ultimate darkness'.

Poet and Statesman: Paul Hasluck

My direct links with the subject of this essay were few and tenuous, but for me, memorable. After returning from Oxford in late 1967 and soon thereafter having a choice, in those days of easier employment, of a diplomatic post in the department of external affairs or a university lectureship, I approached Paul Hasluck, then minister, for his advice. Having drawn from me that my chief interest in external affairs would be to influence foreign policy, he politely but firmly indicated that the best place to shape Australia's foreign policy was parliament. I should get myself elected to the federal parliament and formulate policy there. Alternatively, if I found university teaching satisfying, as I thought I would, the intellectual influence I could have on students and a wider public would be a worthwhile goal too. In coolly and deftly placing these alternatives (and throwing in the wild card, for me, of entering politics), I now realise that Paul Hasluck was recounting some of his own dilemmas of the 1930s and 1940s. Not only had he been relatively uncommitted in a party political sense but he had several vocational options in journalism, university life and international diplomacy before, as he says in his autobiography, *Mucking About*, he 'let them all down and went into politics'.[1] I was especially interested in his reasons for turning down an offer of a position in the United Nations because, as he later remarked: 'I was too nationalistic to be a good international public servant, but largely because I wanted to live in Australia, have my two sons grow up as Australians and not as international diplomatic waifs'.[2]

One of those sons, Nicholas Hasluck, I got to know when we fortuitously shared a cabin on the P&O liner *The Himalaya* en route to England and studies at Oxford—a journey that would re-emerge in heightened imaginative terms in the younger Hasluck's first novel *Quarantine*.[3] Not surprisingly, perhaps, I became interested in the relationship of sons to famous fathers and mothers. My parents, who had both left school in their early teens, and never aspired to public office, seemed in some ways to make it easier for their sons to go their own ways. On the other hand, Nicholas Hasluck had absorbed the legacies of a reading and writing family deeply engaged in Australia's public culture.

My focus here is on Paul Hasluck as poet, but I want to stress his broader concept of the writer. Hasluck had a high regard for good writing in all its forms. He had a higher regard for writing than for mere talking. The telephone, he came to believe, was in some respects a curse: 'The facilitation of communication has been a great benefit for persons with nothing to say', he remarked.[4] On the other hand, poetry, as one of the higher art forms, required expertise in verse forms, a fine control of language and a subject of significance. An old-fashioned Australian democrat in his belief that the poet should not be seen as a special person—a shaman or magician figure—Hasluck believed, as the British neo-classicists did, that poetry should be part of civilised discourse. In his extended essay *The Poet in Australia*,[5] published after he retired as governor-general, Hasluck summarised his Utopian vision for Australian society: 'I will not believe Australia is fully civilised ... until some men will talk as naturally and as knowledgeably about poetry as most men talk about golf and the stock market'.[6]

The targeting of 'men' here owes something to Hasluck's generation's tendency to talk of civilisation as a male's responsibility; but it is still often the case that poetry is thought of as 'women's business', and the civilising of men specifically in this way would indeed be a breakthrough.

As a writer as well as a reader, Hasluck's interests were broad and inclusive, and often surprising. The breadth is evident in his interest in historical fiction, on the one hand, and French poetry of the 'symbolistes' on the other. Morever, like many writers before him, he used his writing to experiment with different selves and ways of seeing the world. Paul Hasluck's presentation of pseudonymous writing selves could not compete with some recent examples (he was never guilty of 'doing a Demidenko'), but when his initials P H were sometimes confused with another writer of his time, Peter Hopegood, he changed his signature as a critic of drama in the *West Australian* to 'Polygon' and used this name subsequently for short stories and historical reconstructions in the *Western Mail* and elsewhere.

The sources of Paul Hasluck's poetic self seem to lie in his late adolescence, between the ages of sixteen and nineteen, when, as he put it in his autobiography, 'confusion came into my life'.[7] The catalyst was his parents' departure from Guildford and their transference from 'the social work of the Salvation Army into the field work', effectively making them peripatetic clergy for the Salvation Army cause. Hasluck increasingly found the 'hot-gospelling and the public practice of religion ... very uncongenial'.[8] As he later saw it, he was:

> living a double life—one centred on the strict and narrow religious discipline of a Salvation Army family and another life centred on school and the comradeship of ordinary boys, bemused by strange dreams and ambitions and hopes, privately and indeed secretly enriched by poetry.[9]

He gradually distanced himself from religion, convincing himself that Christianity was a barrier to intellectual advancement but continually heard the echo of the scriptures in what he read, thought and wrote. The despatch of Christianity from the centre of his life required a replacement. Looking back on this period half a century later, Hasluck concluded that 'What chiefly supplanted religion ... was English literature. Wordsworth gave me more than the Pauline epistles'.[10] Indeed, Wordsworth echoes often through Hasluck's poetry as in his autobiographical recall of solitary walks 'through the Darling Range from the gorge of the Swan River in the north to the vicinity of Karragullen in the south'.[11] 'Bliss was it in that dawn to be alive', Wordsworth wrote of his time of walking and reflection in pre-revolutionary France and there is something of that exhilaration in Hasluck's memories of drinking from 'running brooks' in the

Darling Range in the winter of 1925 and returning to the fireside where he read a Shakespeare play each Sunday evening before going to bed.[12]

Hasluck's reading of English literature during his school and university years was very comprehensive and, in the best sense, personally meaningful. In the great tradition of the autodidact, he read Chaucer, Milton and Shakespeare, George Herbert, Tennyson, Cowper, Matthew Arnold, Shelley, Byron, Coleridge, Browning, Dryden, Pope, Johnson and Goldsmith; but Wordsworth and Keats made the deepest impression. The romantic spirit in Hasluck is one of his least explored aspects and this is perhaps because it is often counterpointed in his writings by a ruminative, ironic and worldly wise voice. Nevertheless, it finds its fullest expression in his poetry.

The Australian poets who came to mean most to Hasluck included Furnley Maurice (Frank Wilmot), Kenneth Slessor and, surprisingly, Christopher Brennan. Hasluck's discovery of Brennan's *Poems 1913* preceded any knowledge of Brennan's work in the English department at the University of Western Australia, and led to a paper on Brennan's symbolism to a newly formed English literature society in 1933 or 1934, soon after Alec King's appointment as lecturer.[13] Interestingly, Hasluck came upon Brennan's work through his interest in French symbolist poetry, fostered by Margaret Clarke in the French department, and fuelled by a 'patriotic fervour' for a more difficult, cerebral poetry in Australia than that of Henry Kendall and Adam Lindsay Gordon.[14] In later years, Hasluck was remarkably balanced in his assessment of the literary and intellectual influences operating at the University of Western Australia in the 1920s, recognising that he had 'grown up in Australia in an old-fashioned community in a part of Australia even more remote from novelty than the rest'.[15] His assessment of the influence of the foundation professor of English, Walter Murdoch, was similarly balanced but with an edge to it: Murdoch was important for his 'personality and influence rather than ... his achievements'.[16] Summing up, Hasluck remarked, 'It was our peculiar blessing that our professors and lecturers had learnt to love books before 1914, just as it is sometimes the misfortune of undergraduates today to be lectured on literature by persons who developed a dislike for books after 1945. Our teachers expounded with joy the merits of their favourite authors; their successors mumble about the defects of those whom they do not appreciate'.[17]

In reading Paul Hasluck's four books of poems published between 1939 and 1991, I am struck by their importance not just to an understanding of Paul Hasluck but also to the art of poetry in Australia. The first of these books, *Into the Desert*, has its genesis in the 1920s and 1930s when Hasluck was fostering a hidden life as poet alongside his more public roles as student, journalist, academic historian, husband, and traveller.[18] As in many first books, the author experiments with a variety of voices and styles. In Hasluck's case, he ranges from poems of contemplation and vision to lyrics, sonnets, hymns and metrical exercises. The opening section of the book, which sets its agenda, is a series of poems about entering the desert and the insights that can flow from this. These poems are not concerned with geographical realism, though one of them locates itself at Cook on the transcontinental railway on the Nullarbor Plain, and muses on the temptations to lose oneself in the immensity of space. However, other urgent voices pull the speaker back to present realities: '... plan the day. Plan better days ahead./Forget the sky. Focus dilated eyes./You dare not look at space or think beyond/The sky and desert edge'. The epigraph to this sequence, 'And He went into the desert to pray', recalls Christ's desert experience and indicates the continuing influence of Hasluck's Christian upbringing even as he sought alternatives to it. The desert thus comes to symbolise both renunciation and a space in which spiritual regeneration may occur:

> The air is singing. We will see life new
> At music's centre, understanding's heart;
> Go calmly from the coast, led by the faith we keep,
> Out to the untouched inland plains.

Against this impulse towards the 'music's centre' is set a deadened suburban mentality and way of life in 'Discontent in the Surburbs':

> The tarred road through the suburb is lined with dying trees
> And grey dried weeds
> Between a palisade of skinny poles and whining wire.
> We know brief repetition, never birth,
> For we have strangled love, dashed beauty from the rock.

Because the quasi-biblical journey into the desert has become a familiar trope in Australian writing from works such as A D Hope's poem 'Australia' (also first published in 1939), Patrick White's *Voss*

(1959), Randolph Stow's poem 'The Land's Meaning' (1962) and Stow's novels *To the Islands* (1958) and *Tourmaline* (1963), it is important to note Hasluck as a pioneer in this field in Australia, although T S Eliot's influential poem 'The Waste Land' (1922) had set the scene by definitively locating the inter-war period as a desert awaiting the life-giving rains of spiritual regeneration.

A D Hope, who was two years younger than Hasluck, provides an interesting comparison. Hope was the son of a Presbyterian minister and spent most of his childhood in rural New South Wales and Tasmania. His poem 'Australia' differs from Hasluck's desert sequence in its bold assertion of Australia as a cultural desert, from which prophets might miraculously spring who would re-orient the national spirit, setting aside 'the chatter of cultural apes', which purported to be civilisation in Europe. Leonie Kramer has pointed out, however, that very little of Hope's own poetry reveals any 'direct inspiration from his actual [Australian] environment'.[19] Hasluck, on the other hand, was closely observant of his natural environment, and had honed his descriptive skills in journalism, as had his Western Australian predecessor, Katharine Susannah Prichard.

Among the various voices and roles that Hasluck was hypothesising for himself in the interwar period was that of the romantic nationalist, singing a song of the land. There were many models for this, but P R ('Inky') Stephensen's *Foundations of Culture in Australia* (1936) seems to have provided some of the ideas and impetus. In 'Songs of Australia' Hasluck switches from a satire against the banks and all city-bred (and therefore un-Australian) hypocrites to the men of the land who are relished for their colour, courage and humour:

> O, give us your hand, digger, dingo, sand-groper, old fossicker, swaggie, cow-cocky, sheep-chaser, mullock-shoveller, crow-eater, boundary rider and farmhand
> For Christ's sake, don't sing; but give us your hand.

'Songs of Australia' suggests the influence of Whitman among others, with its long lines and its expansive, energetic celebration of a national ethos, but there is more humour, ironic understatement and sheer idiomatic pleasure in Hasluck's lines.

Hasluck's audacious combination of biblical-style prophecy with a recognisably Australian vocabulary and speech rhythms was tested at greater length and depth in his ambitious script for radio, 'The Burden of Habbakuk and the Sword of Gideon', which was written in the 1930s but not published until 1969 in the *Collected Poems*.[20] Hasluck himself described this script as an attempt to deal with 'the struggle between individualism and communalism that goes on both inside the personality and in the daily struggles of life in society'.[21] Based closely on the old testament book of the prophet Habbakuk, Hasluck's script is not intended as a dramatic composition but as a monologue—'the tumult of many voices playing around inside a man's mind, the man's mind itself, like that of a troubled prophet in a wilderness, being full of echoes of his own age as well as of all he has inherited from the past'.[22] Although somewhat static, the script has its moments of neatly orchestrated counterpointing of voices, views and attitudes. A narrow, isolationist cultural nationalism, for example, is excoriated as:

> The proud invocations of inbred Aussidolaters
> Searching Lawson and Furphy for something to quote,
> Spinning high romance in the shoddy brutalities of Kelly,
> And making each speech one long peroration
> Hung round with the smell of stale eucalyptus.

To Hasluck, this is not a communalism worth giving oneself up to. Yet an almost mystical communion of the individual with the land is not denied:

> I once stood on a mountain in the morning and said:
> This is my land. I belong to these hills and plains
> And my body escaped from my mind.

The script seems written with a sense of the coming war and is testing (but not fully resolving) the limits of individual self-interest against the requirements of patriotism and the commitment to fight for one's country.

Hasluck's war years were spent not as a fighting man (he was thirty-four in 1939) but initially as a replacement for Professor Fred Alexander, who was on sabbatical leave in 1940 from the history department at the University of Western Australia, and then in the department of external affairs working on the civil side of the 'war effort'.[23] Hasluck had enough poems for a second collection in 1947, which he would have dedicated to the Melbourne poet Furnley Maurice, but he waited until 1969, when the Hawthorn

Press in Melbourne published his *Collected Poems*. The new poems in this book, written as they were in the margins of a relentlessly busy political life, are generally shorter and less poetically ambitious than his prewar verse. While some of these poems have that special imaginative quality that Hasluck himself associated with the best poetry, others have a more journalistic appeal, prompted by experiences at places as far apart as Wyndham, Wagin or a bus in Mount's Bay Road, Perth. In such poems Hasluck's west appears as a place of inwardness and relief from his outer world of politics and anger.

Hasluck's poetic experiments with communalism in the interwar years gave way in the war and postwar years to an engagement with a more solitary, unified speaking subject. Nevertheless, against the backdrop of a busy working life we sometimes see the vulnerability of a thinking, feeling, divided person constantly aware of his mortality. In the fine poem 'At Augusta', Hasluck's persona questions his achievements as he looks out across the 'sandhills and bar and the green troubled seas' as the wind blows in from the 'far Polar waste', offering no peace. Other poems express a frustration with the gap between rhetoric and the speaker's personal reality which is shown to derive ultimately from a faith in the Australian soil and its propensity to regenerate.[24] Such a faith seems a resting-point rather than an occasion for that restless scepticism which Hasluck praised elsewhere in the figure of Montaigne, and which so often characterised his own thinking.[25]

Paul Hasluck's major phase as a poet occurred in his third book *Dark Cottage* (1984).[26] In some respects, the book may seem a throwback to an earlier phase of youthful poetic and personal exploration in the Darling Range. However, although a Wordsworthian romanticism recurs in *Dark Cottage*, Hasluck's poems of his later years have a deeper and more satisfying complexity as they interact with the Australian landscape, European music and English metaphysical poets such as Edmund Waller and Thomas Traherne. The versatile seventeenth-century English politician and poet, Edmund Waller provides Hasluck with the epigraph and title for his third book:

> The Soul's dark Cottage, batter'd and decay'd
> Lets in new light thro chinks that time has made.
> Stronger by weakness, wiser Men become

As they draw near to their Eternal home:
Leaving the Old, both worlds at once they view
That stand upon the Threshold of the New!

Although Waller's topsy-turvey record of switching political allegiances from Charles I to Cromwell and then back to Charles II has no discernible parallel in Hasluck's career, the seventeenth-century poet's image of the 'Soul's dark Cottage' as a site from which past and future might be viewed without illusions, was clearly compatible with Hasluck's outlook. Judith Wright's book of poems from the same phase of her life, published when she was seventy, with similar intent, is called *Phantom Dwelling*.[27] In both of these books the poets have stripped their public egos and modes of address down towards bare, unadorned statement. The idea of stripping the personality of all extraneous trappings is epitomised in Hasluck's opening poem in the image of a mummy being unwrapped in Cairo:

What has survived?
Cracked flesh, dry bone, not even nakedness
And nothing of the vital shell
With which this shape began.

This poem offers an altogether bleaker vision than Dorothy Hewett's youthful romantic challenge to 'walk naked through the world'.[28] No person in Hasluck's kind of public life could show Hewett's kind of temerity and survive. Yet Hasluck's private inclination was towards that romantic world-view which values the *spirit* with which a person lives his or her life rather than their trappings or position.[29]

Hasluck's last poem in *Dark Cottage* restores hope for the unadorned self as the speaker pictures himself in his garden after reading Thomas Traherne's poetry, and echoes something of that English poet's style and sentiment:

Let no alien sound intrude
    Where clear skies bless
With fruitfulness, fulfilment and a mood
    Of happiness
The place that is my home.
    Apples as old as Eden
    Deep in Australian loam
        Burden the bough

Where noisily the parakeets return
    In coloured flight
And here I read Traherne.
    He and the Saxon Sheep are native now.
      This is my sacred site.

This closing declaration in the poem asserts quietly but firmly the writer's belief that the European Australian, like the Aborigine, can have his sacred sites.

That is not quite Hasluck's last word. Like A D Hope in his later years, Hasluck allowed a number of light-hearted spoofs in verse to be published in a pamphlet under the title *Crude Impieties*.[30] The sense of fun in these light verse exercises occasionally leads to a satiric point, but generally the sound of the words, their rhymes and rhythms are centre stage. In his poem 'An Inexact Comparison', Hasluck compares the achievements of two men in 1829, Felix Mendelssohn, who published a symphony, and James Stirling who founded a city. In his later years, Hasluck believed that art, especially music, was a more important achievement than the development of cities and wealth, as his concluding stanza indicates:

Now, tell me, Felix, what did you achieve?
    'I tossed some semi-quavers in the pond'.
And you?—Young Jimmy Stirling I believe.
    'I opened up the way for Alan Bond'.

From his early, intense experiments in verse, which enabled him to make the difficult transition from religion to art, to his later light-verse spoofs, Hasluck managed the difficulties of the double life with great dexterity. His record as a poet, together with his prose writings, across a variety of subjects and styles, establish him as the most developed literary intelligence in Australian political life since Alfred Deakin, and therefore a figure likely to endure in the Australian mind. It is interesting, in view of his later statements about the importance of poetry to the civilisation of Australia, that Hasluck did not publish his poetry while he was in the full glare of public life and that his two most important books, *Into the Desert* and *Dark Cottage* were self-published by the Freshwater Bay Press. Hasluck was fully aware of the capacity of journalists for ridicule and derision, and if he were to lay his heart bare, it would be where and when he wanted. Poetry, then, was a secret vice—and all the more satisfying, and revealing, for that.

Clive James, Humour and Empire

Since his arrival in London from Sydney in 1961 (ten years later than his decade-older friend and fellow writer Peter Porter) Clive James has travelled the world with astounding dash and has left records, not in bottles found on distant beaches but in hastily composed 'postcards' published in newspapers and then books by leading international publishers. The mood and manner are caught in *Flying Visits: Postcards from the Observer 1976–83*, which after appearing in the *Observer* were collected and published by Jonathan Cape in hardback in 1984 and by Picador in paperback in 1985. More rueful, less excitable than James, Porter writes in a poem called 'Anxiety's Air Miles'[1] of himself as a 'frequent flier' after he has 'ringed the globe five times'—a miniscule fraction of James's air travel. James's public life as writer, entertainer and television celebrity might indicate a less reflective persona than we find in Porter's work, but I suggest in this essay that James's range and volume of work does not preclude depth and that the humorous, wise-cracking persona is complemented by a more serious (but not earnest) self who has reflected on the rise and fall of empires, and their legacies.

While Clive James can be accurately presented as an all-rounder in the cricketing sense that he bats, bowls, keeps wickets and fields (often simultaneously), he himself prefers other sports for his metaphoric matrices, including surfing, skiing and racing cars. In later middle-age, he has sportingly learnt the tango. James's *literary* sports include essays, poems, plays, songs, novels and autobiography

together with theatre, television, radio and internet programs. In a
sense, his public life has been a non-stop festival of words. In his
65th year, there were few signs of diminution in the kind of energy
and ambition of earlier years. Perhaps he foresaw this period of his
life in an early rock lyric called 'Senior Citizens', which he wrote for
Pete Atkin. Here is one verse:

> And there'll be time to try it all:
> I'm sure the thrill will never pall
> The sand will take so long to fall
> The neck so slim, the glass so tall.[2]

Among the various genres that Clive James's restless persona has
inhabited are articles in newspapers and journals that most literary
academics would give their eye-teeth to appear in, including the *New
Yorker*, the *New York Review of Books*, the *London Review of Books*,
The Times Literary Supplement, the *Atlantic Monthly* and the *New
Statesman*. The books on which his reputation as a literary critic,
commentator and reviewer chiefly depend are *The Metropolitan Critic*
(1974), *At the Pillars of Hercules* (1979), *From the Land of Shadows*
(1982), *Snakecharmers in Texas* (1988), *The Dreaming Swimmer* (1992)
and *Even as We Speak* (2001). For many people, James is a television
talking-head or is remembered chiefly as the *Observer*'s most brilliant,
humorous and widely read television critic when he wrote there in
the 1970s and 1980s. His three volumes of autobiography beginning
with *Unreliable Memoirs* (1980) have increased his fame as a witty and
thoughtful raconteur of his own life. But James's literary critical
essays and reviews preceded his other work and he has returned to
this genre in recent years. His characteristic wit and humour is
sometimes tempered, sometimes sharpened in these writings, in the
service of a life-long attempt to understand empires and their
consequences.

James's typical approach is not through theory; rather, he gleans
knowledge and insight through the filter of opinion-making writers
and intellectuals who represent aspects of the culture and society
from which they have sprung. Such individuals include Gore Vidal,
Phillip Larkin, Alexander Solzhenitsyn and Les Murray, through
whose work James is able to explore both individual creativity and
significant aspects of America, Britain, the Soviet Union and
Australia respectively. In each of them, and in other writers, he sees
indications of the fate of nations, empires and human imagination.

In an essay called 'Unpatriotic Gore' James observes something Roman in his subject, Gore Vidal, and beyond the Roman empire the current American one which Vidal has so perceptively recognised and satirised:

> Even early on [says James], he was already a Roman—he was the knowing voice piercing the mist at the baths, ridiculing the hypocrisies of a stifling hegemony. As the hegemony crumbled into an age of transition, he became more recognizably a Roman figure than ever, viewing the anabases of the new Caesars with an unfoolable eye.[3]

James notes that Vidal has often been accurate in his prophecies: 'In 1968 he guessed Nixon would be the one. He knew that Kennedy's presidency was an irreversible disaster from the Bay of Pigs on ...'.[4] More recent work by Vidal continues his deft use of historical precedent to represent and analyse political events in the world's most powerful empire. That he is far more politically savvy than Clive James is not to James's detriment: few could match Vidal's political knowledge and insight.

What value could Phillip Larkin, the Englishman, have in consideration of empires? Many commentators and critics have used Larkin as the base from which to mount a criticism of the 'middle England' he seems to represent. But James is cleverer and more sensitive to the poetry than that. In his ironically titled essay 'Don Juan in Hull',[5] first published in *Encounter*, James locates his subject in 'the old mercantile civilisation which Larkin has been quietly celebrating most of his life, a civilisation in which a place like Leeds or Hull ... counts as a capital city'.[6] 'There is another and bigger life', James insists, 'but Larkin doesn't underestimate this one for a minute'.[7] What is implied rather than stated by James is that these cities were active mercantile centres in the empire machine. There is nothing triumphalist or condescending in James's recognition of the 'little England' of the mid-twentieth century that Larkin represents, or its reduced horizons. Rather, like Porter in 'Seaside Resort',[8] James finds a pleasing melancholy in the limited world-view of a departed empire into which Larkin draws his readers. And Larkin's sense of missing out, as Don Juan never did, in the sexual stakes is also one of James's recurrent comic modes. The provincial view is of course what James thought he chose to leave behind in Australia in the early 1960s to become a self-styled 'metropolitan critic'. Yet he is attracted for a time by the siren song of desperation he hears through the Larkin persona, which reminds him of Leopardi—'disconsolate yet doomed to being beautiful'.[9]

Clive James is not attracted with the same force as Peter Porter to 'deliquescent empires', such as Porter found in twentieth-century Vienna—the former centre of the Austro-Hungarian empire, now stripped of its possessions, and living on through the ghosts of its famous musicians, artists and thinkers.[10] Yet the two Australians living in London, now part of Europe—which until the 2003 war on Iraq had seemed to deny most present-day imperial pretensions—both seem attracted to the remains of empire in the form of artistic figures who flourished in its heyday.

When James thinks about Britain, his adoptive country, he is more likely than Porter to defend its institutions, especially the monarchy, as a bastion against the new American empire. This tendency is evident in an essay called 'The Queen in California', which reports for the *Observer* on Queen Elizabeth's visit to the centre of America's entertainment industry in 1983.[11] James presents himself as ironic chronicler of a Royal tour that was almost washed-out, both literally and figuratively. At one point in the essay James describes an 'entertainment' arranged by the American hosts:

> The Royals were seated with the British filmstar colony all along one side of a long table up on stage, like a Last Supper painted by Sir Joshua Reynolds. Before and below them stretched a sea of Americans all staring in their direction. It was a stiffening circumstance in which only Dudley Moore could possibly look cheerful, although Michael Caine was also trying hard.[12]

Like David Frost before him, James is drawn to fame and glitter, but a residual sense of proportion and balance asserts itself as he reports on this out-of-proportion entertainment of an upstart American empire:

> The Entertainment had elephantiasis, like the evening in general. When Hollywood gets beyond energy without taste, it arrives at taste without proportion. Perry [Como] ruffled his hair to prove that it really grew on top of his head, even if it had started its life somewhere else. 'You obviously do not adore me', Frank [Sinatra] sang at the Queen, who if she didn't nod her head, didn't shake it either. The big night out was a downer, but it wasn't her fault. They had put her on display.

In fact she had been had.

The evening was a pay-off for Ronald Reagan's financial backers, who would never have met the stars if the stars had not come to meet the Queen. Buckingham Palace had been hustled into bankrolling the next campaign wagon.[13]

The Queen is here given the role of dupe—a role played by many colonials through the history of empire. Pope's *Dunciad* ends with universal darkness: James here uses his virtuosic comic talents to describe the skies swamping his event with rain, washing away difference, and significance.

James's position is unusual. He is an admirer and defender of the monarchy and of the present Royal Family and has been so since his leading role in the Footlights Revue in Cambridge, where he prevented any sketches about Prince Charles, who was then an undergraduate at Cambridge.[14] Later, however, he wrote a mock epic verse play *Charles Charming's Challenges on the Pathway to the Throne* (1981), which also appeared as a double album featuring James himself, Pamela Stephenson and Russell Davies.[15] Despite Phillip Larkin's criticism of 'the corniness of his [James's] mocking the royals',[16] James's play was generally benign satire, with nothing like the savage attacks on Prince Charles by others in more recent years. James's subsequent espousal of the doomed marriage of Charles and Diana and his enthusiastic eulogy after her death revealed a recurrent strain of sentimentality in his nature.

A different kind of sentiment is evident in James's most successful novel, *The Silver Castle*, which is set in Bombay. The novel traces the rise of the protagonist Sanjay's fortunes from street child to Bollywood stunt-man and lover of a beautiful and famous film actress to his fall, both literal and metaphoric, back to the mean streets as a beggar. Sanjay's sentimental education is gained thanks to his luck, good looks and astute self-management on the fringes of India's commercially successful film industry. Lacking any formal education, Sanjay exercises his considerable native intelligence in learning to read and speak like the Bollywood magazines. James's parody of these magazines and the industry that spawns them never descends to contempt for the romantic dreams they express—what he calls 'the democracy of longing'. Bollywood is no evil Empire.

Despite the corruption and cruelty it embodies, the Indian film industry offers to the public an escape and a relatively harmless focus for daydreams and desire. The popular, commercial culture it represents is not denied by James. Rather, it demonstrates a way in which previous exploitation of India by the British Empire and by powerful Western moguls can be reversed. The computer software industry is another avenue. James's compassionate portrayal of his Candide figure, Sanjay, in contemporary India evokes both laughter and tears. In the end, James tries to look beyond a natural scepticism to a hope that 'the new free enterprise society' may begin to show a 'trickle-down effect' to the poor.

Clive James's political inclinations have been what his Marxist critics would call 'bourgeois', but they are not blancmange. Ian Britain has summarised:

> He has eschewed (at times trenchantly criticised) the extremes of the Thatcherite right, but he has also directed some of his most merciless satiric barbs at the British trade union and Labour party establishments ... Along with many other intellectuals disenchanted with Labour, James imagined he had found a political home for a while with the Social Democratic Party at the height of its short vogue in the early 1980s.[17]

James's promotion of democracy has modest rather than utopian aims. In his view, 'democracy is even more important for what it prevents than for what it provides'.[18] What it prevents, in short, is a totalitarian state.

Although seldom openly political in his public appearances, James's autobiographical remarks in the Introduction to *Even As We Speak* indicate his opposition to totalitarian rule and the evil empires it has spawned:

> The undoubted fact that democracy was currently making a murderous fool of itself couldn't make me forget that totalitarianism was still the enduring and implacable antagonist. I had opinions about what a democratic state should do in the circumstances—pull out of Vietnam, decommission the CIA, put Henry Kissinger on trial for sedition, stop subsidising the kind of dictators who exported their own economies to Switzerland—but it was part of my world view that a totalitarian view was unjustifiable in any circumstances.[19]

We can see something of James's own evolution to this world-view in his various considerations of Nazi Germany and the Soviet Union. In particular, the writings of Soviet dissidents such as

Solzhenitsyn, Mandelstam, and Zinoviev give form and detail to the horrors of Soviet suppression of the individual and convince James that the radical, left-wing views adopted by many opinion-makers in the universities were misguided. James is struck forcefully by his realisation of the radical conservatism of Solzhenitsyn's critique of the Russian revolution:

> Solzhenitsyn ... [traces] the Terror back to the revolution itself ... It is the overwhelming tendency of Solzhenitsyn's work to suggest that the Russian revolution should never have happened.[20]

In his early sixties, James attempted to summarise an approach he derived from Karl Popper whom he described as 'the great deconstructor of Karl Marx's scientific pretensions':

> For a hundred and fifty years, left-wing analysis retained the impetus of Christian revelation. Even after the Soviet Union, its holy land, showed clear signs of coming to pieces, the Marxist heritage retained its prestige. In the Soviet bloc nobody with any sense believed any of it—direct experience had done its work—but in the West there was still a reputation for frivolity to be earned by not paying it sufficient respect.[21]

If James seems something of the slow learner he accuses Australians generally of being when he turns to critiques of Soviet totalitarianism from as late as the 1980s, he nevertheless shows by then an impressive command of Soviet Russian literature and culture, including a reading knowledge of Russian. Moreover, it is difficult to dodge his charge that literary and cultural critics in the universities were even slower to recognise that much of the ideological framework which had sustained them had been proved moribund in practice. While James is right, in my view, to be scathing about the 'waves of pseudo-scientific dogma that had taken over humane studies in the universities, most damagingly in the English faculty', he is more controversial in his attempt to trace this 'vacuous theorizing' and 'obscurantism' back to 'the French left, an obscurantism whose origins could in turn be traced back to the period of the Occupation, when there had been shamefully good reasons for intellectuals to hatch an impersonal language by which history would take responsibility for what they said'.[22] A great deal better than a socialist paradise, he claims, is 'the bourgeois democracy so despised by both extremes', which 'proved, by its power to defend itself, that it was capitalism's natural host'.[23] At such moments, it seems, James gets unusually close to soapbox oratory, forgetting the critical obscurantism also emanating from the right of the political spectrum. Nevertheless, the middling position James occupies on the political spectrum is itself shown to be difficult and contested territory.

How does Australia enter and make its mark in James's international 'bourgeois democracy'? In part, James asserts that this will occur through literary figures such as the poet Les Murray, who gives readers and listeners a 'vernacular republic' within the world of letters. (It helps the case, of course, that one of Murray's books is called *The Vernacular Republic* (1982) and that James reviewed it glowingly in the *New York Review of Books* (14 April 1983).)[24] In James's commentary Murray plays the role of a large figure in a national allegory of a country which seems no longer inclined to 'go on accepting the status of a second-hand country'.[25] However much he might wish to call it something else, James expresses here a post-colonial status for the country of his birth. However, James is careful in his commentary to distance himself from Murray's wish for an actual Australian republic, suggesting that there is nothing 'unimaginative about a wish to keep the monarchist tradition'.[26] (Japan is invoked by James in passing as an example in the Asia–Pacific region of a continuing monarchy; he might have mentioned Thailand. But both are 'home-grown'—not continuations of the symbolism of a foreign empire. Supporters of the Australian Republican Movement, such as myself, can equally invoke the republics of India or Singapore.)

In James's dream-world of an empire of letters, outstanding imaginative writers and other culture-makers are given a status and value not accorded by the unregulated market-place. National broadcasters such as the ABC and BBC are necessary partners in this enterprise. But James wants to think about Australia in world terms. In a *Times Literary Supplement* article called 'Les Murray and his Master Spirits',[27] James praises Murray and his 'forefathers' represented in the *New Oxford Book of Australian Verse*, such as A D Hope, Judith Wright and Gwen Harwood, for playing their international role. 'A culture can never flourish', he asserts, 'as a hedge against the world. It isn't a bastion for nationalism, it is an international passport'.[28] James's is a serious and important voice in such essays, representing a sensible and informed point-of-view in the continuing struggle between local roots, provincialism and emerging patterns of globalisation.

That a new empire of letters is a dream does not deny its validity. James is interested in such dreams and the consequences they make possible. Behind the bluff suavity and witty one-liners, Clive James exhibits hints of what Ian Britain calls an 'awkward sage'.[29] A self-described 'cultural reactionary', he also promotes the intelligent consideration of popular culture and a critical attitude to certain powerful media czars such as Rupert Murdoch.[30] James's version of bourgeois democracy is a troubled brew but more to his taste than the available alternatives. Debate, difference and dissension within the bounds of rationality have their place on his menu; and it is interesting to find that his recent book of essays, *Even As We Speak*, is dedicated to contentious journalist Christopher Hitchens 'in affectionate disagreement'. Clive James's contribution to intelligent discussion of literary and cultural studies, and to the cause of literature in the world, keeps a sense of humour and proportion, while it wrestles with ideas and issues, and empires come and go.

'Nation' and Literary History

How is a nation known? By what its citizens eat? Or write? Or read? The question arises from a recent Japanese judgment that there is no such thing as an Australian cuisine. Although rescinded some days later, this judgment caused some journalistic pondering in Australia, where a food writer, Cherry Ripe, author of *Goodbye Culinary Cringe*,[1] made the following defences of Australian cooking:

> It's not the ingredients—indigenous or otherwise—that makes a cuisine. It's the way they are treated ...
>
> We have certainly developed a distinctive, Australian style in our food which has nothing to do with lamingtons or Vegemite, meat pies or sausage rolls, pavlova or peach Melba. We have potentially the most exciting and eclectic cuisine in the world developing here, one that borrows from everywhere ... Australian cuisine is defined by its very eclecticism.[2]

Against the 'purist' who insists that it takes at least 100 years for a cuisine to develop, and that it has to grow out of a 'peasant and agrarian base', the Sydney metropolitan modern woman whom Cherry Ripe represents, contends that there is an identifiable Australian style. Although she argues elsewhere for 'bush tucker' and kangaroo on the menu, her case for a national cuisine is positively post-colonial:

The one thing we do that is substantially different from the rest of
the (Western) world is the degree of incorporation of Asian
ingredients into our food.[3]

I want to suggest here that the making of a national literary history
also involves cooking up a variety of menus which demonstrate
something of the range, style and characteristics of a country's
artists and their artworks made from a variety of borrowed
materials. The ingredients in which most literary historians are
interested are of course words and their use in a variety of generic
dishes. Moreover, literary history involves nothing less than the
history and geography of word-menus that have been created over
the years presented in the contexts of their production and
reception.

But every metaphor has its limitations. Let me turn to questions
of nation and nationalism in the late twentieth century, which lie at
the heart of most accounts of literary history. The most damning
recent critiques of the idea of the nation and nationalism have come
from Europe, and no wonder. Utopian expectations of a unified
European community were rent asunder by events in Yugoslavia
and elsewhere. The reinstated nations of the former Soviet Empire
have assumed a more positive aura in some (Western) European
eyes. But the identification of nationalism with ethnicity in the
former Yugoslavia, as well as in Rwanda, deeply damaged the idea
of the modern nation state. In spite of this, the southern
hemisphere, in particular the Asia–Pacific region, provides many
positive (if embryonic) examples of Benedict Anderson's concept
of nations as 'imagined communities'[4] which are attempting to
bring together ethnically diverse people. Like Simon During, I find
myself more comfortable with the idea of Australia as a nation
when we have a defensive rather than an offensive cultural posture.[5]
Furthermore, Australia's increasing political and economic alliances
with countries of the Indo-Asia–Pacific should lead us to a broader
recognition of the different expectations in different countries of
centralised control in pursuit of cultural cohesion and individual
freedom. Australia's important but hazardous relationship with
Indonesia is a case in point: however strongly Australians (including
myself) may feel about individual human rights and censorship, it is
difficult to deny the Indonesian desire for national cohesion in their
post-Dutch period of national reconstruction. Australia's well-

justified support for the independence of East Timor should not blur this recognition. At the same time, we are told that a burgeoning middle-class in Indonesia will create demands for less state control, more individual freedom and imaginative licence.

Because concepts of nationality underlie every national literary history, I want to suggest something of their changing character in Australia and to show why they pose one of the most difficult challenges for a literary historian. An external perspective on Australia is given by Wang Gungwu, former Vice-Chancellor of the University of Hong Kong and a Malaysian-born Australian citizen. Of Australia's changing identity in Asia, Professor Wang Gungwu says this:

> What may emerge as the basis of Australian national identity is a consensus that Australia is not part of Asia, nor Europe, nor America, but a country with some of the best modern features of these three continents.[6]

Wang's image of Australia is of a principally migrant society emerging in post-industrial times with a strong British heritage expressed in its being the fourth English-language state in the world after Britain, the USA and Canada. Although post-colonial theory may suggest a lower-case 'e' English language as the proper way to epitomise the world's variety of distinct 'englishes', this Asian perspective suggests an important identification of Australia as a migrant country with a comparative *advantage* in the emergent world language called English. In this context, Australia's links with the British Empire until the 1950s and the USA since the 1960s have led to an enhanced position in the eyes of non-English speakers in the Indo-Asia–Pacific region.

Wang Gungwu's perspective on Australia is one view. Within Australia, the debates between constitutional monarchists and would-be republicans (of whom I am one) indicate the continuing uncertainties about Australia's emergent nationality. Do these movements have implications for the writing of literary history? A purist approach to literary history, which focussed entirely on literary formalism, would not be affected. At the other extreme, a politically activist history might choose literary exampla towards the polemical goal of converting its readers to a republican or some other kind of Australia. My preference between these extremes is definitely 'impure' (i.e. it admits social and political events and ideas as part of the account). However, the direction is not towards a narrow polemicism but towards an illumination of the active role literary texts can play in the propagation of ideas, thoughts, desires and feelings in the public domain. In addition, literary texts contribute to aesthetic appreciation; they can be considered as 'works of art', though without the mystique that used to attach to that phrase. Clearly, in this view, literary texts are more than mere illustrations of general history, though they can exemplify or throw light on the inner logic (or illogic) of events such as wars and conquests or emergent social movements. They can also influence cultural developments such as a country's changing ethnic composition or its neglect of the physical environment, though the complexity of literary texts should normally prevent their being easily subsumed in such thematic summaries.

In his book *Is Literary History Possible?* David Perkins remarks that a function of many literary histories has been to 'support feelings of community and identity'[7] and I consider this to be a valid goal, among others. More recently, however, the structural motif of critique and conflict, or dissensus, has prevailed in Western literary historiography, including Sacvan Bercovitch's *Cambridge History of American Literature*.[8] 'Dissensus may yield a rich harvest', Bercovitch asserts in his preface to *Reconstructing American Literary History*[9] and the contributions to the first two volumes of his eight-volume history show some of the fruits of this approach. Regrettably however, some of the long chapters in Bercovitch's first volume often seem more self-reflexively concerned with their theoretical positioning than with texts and events. Their problem might be termed 'theory-dependancy', which can itself be historically located and explained. However, if this is a necessary phase in the development of literary historiography, I hope that the sophisticated self-questioning of such volumes will lead to breakthroughs wherein briefer, more incisive and widely comprehensible (though not populist) histories may be written.

The most important single challenge to the writing of national literary histories in our time, I believe, is presented by Edward Said's *Orientalism*.[10] Said's theory that Western Europe has constructed an East, or Orient, in order to dominate and control it is as potent a theory in literary and cultural studies as Freud's theory of repression or Piaget's stages of development have been in the fields of psychology and education respectively. We see evidence of this almost paradigmatic theory used (and abused) in essays and theses everywhere. A recent PhD thesis by a Chinese student at an Australian university, however, successfully negotiated and qualified the theory in examining the representation of Chinese people in Australian literature.[11] More difficult to assess is Xiamei Chen's essay in *Critical Inquiry*, in which she explains the use of Occidentalism as a counter discourse in China in the post-Mao years.[12] She argues that:

> [I]n China—and perhaps elsewhere—Orientalism, or the Western construction of the Orient, has been accompanied by instances of what might be termed Occidentalism, a discursive practice that, by constructing its Western Other, has allowed the Orient to participate actively and with indigenous creativity in the process of self-appropriation, even after being appreciated and constructed by Western Others.[13]

She contends that Chinese Occidentalism has served a quite different function from that of Orientalism:

> Orientalism, in Said's account, is a strategy of Western world domination, whereas ... Chinese Occidentalism is primarily a discourse that has been evoked by various and competing groups within Chinese society for a variety of different ends, largely, though not exclusively, within domestic Chinese politics. As such, it has been both a discourse of oppression and a discourse of liberation.[14]

A sign of the potency of Said's landmark study of colonialism is that it is being applied to contexts as different as those of Australia and China, when its principal motive power was the liberation of Palestine and other countries of the so-called Middle East. Like Freud's idea of repression, Said's theory of Orientalism has taken hold of the popular imagination. Yet the danger of a powerful theory—by Freud, Piaget or Said—is that it may override individual, national or regional contexts, thereby rendering them impotent and insignificant. This is the basis of the anthropological case against Said.

As Bill Ashcroft, Gareth Griffiths and Helen Tiffin have noted in *The Empire Writes Back*,[15] it is possible to extrapolate from Said's geographical entities, the Occident and the Orient, to the theory that 'all post-colonial societies realise their identity in difference rather then in essence'.[16] According to this extrapolation, all post-colonial societies are 'constituted by their difference from the metropolitan and it is in this relationship that identity both as a distancing from the centre and as a means of self-assertion comes into being'.[17] Here then is the major challenge thrown out by post-colonial theory to the writers of national literary history. Essentialism—the search for essences of nationality—is 'out'. But what is 'in'? Assuming the validity of the enterprise of constructing the literary history of a nation, the major challenge of a post-colonial perspective seems to be towards a comparative approach rather than a principally inward, ethnocentric or nationalistic approach. The second challenge of post-colonial theory for the practice of national literary history is its emphasis on relations of power between a nation and its imperial metropolis. I also believe a major challenge is to develop viable and effectively grounded sets of comparative literary studies among the 'new' or 'post-colonial' cultures.

But the literary historiography of individual modern nation-states also contains challenges for post-colonial theory and practice. In the first place, national literary histories are generally written by inhabitants of the countries concerned, though there are some notable exceptions such as Europeans like Albert Gerard[18] on Africa and Americans such as Mary Bresnahan[19] on the Philippines. The perils of an imperialist viewpoint in such accounts are obvious. On the other hand, an internal nationalist account of literary history might be too narrowly focussed to provide modern readers with the international perspective they may desire. Aware of this problem, Bob Hodge and Vijay Mishra, co-authors of *Dark Side of The Dream: Australian Literature and the Postcolonial Mind* assert that their reading of Australian culture as 'paranoiac' is not one from outside but within: 'outside and above', they aver, 'is not where we wish to be'.[20]

The question of vantage point, or writing position, is raised in different ways in literary historical studies of the Philippines. Vicente Rafael, on the one hand, accepts nationalism, in Benedict Anderson's terms, as a cultural artefact rather than as an essential quality and examines the formative period of Filipino nationalism in the late nineteenth century as 'inherently complicated, caught between dynastic/colonial modes of apprehension on the one hand and the possibilities of an egalitarian, post-colonial existence on the other'.[21] His study of nationalist representations in 'textualised embodiments of the motherland and the photographed bodies of male patriots' reveals critical problems and tensions in the nationalist project. Rafael's standpoint is that of an expatriate at the University of California, San Diego. From another perspective, E San Juan examines modern Philippine writing and strongly endorses Filipino nationalism as a counter to the domination of US economic and cultural imperialism.[22]

In San Juan's view, US colonialism harnesses the educational system, and especially the use of English in the Philippines as vehicles of 'benevolent assimilation'.[23] English became 'the wedge that separated the Filipinos from their past and later was to separate educated Filipinos from the masses of their countrymen'.[24] According to this interpretation, the Filipino is 'Americanized through language' and internalises a 'decorum of submission'.[25] Thus, to use Deleuze and Guattari, the sign becomes the site of 'deterritorialization'.[26]

So far, this reading may seem readily adaptable to standard post-colonial analysis, dependent on the paradigms of Said (early and late), *The Empire Writes Back* and the author's Marxist standpoint. However, in the later stages of his essay San Juan turns to attack the outlook and methods of *The Empire Writes Back* for failing to give due scope to national liberation movements and ideologies. He resists deconstruction and argues for reconstruction or nation-building. While agreeing with the basic post-colonial theory of a dialectical relationship between metropolitan and peripheral cultures and the impossibility of recuperating 'an absolute pre-colonial cultural purity'[27] he nevertheless disagrees with 'the corollary belief that it is impossible to create a national formation geared to realizing autonomy within the given hegemonic global system'.[28] Whether through mimetic or allegorical modes, San Juan argues that the quest for national autonomy 'seems inescapable'.[29] 'It is not enough', he adds, 'simply to multiply ingenious deconstructive rereadings of rewritings of the European or American historical and fictional records'.[30] To do so, he contends, 'in the guise of unsolicited "friendly" advice' is to resurrect 'the imperial hubris of Western logocentrism and powers'.[31] 'Post-colonial syncretism' of this kind is far less amenable to San Juan than 'a textual practice of national liberation'. The mythic basis on which his case rests is the quest for freedom and independence.

The myths, or master-narratives, that inform literary history require closer investigation, perhaps even interrogation (though not necessarily in the sense implied by the view that the post–second world war American academy was dominated by counter-intelligence values and methods).[32] Some myths may be exposed, questioned and even deconstructed without being destroyed. I believe this is the outcome, for example, when Robert Lecker unpacks Northrop Frye's concluding essay in the latter's *Literary History of Canada* and discovers in it 'a quest for the peaceable kingdom':[33]

> Only by evoking a pastoral myth can Frye approach the true object of his quest—an ending that finds human beings not exiled from the garden and at odds with their world but nursing the peaceable kingdom that Frye has been seeking.[34]

Lecker's interrogation of this mythic underpinning of Frye's conclusion to the *Literary History of Canada* draws attention to what the pastoral vision denies in Canadian literature and history: garrison mentalities, and themes of isolation, survival and national identity. Most significantly, perhaps, it indicates a romance narrative of Canada, 'a metaphoric conception that is transhistorical, autonomous and distinctly literary before it is cultural'.[35] What is needed, perhaps, is not so much a dismantling of such myths as a comparative placing of them in relation to other equally validly induced mythic constructions. In Australia, the special challenge of our time is to allow an interplay of Asian with Australian myths. Lloyd Fernando has remarked: 'We should ... take more account of the alternative artistic conventions and mythologies found in Asia and bring them into complementary relationships with those so thoroughly explicated in the West'.[36]

The challenge for me, as a contract builder of Australia's national literary history, is to steer a course between my desire for a strong and relatively independent Australian culture with the recognition of intertextuality and interdependence. I am happy to begin with a local and national perspective and declare the position from which I write as an Australian. At the same time, I must try to recognise the scope of this imagined community with all its regional and multi-cultural variations. But I prefer this task, this search for community in my country to the ungrounded discourse that sometimes characterises post-colonial and post-modernist modes of writing. As Ann Paolucci has pointed out, 'the egocentricity of individual national literatures and cultures is perfectly understandable'.[37] Indeed, the practice of Paolucci's *Review of National Literatures* recognises that an historical understanding of national literatures is the necessary foundation of meaningful comparative studies. There is a need, she asserts, for literatures as 'national voices, expressing distinct cultural identities'.[38] This she describes as the 'vertical' dimension, represented in the American academy by area studies specialists. The 'comparatists' (a word which does not appear in the *Macquarie Dictionary of Australian English*) provide a 'horizontal' dimension which they weave into the 'vertical cultural mosaic'.[39] Cooperation between comparatists and area specialists is crucial in development towards the goal of 'a totally new configuration of comparative studies, synthetic overview of cultural units and their national/political roots'.[40]

I see something of this kind of fruitful development in Diana Brydon and Helen Tiffin's co-authored book *Decolonising Fictions*,[41] which compares aspects of the literatures in English of Australia, Canada and the West Indies. Instead of an apparently random discussion of many texts from many contexts, *Decolonising Fictions* grounds its discussion of a limited number of selected texts in significantly detailed contexts. However, because this book by Brydon and Tiffin was published by a small, non-metropolitan press (Dangaroo) its impact has been far less noticeable than *The Empire Writes Back* or other books published in London, Paris or New York. Thus, although certain texts may be demonstrated to be subversive and restitutive (and therefore post-colonial) in a well-grounded set of comparative readings, the impact of these readings and their influence remains severely circumscribed by the mode and place of publication. The pattern of colonial domination whereby colonial authors gained their authority by conversing with each other and their audiences chiefly through the metropolis seems in these instances to be repeated, though I do not want to suggest that local and regional publishing have failed entirely to build a clientele and networks whereby native views and expectations are aired. Moreover, multi-national publishing companies such as Oxford, Cambridge and Penguin are usually strongly based in their host countries. Nevertheless, the pressures towards cultural deracination through international publishing practice remain strong.

Where then does this leave the enterprise of national literary history-making? In my view, the main value of comparative (national) literary studies is not just that they lift the sights beyond mere ego- or ethno-centricity, or that they excite international curiosity, but that they provide in-depth insights into the nature and quality of one's personal and national self-interests. National and personal self-interest should not be obliterated but recognised as natural and built upon, developed, made responsive to international conditions.

Can the literary culture be left alone in these circumstances? Literary nationalists, like their economic nationalist allies, are interferers and resisters, contesting the notion that the market will automatically self-correct and produce the best 'rational' outcomes if left alone. Nor is this analogy with economic history merely theoretical. The literary and cultural history of a nation such as Australia cannot turn away from economics and politics: it must, for example, acknowledge that Prime Minister Menzies in the 1950s and 1960s thought it would be disloyal to Britain and Empire to have a national arts-funding body and that it was only after Menzies retired that a national Council for the Arts was set up. The hangovers of colonialism remain factors for consideration in modern Australia; and the impact of 'economic rationalists' (and nationalists) on literary culture must be watched closely.

A national literary history should never be an entirely 'inward' story. Even its account of formalist concerns, such as the changing uses of certain genres, will exhibit societal preoccupations (e.g. in the cases of the lyric, satire or social realist fiction). National patterns which reflect or resist international fashions will be revealed. The re-drawing of boundaries in the professional study of literature has increasingly emphasised the socio-political contours of criticism and theory. A national literary history should provide 'windows onto worlds'.[42] But the analysis of cross-winds and currents of ideas, beliefs and ideologies is the glamorous end of literary historiography. Australia is not the only country with a history of colonial settlement in which large amounts of bibliographical and empirically based scholarship remain to be done. Certainly in Australia, more bibliographical studies, scholarly textual editing and literary biographies need to be researched and written to further strengthen the foundations of literary historical scholarship.

Glimpses of India

My first sighting of India was during a day in Bombay off the P&O liner 'Himalaya' on my way through the Suez Canal to study in Oxford, England, in 1964. Previously, my only travel 'overseas' from my base in Perth had been to the island of Rottnest off the West Australian coast. Colombo, and then Bombay, were thus potentially momentous experiences, my first foreign countries, my Himalayan adventures, my entry to Asia. In retrospect, what I saw was framed by my mode of travel and its purpose. I was travelling on a Rhodes scholarship to the heart of the Empire which had made such scholarships possible just as that Empire was dissolving into a decentred commonwealth and Britain was turning its eyes towards Europe. Unlike Christopher Koch, whose protagonist in his second novel *Across the Sea Wall* leaves the ship and travels through India with his lover, I was restricted to the tourist's itinerary. Like Nicholas Hasluck, with whom I shared a cabin from Fremantle to Port Said (not knowing that he was storing images for his Kafka-esque novel *Quarantine*), I remained largely isolated from the countries we travelled through.

The first Indians I encountered on my 'Himalayan' expedition were the immaculately dressed stewards. During my single day in Bombay I saw hundreds of thousands of that city's citizens in their *dhotis*, protected from the pelting monsoon rains by black umbrellas. In the midst of crowds at which, as a West Australian brought up with space as his principal inheritance, I was amazed at the capacity of Bombay street people to block out the noise and bustle and find a place to rest and even to sleep. The other deeply etched image is of the Towers of Silence where vultures hovered above the walled courtyards while waiting to pick clean the bodies brought to them on stretchers by white-clad attendants. Together, these images contributed to a highly selective impression of India as an exotic place largely untouched by the Anglo-Saxon Empire. (I did not then look closely at the Victorian architecture of parts of Bombay). Subsequent meetings with Indian postgraduate students in Oxford modified these views towards a somewhat more complicated sense of India's history and role in the post-colonial world but, like first love, these exotic first images of a foreign country remain.

My gradually developing sense of India accumulated, at first, from people I met, writings and media images rather than direct experience. Such images often came via London and the publishing houses which have 'served' (and been served by) Australians and Indians. A West Australian poet, Alec Choate, sums up one strong tendency, that of idealising India, as he presents himself reflecting on a statue of Mahatma Gandhi in Tavistock Square, London:

> I never saw you, the living man,
> But standing before your statue in Tavistock Square,
> I can believe that bronze breathes, that you are here,
> And were you not withdrawn in meditation,
> Even believe your lips could speak a prayer
> Or ask me who I am to stare at you.[1]

Although this image of one of the world's great statesmen and teachers is situated in London, the poet's recognisably Australian voice is modest, un-imperial: the statue of Gandhi is 'A nonchalant but wistful reminder/Of my own small way to live'.

Other less flattering images of Indians have been transmitted to Australians by British comedians—especially by Peter Sellers—in their satiric renditions of Indian English. However, the Indian poet Nissim Ezekiel has also ridiculed the imitation of British accents and manners, and far more effectively from an insider's perspective in his poem 'Goodbye Party for Miss Pushpa T.S.':

> Miss Pushpa is coming
> from very high family.

Her father was renowned advocate
in Bulsar or Surat,
I am not remembering now which place.

Surat? Ah, yes
once only I stayed in Surat
with family members
of my uncle's very old friend—
his wife was cooking nicely ...
that was long time ago.[2]

Because Australian accents also have a history of (not always affectionate) ridicule on British stage and screen, the burlesques of Indian divergences from southeast England standard forms have probably had a minimal impact in Australia except insofar as some Australians thought Indians were determined to imitate 'posh' English. As Australians, we knew we were 'off key', and some of us were keen to make a virtue of this fact. (My brothers had told me that if I returned to Australia with a 'pommie' accent they would not let me back in the house.)

My only personal encounter with Salman Rushdie was at the Adelaide Arts Festival in 1984, some five years before the *fatwa* directed against him. After hearing Rushdie talk on literature and history (his chief subject of study at university) I was invited to a party for him in North Adelaide. When I arrived I heard two raised voices at the far end of the room, both speaking in identical 'posh' English voices. The speakers' backs were turned to me. Their subject was Rugby—the school not the sport—where both the pin-striped lawyer from North Adelaide and his companion with an identical accent had been educated. On closer inspection, I discovered the companion was Salman Rushdie. The subject under discussion was the cadet corps at Rugby, which the Adelaide lawyer averred had made him the man he was. More quietly but no less certainly, Rushdie explained how he had refused to enter the cadet corps, which may have contributed to the sort of person he was.

Between the extremes of idealisation and ridicule lies the mystery of cricket. An avid follower of this true believers' game, I have never been quite as impressed with the huge run-gathering capacity of Sachin Tendulkar or Sunil Gavaskar or the all-round abilities of Kapil Dev (though I admire them greatly) as with the uncanny skills of Indian spinners such as Bishen Bedi and Erapalli Prasanna. In spite of living in the age of the sceptical Edward Said, I am still influenced by Orientalist preconceptions of the magicians of that exotic India where, in spite of lexicographers' ignorance, the googly must have been invented. (This perception of India as the home of spinners has been altered somewhat in recent years with the emergence of an Australian magician of spin, Shane Warne, but it remains a powerful image.)

Exotic India has appeared in Australia in many guises. Australia's major poet of the inter-war period, Kenneth Slessor, drew on William Hickey's eighteenth-century Indian memoirs for his poem 'The Nabob':

> Sometimes, by moonlight, in a barge he'll float
> Whilst hirelings blow their skulking flageolets
> Served by a Rajah in a golden coat
> With pigeon pie ... Madeira ... and Madeira ...[3]

Such images were also reproduced at a popular cultural level through advertisements for food products and recipes. Indeed, Beverley Kingston has suggested that:

> For most Australians ... India meant exotic courts or international exhibitions, occasional reports of grand imperial gatherings illustrated by gorgeously decorated elephants or howdahs, or dark-eyed beauties in saris—visions which were echoed on their packets of tea and curry powder.[4]

Nevertheless, as Beverley Kingston has observed, a defining quality of Indian tea from the 1870s was that it was produced 'under British supervision'.[5] The supervisory role of Britain over Australians' perceptions of India is everywhere evident until well after Independence.

Polonius suggested to Hamlet that he should 'by indirections find directions out'. After my return to Australia in the late 1960s, my few glimpses of India were decidedly indirect, through conversations with members of what would now be called an Indian diaspora. The earliest of these diasporic Indians whose lives began to intersect with mine were Singaporeans Edwin Thumboo and Kirpal Singh. Together and separately, we arranged seminars, conferences and visits in Australia and Singapore. Images and voices of Edwin Thumboo's father and members of his family, who had migrated to Singapore from southern India, have emerged hauntingly from his poetry. In his poem 'The Immigrant', an iconic figure based on his Indian father is evoked:

> Days and Indian days stretch
> Beyond the grasping of his hands,
> That were the hoe, the sickle in the sun.
> Though his body sweated into fields,
> The seeds kept cruel silence ...
>
> He heard of a place
> of padi, coconut, monsoons,
> Toddy and regular wages,
> Where the jungle was being dismantled.
>
> After that year of summers
> He came.[6]

In 'Grand Uncles: Kang to Sinnathamby at Monk's Hill Terrace', Thumboo recreates in memory the dialogue that is possible between Indian and Chinese in Singapore. In 'Little India', he reinforces the value of the Indian part of his dual inheritance in the new island home and tries to regenerate an ideal beyond the tourist-label reality. He encourages his contemporaries to learn to remember, in the spirit of their communal forebears, the way the gods:

> ... incarnate, diffuse among men, as Rama
> journeys south, as clans refurbish duty for that great
> upheaval, gather at Kurukshetra to purify the Dharma.
>
> *'I am the cycle of the year*
> *which generates everything and dissolves it.*[7]

Other talented writers of the Indian diaspora have also given me glimpses of India transplanted. They include K S Maniam in Malaysia and Satendra Nandan, formerly of Fiji, now of Australia. Maniam's powerful novel, *The Return*, gives vivid impressions of the narrator Ravi's experiences in an Indian immigrant community in Peninsula Malaysia, as he attempts to adapt classical Hindu virtues to contemporary circumstances. The novel is a finely evoked parable of linguistic and moral survival and the mixed fortunes that such survival brings.

Satendra Nandan's first novel, *The Wounded Sea*, evokes a brutal separation from his homeland Fiji following the political coup of 1987, in which Nandan himself, as a Minister in the Bavadra Labour

Government, was ousted from power and gaoled. He later sought
and found refuge as a political exile in Australia. Satendra's voice,
with its strong, continuing commitment to the virtues of Indian
culture and international standards of morality, has been one of the
pleasant compensations of my own less traumatic yet difficult
transplantation from Perth on Australia's West coast to Canberra in
1993. A strong affiliation to Fiji as 'home' for Satendra Nandan is
complemented by his sense of an Indian inheritance and a growing
attachment to Australia. At one of the annual Asia–Pacific literary
seminars which Edwin Thumboo and I initiated and which have
been held alternately in Australia and Singapore since 1982, Nandan
suggested that the stories of the *Mahabharata* and the *Ramayana* may
have been too strongly imposed on his immigrant community in
Fiji, with the result that 'we failed to see the holiness of the Nandi,
the river on whose banks I grew up, because we were so obsessed
with the sanctity of the waters of the Ganges'.[8] Nandan's story is a
parable of the danger of immigrant communities living too long
exclusively in their ethnic and cultural past.

Nevertheless, the *Mahabharata* clearly has its uses in Australia as
elsewhere. As Nandan pointed out, the game of cricket may be seen
as a struggle between the Devas and the Asuras. Responding
perhaps to the awe of Australians such as myself at the magic of
Indian spin bowlers, he added:

> Then the cunning spinner comes in; he is an even more wily demon
> (than the fast-bowling Asura) and his weaponry includes leg breaks
> and off breaks, cutters and even the mysterious googly of a
> Ganguly.[9]

Satendra Nandan's humorous evocation of Indian mythology
evokes the paradoxical triumph of India's master narratives in
different cultural situations.

The glimpses of India offered to contemporary Australians have
come from a variety of sources. During the 'liberation wars' of
middle-class Western cultures in the 1970s and 1980s, for instance,
the Rajneesh movement, with headquarters in Poona (Pune),
presented some Australians with the image of India as a source of
spiritual regeneration allied with sexual freedom. (The 'Orange
People', as they were called, were allegedly stronger in the more
'unbuttoned' cities of Perth and Sydney than in colder Melbourne
or Canberra.) Before the movement's leader, Bhagwan, was totally

discredited, expatriate Australian writer and television critic Clive James had dubbed him 'Bagwash'. If the Bhagwan's 'wisdom' was revealed as a cruel hoax too rapidly endorsed by gullible Westerners, he revived in some Australian minds the image of Godbole in E M Forster's novel *A Passage to India*, in whose figure the boundaries between wise man and fool (as in Shakespeare's comedies) become notoriously fluid. We felt on firmer ground, perhaps, with the films of Satyajit Ray culminating in *The World of Apu*, in which the classic emotions of joy, pity and despair seemed to transcend the conditions of Bengal village life and the slums of Calcutta to attune us to a universal order.

Because my profession weds me to words, most of my vicarious insights into India, until I travelled there in the late 1990s, came from English-speaking writers and academics, some of whom visited Australia. I had the privilege of meeting celebrated Indian writers including Kamala Das, Nissim Ezekiel, Eunice de Souza, Nayantara Sahgal and Vikram Seth in Australia. Through the good offices of Australia's leading Indian literature specialist and advocate, Syd Harrex of Flinders University, and others, I also met some leading Indian academics. The outstanding figure among these was C D Narasimhaiah, known as 'CD' before and after the advent of compact discs. 'CD' was synonymous with the wit and wisdom of India in the field of Commonwealth literary studies, a field in great need of a comprehensive intelligence. More of CD later. There were others I was pleased to meet too, including Shiv K Kumar, Chaman Nahal, Alur Janakiram, R P Rama and R K Dhawan. During an extended research visit to the Centre for Studies in Australian Literature at the University of Western Australia in 1986, Alur Janakiram, Professor of English at the University of Rajasthan in Jaipur, collaborated with me on a project to produce a teaching anthology of Indian and Australian short fiction which was subsequently published in India.[10]

A different kind of memorial was bequeathed by novelist, poet and travel writer Vikram Seth, who took part in a symposium in Perth on the construction and prevalence of *Myths, Heroes and Anti-Heroes* in countries of the Indo-Asia–Pacific region. I have vivid memories of the pocket-sized, mercurial Seth meeting his former teacher from the Doon School in Delhi, Satendra Nandan, and of a picnic at a Swan Valley vineyard, after which we stopped at the upper reaches of the Swan River while Vikram stripped down, plunged in and negotiated these only occasionally shark-raided waters with the adaptive ease of an otter. A young man of many parts, Vikram Seth participated in lectures, readings, and debates in the seductively allegorical Fox Lecture Theatre at the University of Western Australia, but his memorial to this first visit to Australia was a fable of absence:

> They're lecturing at the Fox; the speaker is in tears:
> 'Let me defer my talk; I'll wait till Seth appears.
> He can't have gone too far.' True; but he's too far gone
> Here on the springy grass beside the River Swan.[11]

An earlier symposium at the University of Western Australia in 1987 explored the theme of exile in literatures and cultures of the Asia–Pacific region. Our view was that a sense of exile rather than a sense of being 'settled' or 'at home' was a cultural characteristic which Australians shared with inhabitants of many other countries of the region. There were many fine contributions to this theme and the book from this conference, *A Sense of Exile*[12] received the accolade of the English Association in Britain and was translated into *Bahasa Melayu*. The keynote address at this symposium entitled 'Exile of the Mind' was given by Meenakshi Mukherjee, then Professor of English at Jawaharlal Nehru University, New Delhi and the author of two exemplary works of literary history, *The Twice Born Fiction* and *Realism and Reality: Novel and Society in India*. Meenakshi spoke with authority and conviction of the ways in which an education dominated by a colonial power can result in a double alienation of the local student or writer from the native culture: first by erasing the local language and situation and second by imposing selective elements of the dominant metropolitan culture on the local situation. She raised important questions for Australia and Australians as well as for other colonised countries of the world, concluding that nevertheless 'the exile of the mind may be a profitable strategy for claiming a share in the global culture and delinking oneself from the intransigence and specificity of history.[13] International exchanges of views and ideas should be fresh, original and challenging. All of these criteria were met for me in C D Narasimhaiah's approach to the question of exile. Characteristically, and in defiance of fashionable opinion, he took a comprehensive view of the state of exile:

Both world history and world literature lend support to the view that man lives in perpetual exile—exile from home, community, country, race, from God and sometimes from himself too. In its many variations exile has dominated the writer's thinking in different cultures in different ways, so much so that it has acquired the compulsion of an archetypal truth. In popular use, however, it carries intimations of being banished, alienated, uprooted, disembowelled and in all cases of being deprived and dispossessed. Hence Buddha's lament that the mass of mankind were like fish in a pond which was drying up.

   In the main tradition of India the term has gathered around it a positive tone ...[14]

This perspective enabled CD to speak of the 'gifts of exile'. He argued, with examples from Indian and other literatures that 'time out' in a separate place from one's native country or region may give scope for detachment and a transcending of 'the egocentric predicament of man':

   If exiled lovers live in separation and pine for each other in Kalidasa's *Cloud Messenger* in the manner of the early Romantic comedies of Shakespeare like *Twelfth Night* and *As You Like It*, in his mature play *Sakuntala* over which Goethe went into raptures, the lovers attain a ripeness and even practical wisdom like Prospero in *The Tempest* which is often compared by scholars with *Sakuntala*. To invoke yet another source, Yeats's 'Byzantium' poems may also be cited in support of the theme of exile making for transcendence of 'the fury and mire of human veins'.[15]

This was vintage Narasimhaiah. Taking a humorous sideswipe at Forster and giving a pat on the back to the often maligned Kipling, CD considered notions of exile in writings by Nehru, R K Narayan and Raja Rao before bringing his elegant essay to a close with a consideration of Nayantara Sahgal's novel *Plans for Departure* (1986). His discussion turned on the Danish heroine's temporary 'exile' in India which gave her an expansion of spirit. As a result, she realises that 'there was nowhere she indelibly belonged'.

   The vision of one world may be a distant dream, as C D Narasimhaiah remarked, but he endorsed Nayantara Sahgal's heroine's view that 'we can't even hope for things we can't imagine'. That is the kind of mind and imagination-stretching India to which CD and other Indian writers and thinkers introduced me. I always hoped to go there some day. And later I did.

Inner Landscapes: Peter Porter's Later Poetry

Peter Porter, along with Les Murray, is Australia's most eminent practising poet. But because Porter left Australia for England in the early 1950s, his work has been less closely associated than Murray's with the country he was born in, and his reputation has consequently been split between his adoptive and native countries. Australian reviewers and critics have often expressed ambivalence about his place in Australian literature, in some cases because of Porter's own uncertainties about the country he was born in, and perhaps also because he could not be 'owned' as other 'home-grown' writers apparently could. I have argued elsewhere, in *Spirit in Exile: Peter Porter and his Poetry*, that a sense of exile pervades Porter's life and work, and that this has made him a difficult figure to locate in any nationalist ideology.

Yet since his first return to Australia in 1974, two decades after his departure in the early 1950s, Porter has rediscovered an intense and enduring interest in Australian culture, politics, and society, which his poetry reflects. He has edited *The Oxford Book of Modern Australian Verse* (1996) and has been a mentor, model, and facilitator for many younger Australian writers.

Porter's 'later' poetry is defined here as work published after his first, single-volume *Collected Poems* (1983) and culminating in the two-volume *Collected Poems* published in 1999; that is, poetry published between Porter's mid-fifties and the age of seventy, a period during which his main publisher, Oxford University Press, published six separate volumes of his work: *Fast Forward* (1984), *The Automatic Oracle* (1987), *Possible Worlds* (1989), *The Chair of Babel* (1992), *Millennial Fables* (1994), *Dragons in their Pleasant Palaces* (1997) and the new *Collected Poems*. Despite the fact that Oxford University Press, with its list of over forty poets, of whom Porter was a leading figure, decided to cease publishing new poetry after 1999, Porter's second *Collected* is not to be readers' last point of access to his creative productivity. (Picador have since published the volumes *Max is Missing* in 2001 and *Afterburner* in 2004.) But Porter's reputation in Australia was at its height following an extended visit to his homeland in 1999, during which he gave readings and talks in four cities and received an honorary Doctorate of Letters from the University of Sydney.[1]

The 'inner landscapes' of Porter's later poetry are a metaphor for landmark memories and observations of places, people and their personal associations for the poet. Porter has expressed his preference for the 'Athenian' tradition of city poetry over the 'Boeiotian' or country traditions, but his later work covers a wide range of settings filtered through memory and imagination in a variety of traditional and virtuosic verse forms. A study of these inner landscapes must also include the modes of representation, their tempo and their emphasis, for these are moving pictures of a highly intelligent and active sensibility's responses to the world. They also reflect a self-conscious interest in the metaphors of self which register such responses.

Porter's first volume after the 1983 *Collected* was titled *Fast Forward* and was published in 1984. Some reviewers seemed intent on punishing Porter for not allowing the *Collected* to settle in the public mind before he pressed forward. Typically, the new volume provided biographical points of reference for those readers who like to read his poems in part for their metaphors of self and the personal allegory that runs through his work. A key poem in *Fast Forward* is 'Where We Came In', which records the death of the writer's father in Brisbane, and the son's low-key apocalypse:

> At last I was alone with incandescence
> and did not question the mystery,
> The son was now the father.[2]

This 'incandescence' in the face of death lights up what Porter earlier called a personal 'map of loss'; in a number of later poems, the self-lacerating guilt and self-doubt of earlier phases has diminished.

Dedicated to his London friend and fellow Australian expatriate, Clive James, the volume *Fast Forward* took its metaphor from audio- and video-technology, and the title poem spotlights images of the brain's acceleration into undreamt-of places:

> Left to itself, the brain, circuiting the world,
> Becomes a rapid deployment force
> And blasts ashore on any troubled sand.[3]

A forward-moving rhythm and exhilaration with movement of a different kind emerged in Porter's next book, *The Automatic Oracle* (1987), a volume dedicated to his partner, later second wife, Christine Berg. The poem 'Legs on Wheels' is a playful *pas de deux* on wheels, in which the anxieties and disasters to which Porter's mind has frequently been drawn are caught up in the pleasurable commuting of lovers between their respective homes:

> May we avoid disaster,
> Escaping ever faster
> From all the patent deaths
> (Aids, cancer, madness, meths),
> rejoice we swirl on wheels ...[4]

While Porter's oceanic, or perhaps 'airborne' mind seemed to circuit the world as he knew it with great rapidity in his later fifties and had the capacity to 'blast ashore on any troubled sand', a critical view was expressed that such poems were insufficiently 'grounded'. The claim was made by Neil Powell in a 1995 *Times Literary Supplement* review of Porter's volume *Millennial Fables* (1994). The gist of Powell's criticism was that Porter's concentration on 'intellectual landscapes' limited rather than enhanced his scope as a poet. Although, as its title implies, *Millennial Fables* suited Powell's case better than other volumes—a point that is strengthened by the notes on obscure allusions and references which the publisher persuaded Porter to include at the end of this volume—the more general concern about the elusiveness, difficulty, and 'absence of specific contexts' can be addressed directly with reference to a number of Porter's poems in his later volumes, in which places filtered through memory and imagination play a crucial role.

The first observation is that Porter is not and never has been a 'nature poet'. Some of Porter's most quoted lines come from his 1975 poem 'On First Looking Into Chapman's Hesiod', where he wrote, 'Some of us feel at home nowhere,/Others in one generation fuse with the land'. In the concluding lines of that poem, Porter further identified his inclinations in a much publicised clash of values and outlooks with Les Murray. By contrast with those who can 'fuse with the land', Porter writes:

> Sparrows acclimatize but I still seek
> The permanently upright city where
> Speech is nature and plants conceive in pots,
> Where one escapes from what one is and who
> One was, where home is just a postmark
> And country wisdom clings to calendars,
> The opposite of a sunburned truth-teller's
> World, haunted by precepts and the Pleiades.[5]

Born and brought up in suburban Brisbane, Porter is not the kind of poet to extol agraria, Murray-like, or to present himself entranced, Wordsworth-like, in the face of natural scenery. A later poem, 'Skinning a Skunk', from *Dragons in their Pleasant Palaces* (1997), deals with this issue in relaxed and humorous tones:

> *Skinning a Skunk*
>
> Now there's a taking title. What
> Can I who've only once been on
> A horse compose in verse to show
> My Nature Wisdom: do I know
> The latest Georgics, can I pleat
> Our ancient art to modern song
> And is my skunk-lore sound? It's not.[6]

Porter knows the populist pressures towards being what he calls in this poem 'A Rocky Mountains bard', and resists them. Skeptical of tribalism and provincial ways of thinking, Porter is not, his speaker muses in another poem, a 'feel-good' poet, a purveyor of Hope, one of those 'towering Yea-preachers'. Nor indeed does Porter indulge in evocations of the brute violence of nature, in the popular style of

Ted Hughes or James Dickey, preferring instead to search for scarce hope in humanity's capacity for civilisation, justice, and, above all, art.

Porter's attitude to the physical world is well conveyed in the volume *Possible Worlds* (1989), published in the year of his sixtieth birthday. A number of poems in this book show the poet's location of particular sites as stimuli for the imagining of Utopias or dystopias, in the southern hemisphere as in the north. The topic is opened for inspection in 'A Physical World', in which Porter presents himself as the child he was (and in some respects still is)— an outsider, haunted by images of death, out of touch with his physical surroundings. In these circumstances, preternaturally aware of the deaths in his family after the early death of his mother when he was nine, Porter recognises that his poetic mode was to invent 'the blaze/of extinction: to be such a virtuoso/of yourself that truth remained untenable'.[7] Against these personal imperatives, the physical, material world diminishes in importance, and the saving grace of humans is their art that transcends the physical world. Porter concludes his meditation on the physical world with these lines:

How ridiculous to be Columbus
offering Isabella the earliest gold of America
when you could be da Ponte giving Mozart
his first sight of the libretto of Figaro.[8]

The non-material world of art, in this case Porter's favourite art of music, here takes priority over all the lands and wealth of the Americas. Ironic exaggeration, in Porter's hands, is a mode of truth-telling, which shakes the foundations of conventional wisdom.

When actual places are mentioned in Porter's poetry these are most often launching-pads for memories or further imaginings. In 'The Ecstasy of Estuaries' in the volume *Possible Worlds*, the place evoked in the first instance is Australia's south-west coast, which Porter visited in 1987. Here, where 'villagers saved suicidal whales', he sees 'up-river pelicans' and whiting which 'sketch' their shapes on the sea's floor. These direct observations lead to scenes recalled, with a peculiar plangency, from the writer's childhood, a continent away in Moreton Bay, off the coast of Brisbane:

> To scatter toast crumbs to the gulping gulls
> And let the dinghy flutter on the tide,
> To be reliving what was hardly lived
> When years ago the boat came back at dusk,
> A father and a son, strange strangers, home,
> This is the storytelling of the blood.[9]

The estuaries, Porter suggests, give the sense of ecstasy, but behind the estuaries is a kind of perennial, timeless, changeless tableland, at which humans can only wonder. This lyrical 'storytelling of the blood', with its reflections on permanency and change, is relatively rare in Porter's poetry, though it recurs from time to time in the later verse as observation is distilled through memory.

The naming of places in Porter's later poetry often serves an allegorical function, both personal and social. Thus 'Woop Woop', another poem in *Possible Worlds*, names the mythical Australian outback, and is presented as a serious joke invented by city-dwellers as their necessary other:

> Out of its famished acres come anecdotes
> Of men with recipes for 'cockatoo-au-vin',
> Of fossickers in muddy dams taming Irish tunes
> On one-string fiddles—rumours started
> here sell beer ten thousand miles from 'Truth to Tell'.[10]

The actual Australian place-name Porter's Retreat, signifying a town west of the Great Dividing Range in New South Wales, offered too good an opportunity for Porter to pass up. His poem with that title is a humorous personal allegory that highlights the arbitrary but influential power of names:

> Here by Disappointment Bluff, gaze
> across the Vale of Sixty to Uncanniness;
> beyond the rock-strewn creek
> is an escarpment called Incalculable
> and the fields are more elided than Elysian—
> mark this tree the point of going back
> and set it on the map—Porter's Retreat—
> the place at which all further progress
> ceases to have consequence.[11]

Such poems are reflexive, relaxed, and humorous, but they are never merely self-oriented: Porter uses the self and its associations as sources of insight and reflection for wider social, political, or metaphysical concerns. Such poems are seldom merely 'intellectual', but irony and humour preserve their sentiments for inspection and further consideration.

Porter's re-engagement in his later verse with the ironic and satiric social critic of his angry-young-man phase of the 1960s is evident in his poem 'An Ingrate's England' (*Possible Worlds*), in which the speaker presents himself as a malcontent in Margaret Thatcher's Britain of the 1980s. He looks behind the attractive architecture and apparent civilisation to the histories of those who have suffered and been destroyed to build cathedrals and other signifiers of civilisation. A conservationist ethic underlies the images in this poem of the betrayal of the natural environment, the selling-off of water supplies and even graveyards for profit, the development of England as a theme-park for tourists. Perceptions of nature are inevitably influenced by the rampant commercialism of contemporary city-dwellers, he suggests.

In a later bird poem, 'Pigeons, Gulls and Starlings' (*The Chair of Babel*), Porter stamps himself as a very different poet from Judith Wright, for instance, when he remarks with casual sardonicism: 'Imagine a heaven where every one of these/is known by bar codes on its wings or tail'.[12] The terms of contemporary commercialism are as integral to Porter's art as 'other world' alternatives signalled by biblical, musical, or poetic modes of communication. As he reminds us in another poem, 'trade goes on/Beyond Apocalypse ..., [13] but that does not give it a necessary primacy in the imagination.

The great good place of Porter's later poetry is Italy, a country the writer's Australian-bred Anglican and Protestant scepticism has learned to embrace since he first visited that country in the early 1970s. Two poems of Porter's later phase locate the little Tuscan town of Campagnatico where fellow Australian writer David Malouf had his second home. 'The Cats of Campagnatico' and the 'Cocks of Campagnatico' refer to the Tuscan landscapes that appeal to Porter's imagination. In 'The Cats of Campagnatico', Porter's speaker places himself among those who love Italy, praising the '[r]ational landscapes, dotted with walled cemeteries'; and then, as he enters the village:

> Now, coming through the gate,
> The view is a pastoral benediction for those
> Who have never lived in Arcadia. *Thank God,*

Grâce à Dieu, Gott sei dank—we are
As international as an opera festival,
We who love Italy. We have no home
And come from nowhere, a marvellous patrimony.[14]

The cats give the speaker his 'sudden vision of belonging' in this place. The later poem, 'The Cocks of Campagnatico', admits a temptation to draw a 'moral landscape' from the village: 'Ignore mere detail says the ageing Conscience,/Encourage emblems any mind can hail'. As if to answer his call, a chorus of roosters strike up, 'Propose and repropose the Resurrection'.[15] This is one mood, one celebratory perception of a loved place to set against the mood of 'A Short Ballad of Unbelief' or 'A Dance of Death', which nevertheless face last things with more equanimity than some of Porter's earlier poems on these subjects.

One of the great cities of Porter's pantheon is Rome, which was enhanced in his imagination by a number of visits there to his older daughter Katherine and her husband in the mid-1990s. Many grounding details are provided in 'The Pines of Rome', but typically the poet's reflections on these trees are shaped by a musical score:

Rome is all in bad taste and we are no exception
is their motto. Small wonder that Respighi, 'the last Roman',
adds recorded nightingales to his score *The Pines
of the Janiculum.*

And the scent of pines as we dine at night
among the tethered goats and the Egyptian waiters
is a promise that everything stays forever foreign
which settles down in Rome.[16]

The combination of foreignness and familiarity in a crumbling former centre of Empire recalls earlier poems on Vienna and London, but the cityscape of Rome has a special place in Porter's memory-bank for its unique mix of romance and horror. Porter's version of post-colonialism is to celebrate the semiotics of lost power in former centres of Empire, which appeal more to his imagination than present-day power bases such as New York, Tokyo, or Beijing.

Much of Porter's later poetry presents places, people, and ideas perceived within states of half-wakefulness or dreaming, wherein moments of insight or truth emerge as if accidentally from a variety of unlikely contexts. The harmonies of sleep are lyrically conveyed in the poem 'Encouragement to Sleep', where the repeated phrases evoke an air of hypnotic enchantment spiced with moments of dread. *The Chair of Babel* is Porter's later 'dreams volume', and its title poem juxtaposes the outer reality of a conference of psychoanalysts in Italy with the poet's bizarre, cross-cultural reveries:

> I say to my neighbour,
> daring to speak to him at last,
> 'Is yours a big department?'
>
> 'We have Gossip, Pentecost,
> Green Vocabulary,
> Eye Utterance,
> and Cultspeak', he replies.[17]

'Bad Dreams in Venice' calls up again the personal trauma of Porter's first wife Jannice's suicide, and his sense of guilt at the 'cold and wounding' words he had spoken to her during a holiday in Venice. A companion-piece, 'Bad Dreams in Naples', recalls the same relationship in a different place, but again with the special, deeply etched distortions of guilt:

> A terrified and dying man
> Is seeking his estranged wife's hand.

And later in the poem,

> They're packing me into my shroud.
> I recognise it as the cloud
> Always above Vesuvius.
> My soul hangs round for God to suss.[18]

The bad dreams departments of Porter's later poems are counterpointed by a number of wish-fulfilment reveries, as in 'Wish We Were There' (*The Chair of Babel*), which offers a surreal reconstruction of the Australian suburban paradise of childhood, which was suddenly cut short by young Peter's mother's death, thus contributing to its preservation in aspic for later dreams:

> It would be our garden of scents and Spitfires,
> it would be our yard for exercise,
> it would go on for ever (and ever),
> it would, of course, be Paradise.[19]

Such plangent images from Porter's interior landscape are never merely sentimental and are generally brought to earth by the writer's sardonic rationality. Thus his paradisal garden contains the lines:

> Mother and Father in frayed straw hats
> and swathes of angelic flannelette,
> the nimbus of childhood spreading wider,
> the milkman trying to place a bet.[20]

Such vivid images contribute to what has been called the *roman fleuve* of Porter's writings,[21] a personal allegory which can be traced along the water courses and banks of this writer's river of life. If not always 'anchored', such images nevertheless earn recognition in this writer's interior landscape.

In *Fast Forward* we saw Porter's persona, in his mid-fifties, proposing an acceleration of the brain, 'circuiting the world', becoming 'a rapid deployment force'. In *Dragons in their Pleasant Palaces*, produced in Porter's late sixties, the poem 'Anxiety's Air Miles' shows a self still circuiting the world, but carrying with it those memories of pain and vulnerability which guarantee its continuity; however, time and distance have threatened to 'dumb down' the conscience 'till plain grief has lost its way' and a 'dumb impersonality takes over'. Porter links these observations with the single most painful experience of his life—the death of his first wife Jannice, whose ghost has haunted his writings as Hardy's wife's death haunted his. Has a 'dumb impersonality' overtaken the poet, as it seems to have overtaken contemporary society? In a global communications network in which interviewers from CNN and elsewhere offer 'disposable catharsis', what can endure?

> This is the stunted world we have to live in
> And I who've ringed the globe five times since that
> Eclipse now see myself a frequent flyer
> Topping up his helplessness with speed.[22]

The 'advanced' Western democracies promote the dominance of technology, but Porter asserts the primacy of personal experience, of which anxiety dreams are one guarantee. 'Dreams', he asserts, are 'twice as fast as Boeings/And visit more appalling shores'. His register switches to the personal and particular:

> ... Love is the good which died
> That Winter night and with its death became
> The wide-winged world ...[23]

Love and death are the twin compulsions of Porter's interior landscapes, and his poetry continually reveals a human voice that is set to endure the ravages of nature and technological change.

The Poet as Traveller:
Edwin Thumboo

Singapore's premier poet of the post-independence period, Edwin Thumboo, is often perceived as a nation-building citizen-poet whose main task is to set a tone and imagery for citizenship in his island home. The widely quoted title poem of his third volume, *Ulysses by the Merlion* (1979) seems to invite readings which stress the returned traveller rather than the man at sea. Yet Thumboo's self representations as a voyager in foreign places and situations are at least as revealing of his values, beliefs and literary art as his home-based poetry.

Thumboo's second volume of verse, *Gods Can Die* (1977) reveals an author intent on exploring the proposition that every immigrant is also an emigrant. His poem 'The Immigrant' opens with the lines 'Days and Indian days stretch/Beyond the grasping of his hands/That were the hoe,/The sickle in the sun'. The man's tools are an extension of his body and he is an extension of the Indian land that bred him. But the poem's narrative moves from the rooted peasant existence in the cruel heat of Indian summers to rumours of Singapore ('a place/of padi, coconut, monsoons,/Toddy and regular wages'); it ends with the arrival of the immigrant who becomes a symbolic guarantee of Singapore's multicultural environment. But other poems by this Singaporean poet of mixed Indian and Chinese inheritance project the figure of the traveller, whose principal experience is to be neither coming nor going but rather to be *away*, in a state of flux and possibility, between places of fixed abode.

The first 'foreign' country in Thumboo's poetry signifying an 'away' zone is Africa, where Thumboo travelled in the late 1960s to pursue his research interests in poetry and nationalism in Commonwealth countries. In the period following British Prime Minister Harold Macmillan's 1963 'Winds of Change' speech and what has been referred to, from a British point of view, as 'unscrambling an Empire', inhabitants of former colonies were flexing their muscles as they surveyed the gains and losses of national independence. As an Asian in Africa, Thumboo shared some African outlooks but also felt confronted by the brutal directness of African liberation struggles compared with the more subtle indirections of most of his Southeast Asian counterparts.

Two poems in the *Gods Can Die* volume, 'In Africa' and 'A Brother', show Thumboo's poetry at an interesting level of engagement with his experience of Africa. 'In Africa' refers principally to Freetown, Sierra Leone, but it relates more widely to all newly independent nations which struggle to recognise a meaningful past beyond colonialism, and try to modernise. The flag is a key signifier of new pride and a fragile hold on national identity:

> The country's flag is new
> Unfurled just modestly.
> An old colonial cannon sits
> Just quietly
> But hear the trucks and tractors, busy with the earth,
> Push the trees quite out of sight,
> Dismantle the frame of land,
> The green-red flowers.

The disruptive effects of a modernisation which Thumboo came to see as necessary in his island state of Singapore were interacting with his view of one of the smallest West African countries, which gained independence in 1961 and republican status in 1971 and has seen much violence since then. The natural world, the land and its creatures, is signified in Thumboo's poem by a 'nocturnal lizard' which, thanks to the trucks and tractors, finds itself in glaring daylight and symbolises the displacement of 'this feverish century.'

Such sentiments about displacement and its effects recur in Thumboo's poetry. In 'A Brother', Thumboo moves from West

Africa to Nairobi in Kenya, but makes a pan-African gesture in the
ironic opening lines:

> The African can be my brother
> When he is most himself.
> But some have learnt to mini-laugh,
> To adjust their tie before they give a hand,
> Or make cold assessment as you stand,
> Greeting most efficiently.
> These are not themselves,
> And not my brothers.

Thumboo's cross-cultural understanding does not here collapse
under a sentimental assertion of international brotherhood. His
instincts are towards friendship and brotherhood—a much stronger
notion in Thumboo's writings than mere 'fraternal relations'—but
he retains a critical distance which enables him to distinguish
sincerity from mere formalism. The African mimic men represented
in this poem have learnt distance and reserve from their former
colonial masters, summarised in the succinct and expressive phrase,
'Greeting most efficiently'. While 'efficiency' is a hallmark intention
of the civil services in newly independent nations, it is ridiculous
when misapplied to personal greetings, as to many other aspects of
human relations. Thumboo, who had worked as both a civil servant
and a university teacher in the humanities in the 1950s and 1960s,
was thus a highly effective satirist and critic of mismatches between
bureaucratic rules and human relations. Fully aware of the
bureaucratic mindset, he was better able to perceive its incongruities
and absurdities when misapplied to issues of race, belief and
personal relationships. His poetry, early and late, contains many
instances of businessmen and government officials who mistake the
trappings of their professions for the reality of a way of living.

A different kind of traveller's perspective in Thumboo's second
book, *Gods Can Die*, occurs when the visitor to a foreign country
feels in touch with the spirit of the place. By the 1960s and 1970s,
Thumboo was a regular traveller to other ASEAN countries. One of
these, Thailand, had never experienced colonialism of the kind he
saw in Africa and other Asian countries. The poem 'Khan Tok in
Chiangmai' thus bypasses critiques of mimic men or quaint colonial
legacies to engage in a lyrical, Yeatsian dialogue with a timeless
Thailand evoked in traditional song and dance:

When the sun has kept itself
The daughters of the moon arise
Upon the musings of a flute.
Player and instrument are led
By ancient tribal song ...

Women rather than men offer the visitor a brief but intense experience of sensuous continuity through time, and the poem's speaker is temporarily abstracted from the busy workaday life which has brought him to this place:

As the rhythm conjugates its mood
We feel simple, undetailed,
Move into another time
Where nagas brood.

Typically, this poem offers brief, dislocated movements which highlight the rare moments of lyricism in a context of generally mundane activity.

One of the least noticed contributions to Thumboo's third volume, *Ulysses by the Merlion* is 'To Moresby on Conference', which brings together the satiric and lyrical streams in a single poem that celebrates Papua New Guinea. Like one of his principal models, W B Yeats, Thumboo names friends as icons in his verse, memorialising them in relation to the countries and cultures they inhabit. This is a potentially dangerous technique, risking the alienation of general readers who do not know the individuals named. However, the litany of names at the beginning of this poem is soon succeeded by the speaker's memories of a previous visit to New Guinea. The memories are recalled in a mood of romantic, Wordsworthian wonder:

I stand again among
The winds sliding up each valley,
Remember with that other half of memory
Flowers brighter than colour,
Those quick, unbelievable birds of paradise.

The mood here is playfully inflated, for it is destined to be punctured. The puncturing agent is appropriately from Australia, the country which acted as quasi-colonial ruler in Papua New Guinea until self-government in 1973 and full independence in 1975. Australia's national airline, Qantas, is supposed to take the poet to a conference in Port Moresby, but a strike intervenes and he is stranded in Sydney between his small island home and his destination on the world's second largest island. Like Ee Tiang Hong, in some of his Australian poems, Thumboo evokes the comedy of the situation through the direct speech of his Australians:

> Anything to declare;
> Visited a farm recently;
> Had contact with animals;
> Been ill? We have to be careful
> Of foreign bugs. None?
> All in order sir:
> Have a good stay.

The Australia Thumboo presents in this poem is at best a place of transit:

> This is Sydney in July:
> While the cold marauds
> Under a grey, biting sky
> People shrivel and roll along
> The streets. Those you meet, like you,
> Wish to be somewhere else ...

Known in Singapore for its industrial action and strikes, Australia appears as an amusing irritant on the way to Moresby. Finally, approaching Moresby (by Qantas), the shores seem to beckon and welcome him:

> As we descend, atolls form.
> Out-riggers beat down the waves,
> Their sails powerful crab-claws
> Jousting the wind.
> Below the fishes play
> Upon the sea's rhythm.
>
> Great clams lie waiting.
> I hear the polyps sigh,
> The pearl within the oyster
> Meditate upon itself.

And the 'Qantas man', at last, is thanked. The poem's moods are mixed and the lyricism and light satire make an effervescent cocktail.

Travel poems of the kind described above might lack the *gravitas* of canonical poems by Thumboo such as the title poems of *Gods Can Die* and *Ulysses by the Merlion*, but they reveal an important, lighter side to Thumboo the internationalist. It is not surprising that the fine, subtle and complex poems that have been taken up as Thumboo's major works by the educated elite in Singapore should refer principally to his island nation's preoccupations of nation-building, identity formation and economic success. What is less acceptable is the view that Thumboo is therefore 'owned' and controlled by some such imaginary conglomerate as Singapore Inc. To an outsider, like myself, Thumboo's post-colonial voice fully acknowledges his national and multicultural inheritance in independent Singapore in major poems such as 'Gods Can Die', 'Ulysses by the Merlion' and 'Island', but his work is not contained or circumscribed by these poems. His generally underestimated travel poems reveal the poet, with no lesser sense of responsibility, but with an observant eye and a light touch, ruminating on his major concerns as a human being and a poet.

Although it is not strictly speaking a travel poem, Thumboo's poem 'Krishna' from the 'People and Places' section of his fourth volume, *A Third Map* (1993), shows his belief in travel as a form of searching, or quest:

> Before he became a god
> To tidy up the world, Krishna
> Searched a thousand years,
> Along the peaks, the lesser hills,
> Each sudden, plain, persistent star,
> The columns of his thought ...

Travel for Thumboo, then, is not merely touristic adventure. When it is recorded in verse, at least, travel becomes a testing of the poet's beliefs and outlook and a search for brotherhood or love. Direct observation or naming of places or people visited is often juxtaposed with perceptions of others' lives and the puzzles they produce. Thumboo's poem 'After the Leaving ...', for example, is dedicated to Malaysian poet and friend Ee Tiang Hong, who migrated to Western Australia in 1975 (see Essay 5). The 'double vision' which Ee managed to produce from his state of voluntary exile for his final volume *Nearing a Horizon* (1994), is admired and wondered at in Thumboo's poem:

There are two countries here:
One scarcely meets the eye;
The other binds your heart.
This is Perth, and yet Malacca.
Outside, suddenly spring arrives
In many wild, surprising flowers.
But no chempaka, no melor
Show that beauty of the heart.

Having chosen to remain in Singapore, Thumboo is not as divided at heart as his friend, but he empathises with the view of the displaced migrant, observing its pitfalls and pleasures, the shared memories and the new openings:

Remembering ... your ukulele
Mastering the restless crabs,
Sunset upon the brow of Panteh 2;
Our shared tobacco; images of
Heroic days, court and kampong;
That great Tranquerah mosque,
St Paul's Hill, Sam Po's Well,
And other abodes of our gods.

Against these memories are juxtaposed an already mythologised Australian present:

But here the roads are happily
Waltzing with Matilda, leading
Through miles of bush to Laverton,
Abandoned mines, receding purple hills.

Typically, the heart of Thumboo's understanding of Ee Tiang Hong's divided fate is expressed in terms of dream-visions, with a strong literary and historical dimension to them:

And as you hear the recurring
Soul of Voss adventuring Ayers Rock,
The Dream-time, purifying deserts,
Shore, sky and hinterland are yours.
But you return to Heeren Street,
Ancestral rooms, intricate histories ...

Unable to leave behind the seven generations of family memory in Malacca, Ee was for Thumboo an image of the eternally divided soul, for whom returning to the homeland in spirit is a far more powerful emotional attraction than full engagement in the life of the adopted homeland.

Thumboo's traveller's eye continually seeks the unique spirit of a place, but the process is also one of self-examination. Thus a visit to Kangaroo Island off the coast of South Australia moves from observation of topography and architecture to reflections on memory and the shaping mind:

> Earth-Water-Air await
> Combustion. Landscapes grip your senses.
> Capture is release. Make small philosophies;
> Associate, link. Inspect, if you wish,
> The mind's sequence ...

Thumboo traces his own thought patterns as a musical accompaniment to the sounds of booming surf:

> A thought moves insouciant among
> Waves grown amiable below arc silences.
> Socrates would have liked Lao Tzu and Plato
> Confucius when it came to Government; the
> Sermon on the Mount undivides, is access
> To Divinity ...

This is philosophy lightly applied, the chief purpose of which is to show the mind seeking patterns of reconciliation, accommodation and redemption. Eastern and Western traditions meet in these lines, but the setting in which they do so is never immaterial; indeed Kangaroo Island is presented as a material instigator of these tentative graspings towards a genuinely international philosophy, which could transcend the divisions between men and women and the nations they inhabit. This is typical of the quests which Thumboo's self-fashioning as traveller produces. The relationships of individuals lie behind everything; but such relationships move out in widening circles to inform place, region, country and the world. Individuals are not mere figures in a national allegory, nor are they restricted to their historical place and time. The engine of their transcendance is the imagination, which Thumboo reveals as especially fertile in the figure of the traveller.

13

Home and Away: Reconciling the Local and the Global

An annual event in the small inland city where I live is regularly advertised as 'Around the world in half a day'. The city is Canberra, Australia's 'bush capital', a city of some 350,000 people located in a sub-alpine region between the country's largest cities, Sydney and Melbourne. Canberra is blessed with a beautiful lake, clear air, a national library, a national gallery, the national parliament—and the embassies of the world, or at least that world with which we Australians have official ties. The opportunity to travel round the world in half a day is offered by these embassies, which open their doors to the public on a certain day each year and show visitors films, photographs, maps, artworks and other aspects of the countries they represent. I am a devotee of these rapid world-trips, though I realise that what I am seeing is not much more extensive than theme parks, and that such trips probably seem a quaint activity compared with the 'real world' alternative of surfing the Net, which keeps many of these inland Australians in their homes on weekends.

Perhaps my view of matters global has been influenced by my upbringing in Western Australia, where I lived—except for various prolonged excursions overseas to places such as Oxford, London, Jakarta and Singapore—until 1993, when I moved to my present position in Canberra. Western Australia has been known variously as a place of 'sun, sin, sand and sore eyes', the 'Cinderella State', and the most isolated part of the world. This latter notion, that I lived in some kind of radical isolation, used to alternately intrigue, appal, enrage and delight me.

I still hear it said, very often by Eastern Staters (once known as 't'othersiders' by traditional West Australians) that the West is beautiful but too far away, that it is 'out on a limb', that its main problem is that it's separated from the Eastern States, where the larger populations of Sydney and Melbourne tend to dominate the airwaves, and views of national identity. Carrying this residual West Coast inheritance with me, I treasure a sense of space which is now interiorised, and transportable. Canberra too, I have come to realise, has something of that ambiguous sense of isolation. When fog sets in at Canberra airport, for example, and prevents flights in and out, I think that's good, we are separate, out on our own, as I did when the Nullarbor Desert stood between me and the eastern capitals of Australia. And I applauded Paul Kelly, former editor of the *Australian* newspaper, who remarked in the early 1990s how ironic it was that Sydney businessmen should criticise Canberra as being isolated from the rest of Australia when these same men had been brought up on Sydney's North Shore, had been to the same schools, wore the same brands of suits and thought in the same ways. Canberra, indeed, like Perth, has its own ethos, with which I like to identify even as I travel the world, embassy exhibitions, or the Internet.

* * *

While I have no doubt that global concerns are more with us than ever before, through television and computer technology, especially, I am interested in those kinds of literary and human sensibilities which, while recognising what E M Forster, in a previous era, called the world 'of telegrams and anger', still seek a quieter, contemplative space in which human desire can express itself in local environments, in an individual, independent way. For me, an epitome of such a recognition is Virginia Woolf's novel *Mrs Dalloway* (1925). The setting of this novel is central London in the early 1920s, the centre of empire in the early post–first world war years. The local environment is a city where big political decisions are made and where people return from their travels to be at the centre of things. Yet Virginia Woolf's genius in the novel is to highlight not that outer world (though there are continual hints and indications of its presence) but the inner worlds of her characters' hopes, fears and desires. When a day in the life of Clarissa Dalloway, a conservative politician's wife in her early fifties is transformed by the return of her former lover, Peter Walsh, from India, the crevasses inside and between individuals are revealed:

> 'I am in love', he said, not to her however, but to someone raised up in the dark so that you could not touch her but must lay your garland down on the grass in the dark.
>
> 'In love', he repeated, now speaking rather dryly to Clarissa Dalloway; 'in love with a girl in India'. He had deposited his garland. Clarissa could make what she would of it.[1]

The characteristic rhythmic hesitancies of Woolf's prose contribute to a stream of consciousness mode which the e-mail is again reviving some eighty years on, though generally with less finesse.

In spite of the shock of Peter Walsh's assertion of his love for another woman, the progress of the novel shows an increasing entwinement of his memories and desires with those of his real love, Clarissa; to the extent that, at the novel's end, Peter's vision of Clarissa is not that of a society hostess but of the visionary woman who makes all others real to him:

> What is this terror? What is this ecstasy? he thought to himself.
> What is it that fills me with extraordinary excitement?
> It is Clarissa, he said.
> For there she was.

In her turn Clarissa is entwined in the physical, social and metaphysical dimensions of the city she inhabits. But her apprehensions, her momentary epiphanies, like those of the other key characters in the novel's fragile community, are their surest signs of significance.

Unfulfilled love, broken memories and desire for completion are universal qualities which can be most fully explored in the local and particular circumstances of individuals in their moments of aloneness. Such isolation, while given encouragement by an open environment, can achieve a certain intensity also in the cities of business and world affairs, as Virginia Woolf shows. Indeed, it is perhaps the case that crowded places increase the urgency of those contemplative moments that constitute the core of many literary works.

Certain kinds of lyric poetry can especially touch these chords of feeling and lead to international comparison. For example, Australian poet and novelist Randolph Stow and contemporary Danish poet Pia Tafdrup both illuminate the aloneness of the individual against the elemental conditions of their very different environments—the hot Australian desert winds for Stow, the snow and silence for Tafdrup, whose love poem 'On the edge' shows the necessity of isolation but also its reminders of death:

On the edge

Our lit bodies
talked of possible
limits and we were
recklessly alive
somewhere softly near
the heart's fiery region
we were flesh with all nights
on the longest night close to greedy brutes
when we came out to the edge where the world was
and the words wanted to leave us just there
not come to a sudden stop wanted
further further still but
crashed themselves against
a wall of white the
poem can speak now
about sparkling
silence.[2]

Love and death are of course traditional themes of literature and they weave themselves, somehow, into, around, and beyond the concourses of business in the global marketplace. While the doom-mongers are busy proclaiming the end of localism as the Internet, email and other aspects of the communications revolution seemingly channel us into the vortex of a decentred, global arena, I notice a countervailing interest, in Australia especially, in local and regional literature, and films of place. In a regional anthology of South Australian writing, editor Phil Butterss contextualises the situation in this way:

> As global media networks make increasing inroads into our lives, the boundaries between nations—not to mention states within nations—are rapidly being broken down. Why, then, at a time when spiralling numbers of Australians are opening their homes and

offices to the rest of the world via the Internet and pay television, this collection of essays on South Australian writing? The trend towards globalisation is itself, in part, responsible for continuing assertions of the importance of the regional and local.[3]

These 'continuing assertions' are not, however, inevitable, like some physical law requiring equal and opposite cultural reactions to any trend or tendency. They represent, on one level, a humanistic response to the apparently dehumanising tendency of what some would call a progressive postmodernity; an attempt, as in Green politics, to retain a degree of identification between individuals, communities and physical land- and sea-scapes. Their principal motivation is the conservation of the physical environment. At another level, these 'continuing assertions' represent attempts to keep critics and commentators honest by not rejecting the local as they dabble in global interests and affairs. I remember Meenakshi Mukherjee's explanation of the purposes of the Indian Association for Commonwealth Literature and Language Studies (IACLALS) conference in Shimla in 1994 being in part to 'interrogate post-colonialism' by reconsidering with a sceptical eye the way in which critics had moved from engagement with local or national issues to being proponents of commonwealth literature and then post-colonialism, and becoming in the process 'confident global intellectuals, part of a highly visible international fraternity or sorority who are redefining the notion of the text—equally at home in Sydney, Singapore, San Francisco or Shimla'.[4] In these astute remarks, we see a proper scepticism about global ambitions which can so easily obliterate local needs and realities. In spite of technological advances, half the world's population have never made a telephone call in their lives.

* * *

Personal reflections may not be irrelevant to these issues. I am not by any means an extraordinary Australian, and my kind of experience would be reflected by many others. My parents, born in Western Australia, each left school in their early teens and started work. Each knew the country towns of Western Australia, where they obtained jobs varying from timber yards to stock companies— and, in my father's case, later a bank. Neither of them had travelled outside Australia when my father volunteered for the Australian

Army in the second world war and spent several years on the tropical island of Morotai off Borneo, where the Australians, like the Americans, were charged with blocking any further southward advances by the Japanese.

Although only a few Japanese bombs were dropped on the island and he seems not to have been in great physical danger, my father's experience dominated the mythological imagination of my two brothers and myself. My mother's home-front experience of giving birth to three sons and bringing them up between 1941 and 1945 paled into insignificance. Like our parents, my brothers and I were 'home bodies', for whom 'transport' generally came through books, radio and, in my late teens, television. (We had no car and always used buses or bicycles.) We revelled in the beach, the outdoor life, football, cricket, and the powerful idioms of West Australian parochialism.

Apart from my father's war years, I was the first in my family to leave our native shores when, in the mid-1960s I found myself the surprised recipient of a scholarship donated by that rogue bull of old Empire, Cecil Rhodes, and sailed on the P&O liner, the *Himalaya*, on a four-week voyage to England, stopping at exotic places like Colombo, Bombay and Port Said. Oxford, for me, was another kind of province, but one where I could more easily leap off for exotic adventures in London, Paris, Rome, Madrid, and even Moscow. Amongst other things, Oxford, and Rhodes House especially, brought me into close contact with the commonwealth— with Indians, Pakistanis, Africans, Canadians, Americans, New Zealanders—and Australians from other States. I suppose I was 'broadened' by the experience. I was elected president of the Ralegh Club, which invited key commonwealth leaders to address issues of contemporary relevance. I also learnt there to value my Australian-ness, and read books by Patrick White, Randolph Stow and others which had not come my way as a student at the University of Western Australia.

This is not an unusual story, though the details may vary: the discovery, in a foreign country, of a belated but deep identity with the homeland. The usual post-Oxford temptations were there too: Yale was suggested to me; I flirted with the idea of joining the Australian Government's Department of External Affairs to the extent that I was interviewed and accepted for a position. But when a University lectureship was offered and I enjoyed the teaching, reading and writing, I embarked on a project to introduce full Australian literature courses in my home university. In that way, I fancied I was establishing my rootedness in my local and Australian community. I edited the local literary magazine *Westerly*. I felt 'responsible' for my local culture; and subsequently, as my reading and experience grew further, I tried to extend notions of regionalism which I had been developing in Australian terms to the neighbouring countries of Southeast Asia, whose cultures, like those of Western Australia, and Australia itself, had been too glibly passed over. This regionalism I saw as extending parochial horizons rather than as an all-embracing universalism, about which I have always felt uneasy, partly because of its tendency to obliterate local concerns and differences and because it had been so blatantly abused by British colonialists to co-opt Australians into their own expansionist ambitions.

Looking back on those Western Australian years after a number of years in Australia's capital city, I can now see conflicting tendencies. On the one hand was a somewhat cautious nativism, which only in the later years (as a director of the Black Swan Theatre Company) took proper and serious account of the creativity of the 'real' natives, Australia's indigenous people, the Aborigines, in the creative arts in Australia. I never held a view of myself as a 'citizen of the world'—a concept that seemed altogether too grandiose for a local boy who liked to travel. I had a strong sense of 'home', in a conventional sense, as house and family, and more broadly as Western Australia, or 'the West', though I only ever occupied a tiny portion of the South West of it. Local writers, whose work I discovered for myself enabled me to dream in, and of, what I thought of as my own territory, by making it both familiar and strange to me. The place became more habitable imaginatively as I read more widely the autobiographies, stories, poems, plays and essays of men and women who had experienced that country as natives, immigrants or travellers. I co-edited an anthology of West Australian writing called *Wide Domain*, indicating a sense of imaginative expansion as well as of geographical space.

In retrospect, I was looking for unsettling experience as much as a settled sense of identity. I became fascinated with an anticipatory—or almost already experienced—sense of expatriatism and exile—of living on the edge; and it is a theme which I still find compelling. My book of essays *An Australian Compass: Essays on*

Place and Direction in Australian Literature attempted to explore the promises, claims, tensions, ambiguities and disappointments of the notion of 'home', and a sense of belonging. My critical biography *Spirit in Exile: Peter Porter and his Poetry* located the key to this Australian-born Londoner in the writer's felt sense of incompleteness or, more strongly, as a sense of exile. At one point, I try to encapsulate Porter's spirited response to his inbuilt sense of exile:

> Whether this sense of exile is projected in dramatic monologues, or through literary figures, such as Cain and Orpheus, or in the fates of exiled painters and musicians, Porter's discontent smoulders, flickers or flares, lighting up a personal 'map of loss'. Irony, humour and ridicule are as much part of this process as tones of tragedy or pathos. In more directly autobiographical ways, too, as in the image of a husband grieving for his dead wife, or a lover separated from his loved one, this sense of exile is evoked.[5]

The literary correlative to my interest in questions of identification with place and belonging, then, may be found to some extent in their opposites, that is, in displacement and deracination. The figures of the expatriate, or exile—and these two figures need not have the same set of identification marks at all—are of interest to me because they open up gaps, or spaces, that the writer seeks to fill. As Kateryna Longley has pointed out, the figure of the migrant, too, is often engaged in 'reconstituting home-spaces in memory and in story telling'. Every expatriate is also, of course, a migrant: whichever the direction of travel, or the degree of displacement, one of the major creative impulses seems to be the construction of a 'home-space'; and these imagined places, though they may expand to include regions or nations, are often couched in more intimate terms. Thus Peter Porter returns to the houses of his childhood in Brisbane; as does David Malouf in *12 Edmonstone Street*; Mena Abdullah in *Time of the Peacock*; and V S Naipaul, in an extended, imaginative sense, in *A House for Mr Biswas*. (As Peggy Nightingale has pointed out, Naipaul's novel both reveals 'the nauseating aspects of Trinidad from which Naipaul fled as a young man, and reinforces the reader's awareness of the central impulse of the book, the intensity of Mr Biswas's longing for a home at once private and secure'.[6])

Yet the role of expatriate or exile remains a difficult one in Australia, as in other commonwealth countries. The mixed receptions of Salman Rushdie's and Arundhati Roy's novels have been affected, in part, by their perceived relationship to the writers' homeland India where they have been more stridently criticised than in the West. At a recent Melbourne Writers' Festival in Australia, novelists Peter Carey (who had lived in New York for seven years) and Frank Moorhouse (who had spent four years in France researching his novel *Grand Days*) found themselves defending their choice to live outside Australia and denied the charge of 'cultural treason'.[7] At the same conference, Moorhouse remarked: 'Australia is a pioneering country ... There is this sense of an obligation on people to stay and build the culture ... As if going away doesn't build culture. As if Peter Carey doesn't keep building upon our sense of self'. Carey for his part, pleaded with Australians to end their 'obsession' with where writers choose to live. Answering questions of 'cultural treason' was, he said, 'alarming and difficult'; Australia's concern with artistic drain revealed a country that still harboured 'a very frail sense of self'. Still speaking as an Australian, to his Melbourne audience, after seven years in New York, Carey remarked that 'this predicament of being away from one's home can be very fruitful'. And certainly his novel, *Jack Maggs* (1998), which 'writes back' to Dickens's *Great Expectations* by presenting Carey's version of Magwitch the convict as the central character (and subsequently his *True History of the Kelly Gang*, 2000), are resonant with individually realised senses of the difficulty and ambiguity of finding a home. Ironically, the place where Maggs eventually finds his place of settlement and belonging is not the London he had dreamed about but the Australia of his former bondage.

* * *

An interesting question for post-colonial countries such as Australia and India is whether the historical moment of such furores over expatriates and expatriatism is nearing its end. Can we envisage a postmodern paradise wherein authors' places and communities of origin are expunged from the record and they become free agents in a global literary interchange? Travellers rather than migrants? Individuals who exist beyond nationalism, patriotism and regional loyalties and affiliations? These issues have been raised by the publication of Ian Britain's book *Once an Australian* (1997), a study of four celebrated Australian expatriates, Barry Humphries, Clive James, Germaine Greer and Robert Hughes. The title of Britain's book, *Once an Australian* invites the rejoinder 'always an Australian', and the book places great stress on the Australian origins and backgrounds of its major subjects.

During the research for my critical biography of another expatriate, Peter Porter, I discussed with the poet his ironic verse poem 'Essay on Patriotism', in which he highlights the hypocrisy and deception of various patriotic proclamations, ranging from those of the Boer War to Vietnam and including the macho protagonist of the American *Rambo* films of the 1980s: 'no wonder/Rambo gobbled up gooks/if he had such voices in his head'. True, I thought (and said to Porter) but patriotism has its uses, too, in focusing a feeling for the land, for example, a known and loved territory and community of belonging; or in encouraging the development of interest in a home culture which has been depreciated or ignored during colonial control. Patriotism does not have to be ugly, brutal and possessive. We agreed to differ on this matter, as on others, in what, for both of us, has been a relationship where we have a full and frank exchange of views and opinions.

It was therefore with great interest that I read Porter's extended review of *Once an Australian* in the *Australian's Review of Books*. Like much of Porter's writing, this review is full of contentious and interesting observations including the following:

> The distrust of expatriates is a special kind of chauvinism, one that seems endemic to the newer empires. Even within what is now the Commonwealth, the irritation felt by those at home viewing their fellows' activities abroad is greater in the white dominions than in the former colonies of the subcontinent or Africa. Countries that did not have to fight for independence but gained it by democratic negotiation seem to produce a bitterer form of dislike of expatriatism than those which were truly colonial. Thus Australians, Canadians and New Zealanders feel such emotions in ways that Indians and Africans don't. This may be because, as we notice among families, emphasis is placed on differences among members rather on similarities and any common heritage.[8]

While this argument undoubtedly contains some grains of truth, I would question Porter's 'family' metaphor and wonder if the remark about African and Indian indifference to the criticism of expatriates would apply to Wole Soyinka's impassioned attacks on the Nigerian polity from Harvard (after what he called his 'Rambo departure from the Nigerian nation space'): or indeed Rushdie's satirical recreations of Bombay from his British hideaway. Moreover, Porter's sense of (post) modernity sounds somewhat utopian when he remarks that 'the world is wired to the Internet, a network where universalism and local interests perform side by side'.

This utopian vision may seem ingenuous when it is linked to the media events surrounding the death of the former Princess of Wales. Universalism and local interests working side by side? While Diana's death and subsequent funeral attained instantaneous world coverage, the roots and origins of her media imagery and 'personality' derived from the massive investment of the British people in their principal symbol of national sovereignty, the royal family. Indeed, in one of those ironies which seem endemic to such occasions, the events were used unashamedly by the British government and media to reinforce the role of Britain as a tourist destination where a recent tragedy could be married with a long and colourful history of earlier tragedies. If the Ritz in Paris seemed to attract an excessive amount of publicity as Diana's temporary 'away' base, the funeral route from Westminster Abbey to Althorpe in Northamptonshire derived a massively multiplied interest dividend for her 'home' country. Although a 'world' event, in terms of the number and geographical range of those who viewed, heard or read about it, Diana's funeral reinforced, among its many variant narratives, one of the most urgent stories of our time, the troubled relationship of individuals to their countries and places of origin. A further irony is that, according to the usual reliable 'sources', Diana had developed, in previous years, a personal mythology of 'away' (in Europe or North America) as a refuge and sanctuary. Although Princess Diana's funeral was undoubtedly one of the world's major media events, ranking alongside far more significant world events such as the demolition of the Berlin Wall, the Tiananmen Square massacre, or indeed the death of Mother Theresa, it did not expunge, either in the life of its principal subject, Diana herself, or for the wider British population, the dilemma of belonging, of home versus away.

* * *

Some of those who embrace the new technologies with uncritical enthusiasm may be in danger of equating their natural excitement about change with the prospect of an emergent postmodern utopia. Let me put the positive side of the ledger first. As McLuhan accurately observed, television first made the 'global village' a possibility. The Internet, a generation later, seemed to confirm it. Email has replaced snail mail for many people in office complexes, universities and even homes. For those who have access to them, these technological advances seem to have made it more possible than ever before to live one's life in an almost perpetual state of 'awayness', plugged into a global network of communications and other people's 'home pages'. The shift in one generation from local to global has been astounding. In the culture of literary criticism and theory, this shift has been signified by a move from an interest in physical 'place' or 'setting' to notions of a 'site', where ideologies clash and compete, to the cyberspace 'syte', where a simultaneous interactive theatre of gossip, opinion and compared impressions of what is 'new' occurs. Information overload is a common complaint, along with an alleged loss of historical perspective. We can live increasingly in such virtual 'sytes', if we, or our institutions, have the resources and we wish to do so.

Underlying many discussions of the developments I have just outlined is an ideology of Progress, which the speaker is either for or against. One of Australia's leading cultural studies specialists, Meaghan Morris, has graphically described the ideology of Progress as it has related to one of the city of Sydney's main landmarks, Sydney Tower, which was completed in 1981. Morris admits to an annoyance at the changes that had occurred in the Tower's semiotic functions—from 'the Eiffel Tower of the southern hemisphere— only higher ... an annunciation of modernity' which would enable Sydney to 'grow up' and become a 'world city' to, a decade later, 'a remodelling of local cultures to meet the needs of a tourist economy',[9] which 'celebrated neither Sydney nor the Tower, but only the possibility of *going somewhere else*':

> There was no narrative (offensive or otherwise) of the founding of the place, and no specific address to Sydney residents. Instead, the images appealed unambiguously to foreign tourists: perfunctory ads for duty-free fur and opal shops, representations of tourist transport systems (trains, boats, hydrofoils, even a picture of a

charter bus drawn up right next to a Qantas jet) and of their destinations—anonymous motel swimming pools, distant tropical and rural resorts.[10]

Faced with the discovery that her 'founding' site of analysis has 'changed utterly', this cultural analyst and proponent of modernity finds herself toying with nostalgia and conjecturing about 'the *relative* rates of renovation or dereliction, as well as a distinctive present, and a local past, in each'.[11]

Meaghan Morris deals with changes in her cityscape quite pragmatically compared with Peter Read's subjects in his book *Returning to Nothing*, who describe their reactions to returning mentally or physically to vanished places, such as Lake Pedder after it was inundated by the Hydro-Electric Commission of Tasmania in 1972, or Darwin after the cyclone of 1974. The places these people hark back to, nostalgically or otherwise, often represent a sense of community lost. As a resident of the former Darwin said on returning to the rebuilt town: 'When you come back it's no longer your town, it's been alienated, you've been alienated from it'.[12] Similarly, the vanished homelands of migrants or exiles in Australia, as elsewhere, are often represented as tragic tales of separation from childhood, family and particular places, as in the case of a Vietnamese immigrant in Australia, quoted by Read:

> Now I live as if I am living in a dream. I feel as if I have freedom, and every material thing I could wish for. I was lucky to be able to choose Australia as my second home. But I feel I love my people, my family, everyone who stayed behind ...[13]

Places often stand in such memories and statements, for people and relationships left behind.

In putting the case, as I have in this essay, for a literary and cultural recognition of the local and particular in people's lives, I do not wish to undermine the benefits of modern pluralism or the benefits of global communication. Reading literature has always offered a pre-eminent transportation to other worlds, freeing us, however temporarily, from the constraints of present existence. It has also enabled us to rediscover the local by presenting it to us as fresh and strange. One of the problems of the binary presented to us as the local *versus* the global is evident in the title of Benjamin Barber's book, *Jihad vs McWorld*.[14] Although both sides of the binary suffer from such caricaturism, it is the linkage of localism with ethnic tribalism under the banner of the extremist Islamic Jihad that suffers most. The notion of a kind of McDonald's global corporatism looks positively benign beside it. Variety, difference and identification with local endeavours are clearly threatened by American corporate dominance to which some economies and cultures have had to assume an almost feudal subservience. Clearly, there is a need for hybrid versions of these too-stark alternatives, including a kind of international regionalism which incorporates the benefits of global communications with those of primary identification with a place, region and community. There should be room in this dynamic too, for an 'enlightened nationalism' of the kind promoted by Prime Minister Tony Blair in Britain, in which the notion of regional and national communities can co-exist with a special relationship with Europe and with the world more generally.

In this new cultural dynamic which we, in Australia as in India and elsewhere, are working out in our different ways, literature may play a substantial but not a dominant role. In Gore Vidal's memoir *Palimpsest*, he remarks on how difficult he finds it to believe, in the last few years of the twentieth century, that he once lived at a time 'when writers were world figures because of what they wrote, and that their ideas were known even to the vast perennial majority that never reads'.[15] That time may have passed. But with whatever permutations of the communicative arts we inform ourselves in the future, it is likely that David Suzuki's injunction to 'think globally and act locally' will continue to inform those of us who view literature as a major source of replenishment, and support, in our continual oscillation between these perspectives. A major goal for educationists should be the conservation of human personalities that are not too spaced-out in global concerns to appreciate, and contribute to, the local and particular circumstances of their daily existence. At the same time, the daily round should be continually enriched by engagement with ideas and images of the wider world to which we are increasingly linked. Whenever I can, I will continue to travel around the world in half-a-day at Canberra's embassies, and when there's time, check my email and surf the Net too. But I will try not to do so at the expense of the local literary community, its readings, festivals and meetings. To join with them is not to join Jihad at the expense of McWorld: it is an attempt to balance, in a particular way, the competing demands of localism and globalism that increasingly influence cultural attitudes and behaviour in many parts of the world.

14

The Trader's Eye: Louis Becke's South Pacific

... trade goes on
Beyond Apocalypse
    (Peter Porter, 'Paradise Park')

The prospect of profit, real or imagined, which precipitates commercial enterprise, leaves few formal records, and innovative commercial activity is usually pursued with as much subterfuge as any intrigue.
    (Margaret Steven, *Trade, Tactics and Territory*)

The first definition of 'trade' in the *Macquarie Dictionary* is 'the buying or selling, or exchanging, of commodities, either by wholesale or by retail, within a country or between countries'. The term 'trader' has two principal usages: the first is human, 'one who trades; a merchant or businessman'; and the second is non-human, 'a ship employed in trade, especially in a limited sphere, as a chain of islands'. That link between men and boats, under the sign of trade, is of special interest in the case of Louis Becke in the Pacific, as we will see. But first a brief a reflection on the relationship between trade and culture or civilisation. When I served on the Australian National Commission for UNESCO from 1985-1990, the islands of the South Pacific were often on the agenda of the Culture and Communications committees as sites endangered by the forces of international (especially American) trade and communications systems. A primary task, as we saw it then, was to assist local people to protect indigenous and local cultures in the Pacific and elsewhere against extinction, and indeed to stimulate local literature, dance, drama, song and the media arts. We were enjoined in a culture versus commerce war, while looking always for those vessels of trade that might promote our cause. In the decade since then, Sky television and the Internet have reinforced the epigraph to this essay by Peter Porter: 'trade goes on/Beyond Apocalypse'. Porter's attitude here is that of a realist, who recognises the perennial power of commerce, but as a humanist, he is appalled by its frequent disregard of human values and significance.

Another dimension interests me as well. Major book-length studies by Australian and New Zealand academics such as Nicholas Thomas, Vanessa Smith and Rod Edmond have demonstrated the resilience and continuity of Pacific societies through the colonial period and into post-colonial times. The 'fatal impact' thesis has been modified to take account of the likelihood that, in many encounters, as Edmond says, 'both sides of a transaction thought they had come away with a bargain and, in their own terms, would have been right to think so'.[1] Do we see here the triumph of Australian and New Zealand pragmatism? A rationalisation of exploitative behaviour? Or a valid account of the mixed economies of all encounters between those that seem strong and those that seem weak, but do not present themselves as victims?

At the same time, I was puzzling over some contemporary developments in dependency theory in politics, which Philip Darby has described as 'more fluid and multi-layered' than previously thought, and demonstrating an 'erosion of the great powers to control lesser powers and to regulate the course of world events'.[2]

These were some of the puzzles that led me back to Louis Becke's stories of the South Pacific written between 1893 and his death in 1913. American academic A Grove Day has written the only biography of Becke, but this and other accounts tend to replicate and reinforce the adventure-romance genre in which Becke principally wrote. Becke gave up his schooling at Fort Street Boys School in Sydney when he was fourteen and took a boat to San Francisco with his brother. Returning two years later in 1871, he stayed in Sydney for only seven months before he stowed away on a barque for Samoa, where he worked in a store in Apia and commenced his peripatetic career of some twenty years as a trader in the South Pacific. Becke signed on in 1874 as supercargo—a

merchant ship officer who manages sales of cargo—with the
American pirate and blackbirder Captain 'Bully' Hayes on the
Leonora, which sank off Kusaie two months later; Becke was
subsequently acquitted of a charge of piracy. These adventures
reveal a certain devilry in Becke's nature but they do not reveal the
trader's perspective as well as some surviving letters to his mother in
Sydney about his way of life and that of fellow traders. As Grove
Day remarks, in ironic understatement, such traders were not all
representative of 'the higher side of European civilisation'. Becke
does not pull punches in a letter to his mother about one fellow
trader named Winchcombe. Becke complains that this trader from
an adjacent island has been there four years but still cannot talk the
language, which Becke has to interpret for him. Becke then
summarises:

> He is a fair sample of too many island traders, fond of liquor and
> never happy without some grievance to relate against the natives;
> these are the men that give the missionaries such a pull over all
> traders. They are no better than the natives—they let their children
> run about wild and devote all their energies to the gin-bottle, but
> still at this present time the general island trader is as a rule a
> respectable and fairly educated man; there are a few left of the old
> class, the dissolute whaler or escaped convict.[3]

The letter is interesting for what it reveals about Becke's sense of his
role as a trader—at least that portion that he is happy to relate to his
mother. Taking a longer historical view, he sees himself in the early
1880s in a transitional phase from the rough and ready traders and
trading practices towards more educated and 'respectable' traders—
as part of a process of gentrification of the trading class. Implicit in
his letter is a hint of 'the white man's burden' which required setting
a 'civilised' example to the island people, or 'natives'. In a short story
published in the *Bulletin* on 22 June 1911, some twenty years after
the letter to his mother, and using that letter as a prompt, Becke
wrote a savage portrait of the trader Winchcombe, describing him
as 'a drink-besotted, unclean creature, illiterate and violent-
tempered'.[4] Winchcombe represented the antithesis of Becke's
notion of what the trader should be.

Louis Becke lived more or less continuously in the South Pacific
for some twenty-two years from 1872 to 1894, when he returned to
Sydney, was introduced by the writer Ernest Favenc to

J F Archibald, founder and editor of the *Bulletin*, and commenced his writing career there. Becke's focus in his stories has been described by H E Maude as 'incidents within his own limited and specialised experience: the relations between the white residents during the 1870s and '80s (usually connected with trading, whether ashore or afloat) and between them and the 'brown men and women' among whom, and with whom, they lived'.[5] But the stories are also shaped to fit the confines of the male adventure romance genre and direct translations from the stories to historical reality should be treated warily, as in the case of Robert Louis Stevenson. At the same time, Becke presents himself as a sceptical, unillusioned author who seems unlikely to be deceived, as Margaret Mead later was, by simplistic notions of a South Pacific world of playful promiscuity or 'free love' without consequences—a myth exposed by Derek Freeman.[6] The cost of casual sexual relationships between men and women, especially between white men and women of the Pacific islands in Becke's stories is often jealousy, anger, physical violence and sometimes death.

The quality required by island traders above most others is a steady, methodical approach to their work. But Becke questions this expectation in his story 'The Methodical Mr Burr of Majuru'. Ned Burr is a 'fellow trader' of the narrator, a slow-witted, methodical man who has remained unusually celibate until his marriage to the daughter of a chief on one of the Marshall Islands. How has this marriage occurred? Ned has 'stood to' (i.e. supported) the girl's people by supplying rifles to them when they were having trouble with a neighbouring king. The white trader is physically unattractive and a misogynist. When two chiefs visit from a neighbouring island, one of them apparently seduces Le-Jennabon, Ned's wife. The methodical Ned shoots him, cuts his head off and forces his wife to carry the man's head around, requiring her to sing the lines of a song he has overheard about her and himself: 'Marriage hides the tricks of lovers'. The fascination in this story is not just with an apparently restrained white man who goes 'wild' and whose savagery exceeds that of the islanders; but Ned sees his actions as cementing his control over his wife, his esteem in the community and 'the esteem of the people generally as a man who hez business principles'. The grotesque irony here cuts both ways—at least as much against assumed Western 'business principles' as against native customs. The story also reveals the savagery beneath the business principles of white men's so-called 'civilisation' in the Pacific, as Conrad later revealed it with greater subtlety and imaginative reach.

What then are the main business characteristics of Becke's traders in the Pacific? Some of them emerge in one of Becke's stronger stories in literary terms, 'The Fate of the *Alida*,' published in *By Reef and Palm* (1894). In this story, Becke reveals himself observing the activities of his character through the experienced eyes of a Western trader. Late in the story, as a trading vessel passes a small, thinly populated island the narrator remarks:

> There was nothing on the island to tempt a trading vessel, and even the sperm whalers as they lumbered lazily past from Strong's Island to Guam would not bother to lower a boat and 'dicker' for pearl-shell or turtle.[7]

The intransitive verb 'to dicker' is a mainly US term meaning to trade or barter by petty bargaining, to haggle. This is the most informal end of the trading process which, over time, becomes a more formal, even ritualised process with more or less developed codes and expectations. While bartering, haggling or trading, the participants learn to play roles.

In the story "'Tis in the Blood'[8] the local traders learn smart 'sales talk' and how to be good buyers with impersonations and clever use of language. Allan, a half-caste *manaia* (Lothario) in Levuka uses these skills to talk Vaega, a beautiful, convent-educated Samoan girl, to leave her 'fat hog of a Dutchman' and give herself to him. Questions of price and value are involved in this. Island women are perceived to lose value when they lose their physical beauty, but white traders like this Dutchman, however gross they are physically, can still buy their beauty and pleasure—or so they think—for a price. However, a competition between those with material resources and those without occurs repeatedly in Becke's stories in the face of 'nature' or natural urges and behaviour. What is 'in the blood' often overcomes money and property, though this kind of triumph is usually short-lived. Thus the Samoan girl Vaega lasts only six months wedded to her Lothario before he is 'captivated' by the daughter of a chief and escapes to marry her. But Vaega is no passive victim and she learns in turn to exploit her beauty, through prostitution, it seems, before rejoining the defeated Dutchman who still wants her back with him. It is because of the close relationship between sex and trade in these situations that the crime of 'theft' so often occurs. But trade has its limits and human passions can undermine or destroy its procedures, with violent revenge and murder a frequent outcome.

Grove Day's selection of Becke's stories *South Sea Supercargo*[9] brings together twenty-two short narratives which feature Tom Denison, Becke's Australian *alter ego*, in a variety of adventures in the Pacific islands. His role as supercargo gives him a particular perspective on Oceania.

An ironic discrepancy between human and monetary value is exposed in 'A Dead Loss,' the opening story of *South Sea Supercargo*. Despite the story's dominant masculinist viewpoint, it reveals the dignity and strength of purpose, in desperate circumstances, of Lunumula, a beautiful young woman who is treated as a chattel by Chaplin, the boat's captain. In a dramatic and desperate act, Lunumula establishes her own sense of value by climbing the topgallant fo'c'sle and, with her white dress flapping against her 'slender figure', she leaps overboard. Denison, the trader with conventional male humanist values of his time, remarks on the 'sad end to the poor girl's life' but the methodical ex-Honolulu blackbirding captain sees it as a sad end to his five hundred dollars which he has paid for the girl in order to sell her for a profit in Fiji. There are other characters and other strands in this story, including a trader who 'goes native' and therefore becomes worthless to his company, and is replaced. But the major theme in the story is a problematic sense of 'home' and its significance for both the white invaders and the indigenous people. In this story, as in others by Becke, those who are isolated for long periods from their island and local community suffer a '*mal de pays*'. This sense of belonging is not idealised by Becke, but he recognises its emotional power.

Louis Becke's Australian trader Taplin, in 'The Fate of the *Alida*', shares with Tom Denison some of the more positive characteristics of the figure of the trader. Taplin is an island-based trader, one of two on Funafuti in the Ellice Islands. Disgusted with his firm's 'unscrupulous method of doing business'[10] he refuses to extend his work period beyond the two-year contract he has signed on for. Taplin is not obviously idealised, but in common with some of Henry Lawson's itinerant bushmen he has 'a curious far-off look' in his eyes, which Becke explains is 'not uncommon' among men who have spent many years moving among the islands of the Pacific— even before he had cut his links with 'the outside world'. Taplin seems to be a man of conscience and humanity also in his relationship with his wife Nerida, a part Portuguese woman to whom he is deeply attached and who wishes to return to her home base in the Carolines. With Nerida 'fretting' to return, Taplin makes the fatal error of travelling with her aboard a schooner with two villains, who murder him, but are thwarted in their attempts to have their pleasure of her. There is no necessary survival for men or women of good conscience and humanity in Becke's South Pacific, but the local woman does survive and marries another sea captain.

One of the favoured outcomes of postcolonial theorists is hybridity. Nicholas Thomas has accurately discerned that, in contrast to many travellers' narratives, Becke's are played out in 'a zone of interaction and hybridity':

> His early stories, in particular, were preoccupied with the often fatal results of liaisons between white men and black women. They also deal with half-castes, with degenerate whites who have assumed the savagery but not the nobility of island warriors, and with natives, who are partially assimilated or acculturated.[11]

Steering a passage between the missionaries' view of Oceania as a world to convert and the colonialist view of necessary Western dominance, Becke did indeed reveal a mixed economy in interactions between 'outsiders' and 'insiders' in the Pacific. There might be more in the description of Becke as the 'Rudyard Kipling of the Pacific'[12] than meets the eye, in view of recent revaluations of Kipling, except that, as an Australian, Becke knew that he could never carry the full burden, or the authority, of Empire.

The metaphor of commerce or trade, which permeates Louis Becke's narratives of the Pacific, suggests continual exchanges of goods, human-resources and services. Robert Dixon contends that:

> Sex, commerce and labour are inextricably connected in these networks of exchange, and the recurring figure of the 'trader' is a synecdoche of the imperial ideal reduced to the profit motive. Most of the stories involve destructive exchanges or sequences of exchange.[13]

While it is true that a number of the exchanges between whites and islander peoples reveal the destructive influence of Europeans and Americans in the Pacific, it is also the case that the cultures of island peoples turn the tables from time to time on those of the whites.

Indeed, some representative islanders survive, and even thrive, by adhering to traditional values and loyalty to place, region and community. Others learn to use Western ways to their advantage.

Louis Becke was not a deeply reflective writer. His genre was the adventure romance and his authorial tone is often briskly dismissive of those discursive opportunities for philosophical reflection which give Conrad's (and sometimes Stevenson's) stories their special flavour and appeal. Becke's recurrent focus, however, is on the modes of exchange—cultural, physical, commercial, emotional—which characterise an early phase of Western trading in the Pacific in the 1870s and 1880s. The Australian's fiction has none of the appropriative impulse that one finds in books like the American Fay G Calkins's memoir *My Samoan Chief*,[14] in which she describes her generally unsuccessful attempts in the 1950s to introduce American institutions such as a credit union, a co-op, a work schedule and hourly wages on the banana plantation begun by herself and her Samoan husband. Like other male Australian writers of the 1890s, Becke recalled with some nostalgia a rough and tough, frontier situation in the Pacific before 'Western' civilisation had significantly encroached on island life, while the 'rules' for intercultural activity were still being written. His two decades as a pioneer trader in the Pacific gave him a set of experiences, and an outlook, both ironic and respectful, which informs his stories. He imagined Oceania principally as a region of masculine adventure and romance. What sustained him, however, was not religion or philosophy but a sense that trade—buying and selling, the exchange of goods and services, and of insults, passions, compliments and blows—will endure beyond particular beliefs and philosophies.

Coda

The world Louis Becke inhabited is now past, with its tyranny (and blessing) of distance, just as Henry Lawson's Australian outback with its open spaces and sparse frontier settlements has been overtaken by jet aircraft and modern communication systems. The leisurely trading schooner calling at island stores looks old-fashioned to a new generation of international jetsetters and futures exchange marketeers. In these circumstances, what can a Louis Becke offer to modern readers in the Pacific and elsewhere? In the first place, his stories indicate a widening of horizons for the white trader/invader.

His short fiction reveals a vivid attention to people, places and dramatic incidents in the spirit of Wordsworth's 'Bliss was it in that dawn to be alive'. But Becke's vision was not in the end revolutionary or romantic. Becke, the Australian, like the Americans and Europeans in their schooners, was a hard-headed trader always on the look-out for profit from the sale of goods. His traders' particular source of power is their capacity to move on when the going gets tough. While this peripatetic life suited Becke and the more or less sympathetic plunderers and pirates of his time, his fiction also shows the strength of the Pacific peoples. These are the people who know their homes and local communities and therefore have a power of endurance beyond the transitory liaisons of the interloper, with whom they will trade and interact only so far as they choose to do so.

Early Prisoners in Australia: Henry Savery and John Boyle O'Reilly

Although some later generations tried to suppress the memory, Australia's origins as a convict settlement have become as important a defining element in versions of 'the Australian story' as Puritan settlement has been in 'the American story'. A memorable commentary on this kind of historiography is provided in Peter Porter's poem 'Sydney Cove, 1788' and the thinking that suffuses and surrounds it. An atmosphere of menace is evoked in the poem's lines that take the reader into a surrealistic perspective that might be shared by arriving convicts and their gaolers:

> We wake in the oven of its cloudless sky,
> Already the blood-encircled sun is up.
> Mad sharks swim in the convenient sea.
>
> The Governor says we mustn't land a man
> Or woman with gonorrhoea. Sound felons only
> May leave their bodies in a hangman's land.[1]

While this poem recognisably arises from Porter's sardonic and angry phase of the 1960s, it is expanded historiographically by his later remark that Australia differs from the United States in being 'born in horror, not in hope, so that the country's progress could only be an improvement, while America has watched its dream of hope disintegrate into corruption and inanition'.[2]

This discussion focuses on the modes of perception and insight in Australia's first and last novels by convicts or ex-convicts, Henry

Savery's *Quintus Servinton* (Hobart Town, 1830-31) and John Boyle
O'Reilly's *Moondyne* (Boston, 1879). Both of these novels have been
underrated when one considers the roles their authors have played
in setting a stage for subsequent Australian narratives.[3]

Two areas of investigation are to the forefront in my
consideration of these novels. First, I am interested in the extent to
which these narratives of imprisonment and escape were dominated
by personal memories and the prisoner's ego, and to what extent the
writers used their narratives to explore wider issues such as place,
region and community. Lying beyond these questions are Stephen
Greenblatt's interlinked concepts of curiosity and a sense of
wonder.[4] To what extent does the prisoner's or ex-prisoner's
narrative, in its historical context, offer a sign of imaginative
freedom and engagement with the wider world? Or does it remain
bound in the cell of selfhood?

With such questions in mind, I am struck by the dominance of
memory in Savery's novel *Quintus Servinton*,[5] a memory pressed into
the service of self-justification and explanation in this thinly
disguised autobiographical novel. By contrast with his often chirpy
satirical essays published in the anti-establishment, emancipist paper
the *Colonial Times* under the pseudonym of Simon Stukely in 1829
and published as a book with the title, *The Hermit in Van Diemen's
Land* in 1829–30, *Quintus Servinton* is a long exposition of a young
man's fortunes and misfortunes, leading to his transportation from
England's West Country to Australia's Van Diemen's Land. The
lighter-hearted, satirical journalism suggests a bolder, more
confrontational author than does the novel. Although the novel is
no Dostoievskian exposition of the marking of men's souls by their
involvement in crime and in punishment, it does offer an account of
the protagonist's induction into crime and his suffering as a result of
it. The allegorical, satiric method of the essays by 'the Hermit' is
periodically present in the novel in figures such as Mr Plausible or
Mr Glossover, and a sententious, *Pilgrim's Progress* style, widely
recognised among literate protestants of Savery's time, is adopted
for ethical or spiritual commentary:

> No person ever yet perhaps, committed a first offence, without
> some contentions with that small, still voice, implanted within our
> breast, by a beneficent Providence, serving, like a light-house or
> beacon to mariners on a dangerous coast, to warn them of their
> danger, and to point out the track, which may be followed with

safety. But the broad and open road to hell, is paved, presenting a gentle declivity to those who tread it; studded with allurements in every shape, likely to attract and gratify the senses, and ever teeming with the sin, that most easily besetteth us.[6]

While this kind of passage recalls conventional confessional narratives, Savery presents Quintus elsewhere as an over-reaching, ambitious man who charms people in the manner of a confidence trickster. But because this is an autobiographical novel, wherein the self under examination is principally that of the author himself, who has suffered the deepest of disappointments and despair, we are not presented with a figure of ramifying interest, resilience and complexity like, for instance, Henry Melville's American protagonist in *The Confidence Man* (1857). We have instead a young English businessman from Bristol and surroundings, tempted, succumbing to forgery, and, most significantly, being captured and sentenced to death, before being given his reprieve in Australia.

Quintus Servinton, subtitled *A Tale Founded on Incidents of Real Occurrence*, is a thinly disguised memoir about the author's upbringing, education and induction into business followed by his trial, transportation and experiences as prisoner and ticket-of-leave man in Australia. (Savery was transported to Van Diemen's Land and arrived in Hobart in December 1825).[7] Savery's evocation of place in the English West Country is more extensive, more detailed and sensuous than the novel's Australian settings, which are stripped bare of specific identifying features, not just because the protagonist's movements are restricted, but also because his psychological state isolates him from landscape and society in Australia; and because, for reasons to be outlined later, Savery transposed his 'real-life' setting of Tasmania to New South Wales. Often prolix and repetitive, Savery's narrative is driven by a brooding and compelling sense of disappointment and despair. The title of a 1984 reprint, *The Bitter Bread of Banishment*,[8] quoting *Richard II*, captures the novel's recurrent dark tone, which is reinforced by the narrator's search for the seeds in his early life of his later 'tree of sorrow'.

A spirit of curiosity is reserved chiefly for the discovery of those 'seeds' that led to Savery's convictions for forgery and counterfeit with intent to defraud, following bankruptcy in business.[9] Trying to abscond from England, the novel's protagonist, like Savery himself, is captured by the authorities on board a boat destined for America, and is tried, convicted and sentenced to hang, before the lesser penalty of transportation to Australia is imposed. A sense of wonder is reserved in the narrative for a compensating romance in the past—the one which led to Quintus's marriage to a London girl called Emily. In the manner of many nineteenth-century novels, the representation of Emily is idealised, but it is an interesting case of idealisation, in which problematic elements of misunderstanding, deception and separation are intertwined. In the early stages of the relationship, as it is presented, the semi-genteel, rural West Country life of hunts and country houses provides the requisite background for a romantic idyll, complicated only by what the writer retrospectively recognises as his own over-weening 'self-confidence, restless ambition and wild speculation', which lead to his later undoing. The 'country Quintus' constructed in this narrative is happier, more secure and a better person than the 'city Quintus', thus building on British Romantic country-city oppositions depicted by Wordsworth, Cobbett and others.

In the later stages of Savery's novel-memoir, leading to the romantic conclusion of the couple's return from Australia to a cottage in Devonshire, it is difficult to avoid a sense of novelistic invention, which distinguishes this narrative from 'straight' autobiography. In retrospect, we know that the 'love-problems', caused principally by the plausible Savery, were indeed irreconcilable. As author, Savery uses both the device of historical distancing, claiming to look back twenty or thirty years to different forms of punishment, and that of the romantic ending. Neither device is convincing in the novel. The author Henry Savery's actual fate reinforces the impression that the distancing devices of romantic fiction were covers, necessary disguises, of his actual fate, which was to persuade his wife and son, with false expectations of his circumstances, to join him in the colony; and for this to be followed by the failure of that reunion within a week and Savery's attempt at suicide by cutting his throat—only to be subsequently reimprisoned, at Port Arthur, on another forgery conviction. It has been speculated, with some evidence, that a complicating factor in Savery's misery was Mrs Savery's shipboard relationship with Algernon Montagu, who was on his way to a job as Attorney-General in Tasmania.[10] Montagu appears as Malvers in the novel-memoir, and is said to be going to the colony of New South Wales, not Van Diemen's Land—thus contributing to the erasure of place as a significant factor in the novel's Australian episodes. Montagu had acted as Mrs Savery's 'protector' on the eighteen week voyage to Tasmania, and there are indications that she and Montagu saw each other frequently during the three months before she returned to England with her son, never to see her husband again. Unable to confront these real life complications directly in his novel, Savery retreated to the easier, wish-fulfilment conventions of romance.

Unlike some other forms of writing, a novel requires sustained attention over a period of months, or even years. From his own account, and from historical deductions, it seems that Savery wrote *Quintus Servinton* during the latter part of his imprisonment at Port Arthur, and after he was discharged and assigned to a farm owned by an army man in the New Norfolk district.[11] For a social being and a charmer, as Savery clearly was, the enforced isolation must have provided some necessary conditions for the long and lonely pursuit of novel-writing. But the narrative itself, together with the circumstances of its composition, contribute to a view that the writer was in a state of depression when he wrote the work. The relative placelessness of the Australian part of the narrative may result partly from this condition as well as from the need to disguise the story-teller's identity. In such circumstances, it is hardly surprising that the author does not 'marvel' or 'wonder' at a new world in the way that Greenblatt's travel writers do in a spirit of confidence, freedom of action and general buoyancy of spirit in which they imaginatively 'possess' new lands. Nor can he respond with the resilient optimism of an escapee such as John Boyle O'Reilly.

From a literary historical perspective, the most compelling sequel to the story of Henry Savery's novel about his alter ego, Quintus Servinton, is the reported meeting, some twelve years later (in 1842) of David Burn, author of *The Bushrangers*, the first play with an Australian theme performed overseas,[12] and Savery, Australia's first novelist. Savery was on his deathbed at Port Arthur prison and seems to have been unconscious. Burn wrote that he saw in Savery's prone figure on the prison pallet 'a sad, a solemn warning', evoking 'the deepest compassion, mingled with horror and awe'.[13] At age 50, Savery would be dead within a month of Burn's visit. Burn had written his play, *The Bushrangers*, a decade earlier, and contributed plays, poems and travel narratives to the regional literature of

Tasmania and Australia. Savery's contribution was of a different kind. His novel dug into the darker recesses of the self, a greater subject for him than the Tasmania he inhabited in body but hardly in spirit.

John Boyle O'Reilly's utterly different novel, *Moondyne*[14]—a product of the last phase of the convict system in Australia—was played out in the historically belated colony of Western Australia which received convicts from 1850 to 1868. O'Reilly was a Fenian who had enlisted in the British army in order to win over his fellow soldiers to the Irish cause. He was court martialled, found guilty and sentenced to death, but had his sentence commuted to twenty years penal servitude. O'Reilly spent time in prisons at Millbank, Portsmouth and Dartmoor before being transported to Western Australia in 1868 on the *Hougoumont,* the last convict ship to be sent to the Australian colonies.[15] In his biography, *Fanatic Heart : A Life of John Boyle O'Reilly* ,[16] A G Evans notes the 'restless, resourceful spirit' of his subject, who had a record of three escape attempts from English prisons before his successful escape from Bunbury, Western Australia, to the United States in an American whaler in 1869. O'Reilly later organised from Boston the escape of six Irish prisoners from Fremantle gaol in 1876—an adventure which is celebrated in the rousing and still popular folk-song, *The Catalpa.*[17] With this successful track record in escapes, it is perhaps not surprising that O'Reilly chose as hero of his romantic and melodramatic novel, *Moondyne,* the figure of a celebrated Western Australian bushranger and escapologist, Joseph Bolitho Jones, better known as Moondyne Joe, who was in Fremantle gaol at the same time as O'Reilly. Moondyne has been described as 'Australia's own Houdini'[18] and he achieved a legendary status in Australia's West which has been taken up in various literary forms including Randolph Stow's book for children and young adults, *Midnite* (1967) and the folk musical, *Moondyne Joe,* at the Perth Festival in 1982.

O'Reilly's novel *Moondyne*[19] begins and ends in Western Australia, chiefly at Fremantle gaol and in what O'Reilly calls the Vasse region of the south-west. The protagonist has two guises: in the first part of the novel he is Moondyne, the convict who escapes from prison, joins an Aboriginal tribe and discovers a goldmine in Aboriginal territory before returning to England; in the rest of the narrative he is known as Mr Wyville, an impressive penal reformer who is appointed in London as comptroller-general of convicts to clean up the prison system in Australia. When he dies in a bushfire in Australia's south-west, the self-sacrificing hero takes the secret of his former identity with him, though it remains known and respected by Ngarra-jil, his long-term Aboriginal companion and friend.

O'Reilly's first biographer and advocate, J J Roche, has noted many similarities between the author and his protagonist, Wyville-Moondyne,[20] and A G Evans, the more recent and more careful biographer, concurs that there is much of O'Reilly in the novel, both biographical and in terms of his social philosophy.[21] The biographies contain some apparently well-founded speculation about O'Reilly's hopeless love for Jessie Woodman, the daughter of his gaoler in Bunbury, which O'Reilly transfers to Wyville-Moondyne's unfulfilled love for Alice Walmsley, a young convict woman wrongly transported to Western Australia for child-murder. O'Reilly apparently attempted suicide when Jessie decided to marry another man. In such transpositions from raw experience to the page, novelists are of course freer to indulge their fantasies and speculations than biographers. The idealised figure of Alice Walmsley is contextualised in terms of the pretty rural village of Walton-le-Dale, near Preston in Lancashire, where O'Reilly lived for some years (1859-63) before he was charged with seditious activities in England, and this setting provides the centre-point of a somewhat complicated love interest in the novel *Moondyne*. First, Alice is courted in her village by two young men, Tom Draper and Will Sheridan, before the deceptive and villainous Draper (who is already married to a woman named Harriet in Calcutta) wins Alice's hand and has a child with her, who is subsequently killed by the jealous Harriet during a return visit from India. Recognising Harriet's feelings and rights as a wife, Alice takes the rap for Harriet's crime, and is imprisoned and then transported to the Swan River Colony. Wyville-Moondyne recognises Alice's innocence in England and becomes her protector, first in England and later in Australia. However, he has to relinquish his hopes for Alice, as O'Reilly did for Jessie Woodman, when another good and faithful man from her home village (Tom Sheridan in the novel) claims her hand. As this brief summary indicates, the tenor here is hope for true love, though its path never runs smooth—a note of hope which is struck with far less conviction in *Quintus Servinton*. Alice Walmsley and the faithful lover of her Walton days, Tom Sheridan, become inheritors of Australia's beautiful south-west. Wyville-Moondyne dies sacrificing his life in a vain attempt to save the unreformed Tom Draper and the wife who still follows him.

O'Reilly's representations of women in *Moondyne* are framed by the generic requirements of melodramatic romance, but they are informed also by his Irish-Catholic inheritance. Alice Walmsley, for example, is a mix of the Madonna and a natural English rose; and the angry and sometimes alcoholic Harriet somehow manages to forgive her errant husband. As O'Reilly somewhat unconvincingly psychologises, 'A woman's hatred is only her love on fire'.[22] By implication, men are the only true haters. In addition to Wyville as protector, Alice is blessed with the tutelary figure of a nun, Sister Cecilia, who travels with her until her release from prison in Western Australia and this is presented as a guarantee of her virtue. The Protestant dominance in the colony is thus redeemed in part by Catholic grace.

Heroics are an intrinsic element in melodrama, and O'Reilly shows flair with the genre in his figures of Moondyne Joe and Alice Walmsley. Joe is a bold and good man:

> Whatever was his offence against the law, he has received its bitter lesson. The worst of the convicts grew better when associated with him. Commonsense, truth, and kindness were Joe's principles. He was a strong man, and he pitied and helped those weaker than himself. He was a bold man, and he understood the timid. He was a brave man, and he grieved for a coward or a liar. He never preached; but his healthy, straightforward life did more good to his fellows than all the hired bible-readers in the colony.[23]

By comparison, one of O'Reilly's Irish compatriots wrote of the author thus: 'He excels in all manly arts and accomplishments in a way that we are almost afraid to chronicle, so like a hero of romance the list would make him seem'.[24] O'Reilly's fictional heroine is suitably endowed with the feminine graces of beauty, innocence and morality:

> Alice Walmsley had been born with a heart all kindness and sympathy. From her very infancy she had loved intensely the kindly, the unselfish and the beautiful. She had lived through her girlhood as happy, healthy and pure as the primroses beneath her mother's hedgerows. She had approached womanhood as a silver stream

ripples to the sea, yearning for its greatness and its troubles and its joys—hurrying from the calm delights of the meadow-banks to the mighty main of strength, and saltness, and sweetness.[25]

The novel *Moondyne* bears the marks not only of O'Reilly's Western Australian and English adventures but also of his decade of experience in North America after his escape, when he was a social activist and editor of the Boston *Pilot*. O'Reilly began his serial story entitled 'Moondyne Joe' in the *Pilot* on 30 November 1878, and the novel was published the following year by Roberts Bros. in Boston. Many of the attitudes and values in the novel were thus in part the product of a decade of freedom in 'the land of the free', largely in the expatriate Irish community in and around Boston. On the broader literary front, O'Reilly was probably influenced in his presentation of masculine literary subjectivity and the natural environment by Whitman, whose *Leaves of Grass* had appeared in 1855 and Thoreau, whose *Walden* was published in 1854. And in his representation of Australia as a place of extraordinary happenings, O'Reilly prefigures Mark Twain's commentaries about Australia in *Following the Equator: A Journey Around the World* (1897), in which the American author typified Australia as 'like the most beautiful lies ... full of surprises, and adventures, and incongruities, and contradictions, and incredibilities ...'.[26] More specifically, the spirit of enterprise and opportunity which O'Reilly imports into his account of the sandalwood trade in Western Australia seems to derive in part at least from his North American experience. O'Reilly introduces a bunch of strong, devil-may-care Irish timber-cutters from Dardanup in Western Australia who break up a cartel of recalcitrant and violent ticket-of-leave 'teamsters' standing in the way of free enterprise and increased trade.[27] O'Reilly's American experience may also account for aspects of his presentation of republican and anti-aristocratic English views that recur, as well as a respect for minorities. O'Reilly was a defender of Negroes and Jews in his Boston journalism, and some of those attitudes seem to infuse his creation of Ngarra-jil and his Maori-sounding Aboriginal Australians. Through his alter ego, Wyville, O'Reilly proffers idealistic reforms which may transmute Western Australia from a 'menagerie' to a fountain of civilisation.

The novel also contains O'Reilly's brave attempt to express a philosophy that rises above tribalism, but which surprisingly raised the ire of Irish critics described by Roche as 'ultra Catholics, who objected to what they called [the novel's] pagan spirit'.[28] Wyville's preference for 'Mankind and Liberty—instead of Patriotism and Law'[29] was an expression of a Christian humanism too broad-based for some of the Irish tribes on America's north-eastern seaboard. Despite O'Reilly's apparently egalitarian sentiments, the new society he envisaged for Western Australia was paternalistic, dependent on a benign autocrat such as Wyville. Such societies need heroes— larger-than-life, self-sacrificing men and women who are prepared to impose their moral authority for the greater good. How they get to such positions as Comptroller-General of Prisons—unless by disguise, as in the case of the former bushranger, Moondyne—is never seriously addressed. (The special authority given to Wyville is said in passing to be based on his record of reform of the Indian Penal System at the Andaman Islands and he was accepted by the French emperor as an authority on the treatment of crime.[30]) The treatment of Aboriginal issues is similarly thin. The land rights bequeathed to Te-mana-roa and his people, giving them 'a certain section of land in the Vasse Mountains' are contained in Wyville's will and registered with lawyers in London. But no general hereditary right is implied by this.

However, we should not expect expert social analysis according to modern assumptions and values in an entertaining and visionary novel such as *Moondyne*. What we are presented with is an adventure novel which, though to some extent ego-driven, also has its eyes set upon actual places and communities in the country of imprisonment. A spirit of curiosity and a sense of wonder are recurrent in descriptions of place and people, and these seem to reflect not only aspects of the writer's experiences in Britain and Australia but also in America in the period of the novel's composition and creation. Furthermore, *Moondyne* successfully addresses the American and British colonial reading publics' hunger for such stories. Unlike his predecessor Henry Savery, John Boyle O'Reilly made his escape from the prison-house of self, as he did from the Australian convict system, and transformed it imaginatively into a land of hope and opportunity, reinforced by growing self-confidence in the colonies following the gold rushes. When Will Sheridan enthusiastically encourages a potential English settler in Western Australia, he strikes a note that is recurrently endorsed in *Moondyne*: 'Australia is going to send out the largest-hearted men that ever owned the earth. You will breathe freely in its splendid air. Oh, I am proud to see such men turn by nature to the magnificent South!'.[31]

Savery and O'Reilly conveniently frame the early and later phases of literary creativity by convicts in colonial Australia. Bringing them together in this way also serves to reinforce the different times, places and circumstances in which, and of which, they wrote. So different are those places, personalities and conditions that it would be foolish to invoke any myth of progress from them.

The interiority of treatment in much of *Quintus Servinton* exposes a dark night of the soul which overflows and pervades the author's account of his protagonist's life, early and late, from his picaresque English West Country adventures to imprisonment in Australia. This gloomy side of Savery's temperament draws on a store of Anglican protestant scriptures together with moralistic texts such as Bunyan's *Pilgrim's Progress* and is evident in summative passages such as the following:

> ... [H]e built his house upon the sand, choosing for its cornerstones self-confidence, restless ambition, and wild speculation, rather than humility and a prudent ascent of the rugged path of worldly gains, and suffering all his advantages of birth, education, talents and connexions to be lost ...[32]

Such sentiments emerging from the protestant tradition, and culminating in Milton's *Paradise Lost*, may indeed be the strongest element in the mental and emotional environment transported with Savery to Van Diemen's Land in 1826, reinforced by the isolating physical and social environments he inhabited there. Yet Savery's resilient journalistic persona, Simon Stukely, is a more buoyant figure, observing his social environment with some of the hard-nosed realism of a Defoe, and capable of mocking it with a well-turned phrase. The oscillation between these states of being—that of the engaged and witty social being and of the miserable isolate—indicates the mood swings which led Savery to several attempts at suicide.[33]

The most obvious social difference between Savery and O'Reilly is that the convict experience of the former was as an English 'gentleman-criminal' while the latter was an Irish political prisoner. While both learned to use the resources of language to establish an image of distance between themselves and 'ordinary' prisoners in

their different environments, they drew on different language
communities and cultures to do this. O'Reilly's Irish Catholic
inheritance, with its emphasis on miracles and a community of
fellowship, gave him access to patriotic songs and verses as well as
to the scriptures. After his first arrest in Dublin in 1866, O'Reilly is
recorded as writing patriotic songs and ballads in prison,[34] and he
went on to write and publish prolific songs, speeches, reports,
sermons and narratives until his death in 1890.[35] J J Roche, his first
biographer, has summarised O'Reilly's inherited discourses as an
integral part of his life, work and reputation:

> In boyhood his imagination feasts on the weird songs and legends
> of the Celt; in youth his heart agonises over that saddest and
> strangest romance in all history,—the wrongs and woes of his
> mother-land, that Niobe of the nations; in manhood, because he
> dared to wish her free, he finds himself a doomed felon, an exiled
> convict in what he calls himself 'the nether world', then, bursting
> his prison bars, a hunted fugitive, reaching the haven of this land of
> liberty penniless and unknown, but rising by the sheer force of his
> genius and his worth, till the best and the noblest in our country vie
> in doing honor to his name.[36]

By contrast, Savery's emotionally reconstituted images and ideas in
Quintus Servinton more dourly evoke Peter Porter's image of a
predominantly protestant 'hangman's land', where the self remains
imprisoned, salvation is an individual pursuit, ambition and drive are
stultified and the boundaries of living are severely limited. From this
state of imprisonment, a greener past in England's West Country is
constructed, as compensation. Savery could hardly have imagined
O'Reilly's thoughtfully audacious hero, emerging in print a half
century later, a bushranger transformed into a prison controller,
who turns the tables on the old penal code and institutes a practice
of kindness and respect based on what O'Reilly calls 'the radical
principles of humanity'.

Sharing National Memories: Literary Histories in the Commonwealth

> Most of the family is there and words are said
> and those who can't attend wait for news of the dead
> as now it is all about memory.

The above lines are by a West Australian poet, John Kinsella, who lives and works in England and the United States. The lines are from his poem 'Funeral Oration' and they refer to the death of the writer's grandmother in Australia. My purpose in quoting these lines in the context of a discussion about literary history is not to argue that all literary history is of the genre of the funeral oration, though it may sometimes assume that role. I painfully recall once showing the Australian poet A D Hope a literary-historical piece I had written about him, to which his response was that he liked the discussion but the contextualising commentary made him feel summarised, classified and boxed-up. It was a salutary warning. In more recent excursions into literary history with Jennifer Strauss in *The Oxford Literary History of Australia*,[1] to which brief reference will be made later, I have been especially aware of the need for literary historiography to establish both the pastness of the past and its continuing vivacity, its 'withness'. It is a matter of concern that literary history can seem monumental rather than an encouragement to appreciate, question and change the world around us.

The memories authors and editors evoke and recommend for consideration from their different geographical and cultural contexts in books of literary history are presented in their own right and, implicitly or explicitly, for comparison with others. Behind such public remembering lie attitudes and assumptions about memory-making and its constant companion, the act (in some cases the practised art) of forgetting.

Remembering, forgetting and inventing. No controversy has had greater airtime in Western countries in recent years than recovered-memory syndrome. After an initial period of euphoria at the power of psychologists to 'help' patients to retrieve memories of child-abuse, experts and media opinion-leaders turned sceptical and threw doubt on the role of certain professionals who were found to 'prompt' and thus to evoke false memories. Hence the concept of 'false memory syndrome'. Another related crisis in the psychology industry since the 1970s has been the rise and fall of Multiple Personality Disorder and its associated experiments in 'multiography', which have been effectively traced by Elaine Showalter.[2] MPD, as it became known, often emerged after patients had been recovering memories in therapy for many years and, as Showalter reported, 'is being exported from the U.S. as effectively as Diet Coke and the Gap'. In 1994, the managers of Psychology's public image changed the name of their 'product' from 'multiple personality disorder' to 'dissociative identity disorder' following the exposure of a spate of competitively-induced, invented abuse narratives in which patients reported 'hundreds of personalities in a kind of competition. Some were claiming lobsters, tigers, chickens or Ninja turtles'. One of the effects of this competitive industry, as Showalter has reported it, was to make the mother 'a central figure in the abuse narrative' and to popularise 'the role of the female therapist as benevolent surrogate mother, in a style very different from that of the bullying or seductive male psychoanalyst of popular culture'. The discovery, and subsequent disowning, of syndromes such as 'recovered memory' and 'multiple personality disorder' may in turn be symptomatic of a widespread cultural fascination with the plasticity of memory and, more especially, with the loss of it, both in personal and in community experience. One of the increasingly named terrors of our times is Alzheimer's Disease, brilliantly portrayed in John Bayley's memoir of novelist Iris Murdoch.[3]

To any historian of literature and culture, the growing interest among psychologists and the wider community in 'emotional intelligence',[4] and the influence of mood upon perception and judgement, must be relevant. Consider for a moment recent thinking about optimists and pessimists, which has a hint of the traditional about it. According to this thinking, people in a positive frame of mind often think more superficially and are more likely to 'rely on pre-existing knowledge and to confuse new information with earlier knowledge'. By way of contrast, people in a negative mood tend to be more 'systematic and vigilant. They rely less on what they think they know and are more sensitive to the actual information in their environment'.[5] Constructed memories, personal or public, are thus emotional as well as cognitive constructs, and one of our tasks as literary and cultural critics is to understand the emotions that underlie and give shape to these artifacts.

The most influential investigation of public and communal memory in recent times has been Eric Hobsbawm and Terence Ranger's *The Invention of Tradition*, first published in 1983 and continually reprinted since then. In his introduction to this book, Hobsbawm suggests that 'invented traditions ... normally attempt to establish continuity with a suitable historic past'.[6] 'It is the contrast between the constant change and innovation of the modern world and the attempt to structure at least some parts of social life within it as unchanging and invariant', Hobsbawm explains, 'that makes the "invention of tradition" so interesting for historians of the past two centuries'.[7]

For those of us in countries of the Commonwealth who had learnt to imagine South Africa's future in terms of a widely predicted apocalyptic revolution, the events before, during and since the first democratic elections there in April 1994, especially the work of the Truth and Reconciliation Commission, culminating in its findings in 1998, have been revelatory in a different way. Aside from the mass of popular journalism that has covered these events, one book stands out in its investigation of the uses of tradition, truth, memory and narrative in this period. This book is a selection of essays called *Negotiating the Past: The Making of Memory in South Africa* edited by Sarah Nuttall and Carli Coetzee.[8] The task of the Truth and Reconciliation Commission, as the editors put it, was to delve into South Africa's grim past; the records of the hearings of the TRC are thus perceived as a major repository of South African memory, a memory charged with emotion. The book is presented as 'a contribution to an ongoing debate about the processes of memory, and about how memory is created and inscribed', but its editors wrote in *medias res* and wisely deferred judgement, admitting that they were 'as yet unable to judge which memories and ways of remembering will come to dominate South Africa in the future'.[9] The purpose of the editors and their contributors was rather to question 'how it happens that certain versions of the past get to be remembered, which memories are privileged, and what the loci are for the production of memory'.[10] While some contributors to *Negotiating the Past* were chiefly concerned with the production of 'truth', others preferred the TRS's role as representing 'healing through narrative'. An important perspective in the book is a set of concerns around 'the drive to reconciliation and unity' which the editors believe 'runs the risk of promoting amnesia'.[11] Should the task of memory be to 'reconstitute and make whole' or 'to reconstitute turbulence and fragmentation, including these painful reminders of what we were, and what we are'?[12] The exposure of remembered pain and fear is seen to conflict here with an impulse towards reconciliation and charitable feelings towards others across racial divisions.

The essays in *Negotiating the Past* offer important perspectives for literary and cultural historians in other Commonwealth countries. If the constituents of a metal are best tested under stress, so too are literary and cultural tendencies. Nuttall and Coetzee's book shows, among other things, that questions sometimes seen as 'aesthetic' in a narrow or refined sense, can play a significant role in social and political reform, as in the emotional set of groups of people towards others in a community. Nuttall's study of autobiography, for example, shows the pressures towards 'redemptive' narratives by those who respond to 'the new, more inclusive, political moment', along with the use of 'confessional' modes, especially by white writers, to show a 'split' self emerging from 'an earlier, politically less enlightened or in other ways unacceptable, version of the self'.[13] The larger picture which Sarah Nuttall draws is of South Africa's coast being '"remade" for the purposes of current reconciliation',[14] not only in Nelson Mandela's magisterial autobiography *Long Walk to Freedom* (1994) but in many other memoirs and autobiographies, including Mamphela Ramphele's *A Life* (1995). A crucial difference is posited between the 'freeing' of personal memories and the bequeathing of a 'model' life. The pressures towards national allegory are great, but in certain autobiographies, such as Ramphele's, a 'writing out of silences', such as of her triangular love affair with Steve Biko, convey a sense of concurrent personal and national liberation struggles, and she succumbs, in Nuttall's reading, to a traditional notion of wholeness as a form of solace, or relief, from traumatic memories of earlier selves. Nuttall astutely observes that 'the practices of psychotherapy ... address themselves to the same contradictions mediated by such narratives'.[15] The challenge she perceives, which may be pre-eminently South Africa's but which strikes at the heart of any literary historian, is to 'create a collective memory that is multiple, flickering with the many meanings that individual experience can collectively bring to it'.[16] This would not represent a multiple personality disorder but rather a sufficiently diverse memory-bank for the story of a modern, complex nation.

Recent literary histories of Australia, New Zealand and Canada help to locate some dynamics of memory and forgetting in these countries and answer the challenges in somewhat different ways. The beginnings of these histories offer a focus of comparison. In his early study *Beginnings*, Edward Said remarked that

> Every writer knows that the choice of a beginning for what [he or she] writes is crucial not only because it determines much of what follows but because a work's beginning is, practically speaking, the main entrance to what it offers.[17]

Thus, the frequent device of opening American literary histories with the Puritans and their world-view and literary output contributes to a narrative of a European redemption sought and recurrently denied. Recent histories of New Zealand, Canadian and Australian literature open with chapters on indigenous cultures, texts and associated mythologies. In the opening chapter to *A History of Canadian Literature*,[18] Bill New remarks how early mythmakers were 'preoccupied (apparently) by the empirical world, but [were] fascinated by the mysterious and the uncertain'.[19] A pre-contact past is evoked, to be followed by a discussion of European myth and a clash of values and outlooks summarised as follows:

> One set of European myths was thus operating to extend Europe institutionally to Canada—identifying wilderness and savagery as the demonic characteristics of the new world, and combating them with religion and a written language, the agents of European civilization. Simultaneously, another set of myths was locating

manners, culture and civility among New World natives, whether in Canada or in other societies lately discovered by European expeditions.[20]

Whereas New's single-author history takes such sweeping, magisterial views of the terrain, the multi-authored New Zealand and Australian histories tend to anchor their generalisations with a closer view of individual writers and texts. Indeed, *The Oxford History of New Zealand Literature in English*[21] is organised generically—the novel, short story, drama and poetry being joined by children's literature, popular fiction, literary magazines, criticism, theory and bibliography. But the book commences with an awkward genre, Maori literature, surveyed by Jane McRae, who immediately draws attention to the many kinds of oral composition including whakapapa (genealogy), karakia (incantations), whakatauki (sayings), waiata (song poetry) and konero (narratives), before proceeding to survey the oral literature in print and twentieth century literature.

The problem of 'getting started' in *The Oxford Literary History of Australia* was apparent quite early to Jennifer Strauss and myself as editors. After much discussion, we decided not to begin on a set date within our broadly chronological framework but to commence with an opening section called 'To 1850', in which the first chapter would problematise the concept of beginnings and origins as it explored Aboriginal contributions to Australian imagining. Our choice of author was Canadian-born Australian, Adam Shoemaker, whose opening chapter connects with a later chapter titled 'Tracking Black Australian Stories: Contemporary Indigenous Literature'. The opening chapter, 'White on Black/Black on Black', locates 'a beginning' in this way:

> The historical dates which constitute what is known as 'chronological time' have often been used to imprison Australia's indigenous people. Terms such as 'prehistory' and 'pre-literacy' carry with them the strongest possible sense of a time before—and a time after. Of course, these dividing lines have been imposed retrospectively upon Black Australians by those who are not members of that culture. Such arbitrary demarcations also imply that the past begins when it is recorded in legible script, not when human beings began to commit stories to memory.[22]

While Terry Sturm's remark that 'there is a much stronger consciousness of Maori culture in New Zealand than of Aboriginal culture in Australian writing'[23] probably remains true, the present *Oxford Literary History of Australia*, as reviewers have noticed, offers a stark contrast to Leonie Kramer's 1981 history,[24] which presented virtually no reference to this aspect of Australia's literary culture. The fulcrum of a change of outlook in Australia to which we responded was the 1960s and '70s, when a combined force of historians, black activists and cultural commentators effectively broke the silence of the previous century. The leading public historian in this re-orientation was Henry Reynolds, whose historian antagonist, Geoffrey Blainey, attacked what he called a 'black armband' view of history which would waste the nation's effort in guilt, remorse and recrimination—a view taken up for a time by the current Australian Prime Minister, John Howard. But the efforts of later historians who took note of W E H Stanner's call to confront 'the Great Australian Silence' about Aborigines[25] have contributed to a climate of thought and feeling in which a genuine sense of national reconciliation might be possible, and in which literature, broadly conceived, will play its part. Such a restoration of memory in the collective unconscious will require an exercise not only of cognition but of what Goleman called 'emotional intelligence'. And the next phase may well be taken up by latter-day representatives of the indigenous people.[26]

The restoration of indigeneity, and its highlighting or denigration in public awareness, has been a factor in histories of most post-colonial cultures. In Malaysia, indigeneity has been a principal factor in the shaping of recent literary history, for example in the privileging of Bahasa (Malay) over English language writing. The different emphasis given to 'indigenous' and 'migrant' perspectives has been influential in the recent history of Fijian culture too. In a different way, Wole Soyinka's interventions in debates about Nigerian culture in the 1970s reveal his attempt to supersede 'the romanticised rhetoric of Negritude' and 'externally induced fantasies of redemptive transformations in the image of alien masters', in favour of a history of the contemporary literature of his 'own people' that offered a 'secular social vision'.[27] Other African countries have promulgated a variety of founding myths with more or less attention given to indigeneity and the indigenisation of imported narratives of origin.[28] Ethnic origins are often a crucial ingredient in such narratives, as they are in accounts of the first trauma, or 'birth', of a culture. The 'birthing', as well as the 'berthing', of such literatures provide loci for the storing and restoration of memories to be shared internationally, and they are often imbued with deep emotionalism, sometimes nostalgic, sometimes violent. They strike at the very heart of personal and cultural identity.

While the vexed notion of 'beginnings', and the role given to indigenous people, present challenges of remembering and forgetting to literary historians of Commonwealth and other countries, so too do the 'critical moments' represented by wars. Rowland Smith has neatly summarised the role of war in literatures of the Commonwealth:

> War, defined in its broadest sense, is frequently seen as a defining feature of the national experience. This applies to many categories of warfare: imperial wars fought by soldiers from the newly created dominions in places far from home; civil wars such as the Nigerian Civil War; wars of liberation or conquest, such as the Anglo-Boer wars in South Africa and the struggle of black movements resisting apartheid in the same country; bitter civil conflicts such as the Mau Mau war in Kenya.[29]

More generally, wars are often remembered, or forgotten (perhaps suppressed) as part of a nation's literary record, according to their perceived value in the invented tradition. And they reveal the workings of public memory.

The perspectives of Paul Fussell's and Jay Winter's major studies of the first world war illustrate a variety of ways in which emotional communal memories can be perceived and reconstituted. Fussell's *The Great War and Modern Memory*[30] argues that the dominant literary mode of the war was irony, because the war 'reversed the Idea of Progress' and was 'a hideous embarrassment to the prevailing meliorist myth which had dominated the public consciousness for a century'.[31] Fussell's narrative requires a pastoral myth which was subverted by major events in the war. He asserts that 'The innocent army fully attained the knowledge of good and evil at the Somme on July 1, 1916'.[32] Fussell notices the tendency of memoirs to call on ironic mis-matches to assist memory:

> In reading memoirs of the war, one notices the same phenomenon over and over. By applying to the past a paradigm of ironic action,

a rememberer is able to locate, draw forth, and finally shape into significance an event at a moment which otherwise would merge without meaning into the undifferentiated stream.[33]

Not surprisingly, the sense of a national literature developed, for Britons and for citizens of Empire countries such as Australia, from these 'national' experiences of war. The reported memories of soldiers leaned heavily on literature, recognising its 'power and authority'.[34]

Jay Winter's more recent study, *Sites of Memory, Sites of Mourning*[35] tackles questions of the 'collective remembrance' of the first world war differently, arguing that the 'modernist' interpretation of the European reaction to the events of 1914–18 of Fussell and many others, is mistaken. Ironic and modernist perspectives preceded the war and continued during it, Winter argues, and the massive trauma of the war should not be represented as a fracture into modernism but as a continuing call on traditional frames of reference and literary modes, behind which lies the experience of personal grief and mourning. These contrasting interpretations of a 'critical moment' in recent European history, which had an impact on many countries beyond Europe, indicate a typical discrepancy to be found in many literary and general histories as they try to construct, or reconstruct, the past: on the one hand, there is a searching of these events for signs of the future (Fussell's modernism); and on the other, the recognition of continuing recourse to traditional forms, a sense of the past represented in Winter's description of communities in mourning, a prevalent nostalgic romanticism and a return of the sacred in wartime and after.

The Oxford Literary History of Australia gives significant attention to three wars—the first and second world wars and the conflict in Vietnam—as critical moments in the public memory through literature, drama and film. The literary record is not construed as mere annals, though those books do provide a chronology of significant literary and public events. Indeed, our contributors were asked to take a critical and evaluative approach to literature and history in their chapters. Thus Adrian Caesar's chapter which includes the period 1914–39 is titled 'National Myths of Manhood: Anzacs and Others' and it questions the romantic and nostalgic nationalism of C E W Bean's mythmaking in his official history and

The Anzac Book. Caesar finds a more heterogeneous set of images and ideas than those posited by Bean, and a set of allegiances to Empire as well as to an idea of Australia. Jennifer Strauss's coverage of the same period shows ways in which the literary culture, both in popular and more high-culture writings absorbed the shock of war on the 'home front'. In her chapter titled 'Battlers All', Strauss argues that the writings most often preserved were those which displayed 'a disillusioned stoicism which sees itself as obliged to soldier on, accepting the cards dealt out by an indifferent chance'.[36] Her judgment is proleptic, the culture of post-war producing the figure of 'the little Aussie battler' who accepted and survived the privations of the Depression years.

My chapter 'Literary Culture since Vietnam' contends that a different dynamic was produced in the years after 1965, when Prime Minister Menzies sent Australia's first battalion to support South Vietnam and the Americans. The chapter does not posit literature as a 'pure' or discrete category, but links events such as the public demonstrations of the late 1960s and early 1970s with literary texts and attitudes in sentences such as this: 'The demonstrations focused a public expression of a youthful Australian counter-culture which, even as it expressed its solidarity in strongly anti-authoritarian and anti-American sentiments, paradoxically found itself imitating American modes of expression'.[37] The often ironic chronicling of these years in Australian cities, in fiction by Frank Moorhouse and Michael Wilding, combined the spirit of protest with a sceptical, cosmopolitan and libertarian set of values. Anger and impatience were prevalent, as publicly expressed feelings, but these were tempered by the irony and humour of a more highly educated population than during previous wars.

The episodes of war and its aftermath have also been profound in other national literary histories of the Commonwealth. Leong Liew-Geok has argued that

> No event in Singapore and Malaysia (then Malaya) has inspired so abundant a literature as the Pacific War. The Japanese occupation of Malaya and Singapore began with the British surrender of these territories on 15 February 1942 and lasted until the Japanese surrender, also in Singapore, on 12 September 1945.

> Embracing a range of genres—historical testimony, narrative, autobiography or memoir, and fiction—the literature testifies to the creative pressures of history on writing, most of the authors having suffered through the war.[38]

Leong stresses the war's alienating effects on the psyche, but also the survival narratives in prisoner-of-war tales and the desire for freedom in escape narratives.[39] Her interventions into the literary history of this region lead her to the observation that 'the circumstantial determinants of courage, and heroism, do not lie in aggressive military action, but in individual and group reactions to defeat, specifically in the chaotic processes of evacuation and its aftermath, where heroic endeavours of otherwise very ordinary men are compelled'.[40]

This essay began with reference to a funeral oration, and drew attention to some of the mysteries of personal and communal memory-making and the powerful emotions that often underlie it. Taking a cue from recent events in South Africa, political and literary, we have been led to consider the twin but competing demands of 'truth' and 'reconciliation'. As diverse public policy-makers and writers of literary history give priority to certain narratives over others, different social and cultural formations may emerge. For example, if Australians transferred their interest in war history to international cooperative endeavour, how would the national memory-bank be altered? Or if Malaysian cultural historians transferred emphasis from the narratives of indigeneity to stories of migrancy, how would attitudes and values, and the emotions which inform them, be altered? Would a culture of reconciliation be encouraged? Would 'truth' be jeopardised? Would 'nationality' be understood differently?

The stakes are high for the sharing of such memories. Understanding ourselves and the world we inhabit depends upon it.

A Family Closeness?
Australia, India, Indonesia

In Christopher Koch's widely cited essay 'Crossing the Gap', he incorporates his own biographical journey into an allegorical trip for Australians from their Anglo-Celtic inheritance to a closer engagement with the countries of Asia. What interests me especially about Koch's essay, as I try to engage with India and Indonesia, is his speculative vision of a 'family closeness' among these three countries. This is how he puts the case:

> Our consciousness [of inhabiting the same spiritual region] may well increase, rather than decrease, as time goes on, since our course [as Australians] has only just begun, and a people needs a sense of origins and continuity as it needs dream and myth. No one needs it more than a country's artists. Without myth, the spirit starves, and in post-colonial Australia, we are going to have to build a new myth out of old ones. And I would suggest that these old ones will not belong simply to the European zone, but to the Indo-European zone, of which India and Indonesia are both inheritors, as we are. Other great cultures, such as China, we may admire, we may gain from, but we will not find such family closeness with; the sense of common roots.[1]

I heard the alternative hypothesis about Australia's future with Asia a decade earlier, in a lecture at the University of Western Australia in 1977, when Stephen Fitzgerald argued memorably that by the beginning of the twenty-first century the predominant influences on Australian cultural and economic life would be China and Japan. My purpose here is not to arbitrate between these two views, which both rhetorically express certain acute observations about directions in Australian culture and society, but to explore principally through some recent literary texts, the nature and quality of the potential 'family closeness' that might be developing between Australia, India and Indonesia through the experience of certain diasporic writers from these countries.

Such an inquiry might draw to some extent upon concepts developed by post-colonial theorists Edward Said and Homi Bhabha such as 'othering', 'hybridity' and 'mimicry'; it must also confront some of the paradoxes of nationality and globalisation. Furthermore, it might test Shirley Lim's challenging notion that 'in an international perspective, paradigms of diaspora tend to overlap, destabilise, or supersede paradigms of immigration'.[2] But my principal interest is in testing the cultural purchase of a notion of 'critical regionalism' among the three countries I have named which might develop through cultural and educational relationships even ahead of economic imperatives. In what ways could such a 'family closeness' be envisaged?

The texts that envisage such a 'family closeness' are Yasmine Gooneratne's volume of stories *Masterpiece*, Safina Uberoi's feature film *My Mother India* and Dewi Anggraeni's *Stories of Indian Pacific* and *Neighbourhood Tales*. These three first-generation women immigrants from Sri Lanka, India and Indonesia respectively give attention to the domestic as well as to the wider public life; and they give great currency to the emotions, the springboard to intimacy between people and societies. They each explore subterranean motives and feelings and reveal the complex inheritance of diasporic South Asians and Southeast Asians in Australia.

A book from Pandanus Press in Canberra, *Weaving a Double Cloth: Stories of Asia–Pacific Women in Australia*,[3] indicates the range of insights that ten apparently ordinary women from what is called the Asia–Pacific (but more accurately might be called the Indo-Asia–Pacific) can produce. The editors of these stories, which were put together from interviews with the women, observe that some of these 'talking stories' are 'event-driven or narrative in style' while others are 'more introspective and reflective'. Leading themes are 'upheaval and dislocation as a result of political turmoil in their countries of birth'; and all engage with the knotty questions, 'where is home, what is home?'[4] Issues of identity are never far below the surface. Similar issues and questions inform the texts to be considered in this essay.

In 'The Writing Life', her introductory essay to *Masterpiece and Other Stories*, Yasmine Gooneratne indicates that the chief source of any 'family closeness' she has felt between her native Sri Lanka and Australia lies in the English language and its literatures. The nature and quality of Australia's and Sri Lanka's shared pasts as members of the British Empire is explored comically and satirically in her novel *A Change of Skies*.[5] In her essay 'The Writing Life', she recalls both the physical landscapes of her homeland and an equally precious inheritance—'an echo-hall of voices that spoke in at least three different languages and used an idiom rich in salt and savor'.[6] But English was the passport to a wider intellectual world. She describes the 'good fortune [of] an English literary education (which, despite the stigma it carries in some parts of the world because it was once part of the process of colonisation, remains an immensely valuable possession)'; for her, this is a 'priceless heritage which not even the deracination wrought by exile and expatriation' can take away.[7]

Under the partial influence of an English literary tradition, Gooneratne recalls in Ceylon 'an Arcadian Golden Age of innocence and high endeavour that ended, alas, all too soon as politics entered our Eden in the mid-1950s and contaminated the cultural life from which so much had been hoped and expected'.[8] When Gooneratne moved from Sri Lanka with her husband to an academic job in Sydney in 1972—the year of a new constitution and a change of name from Ceylon to Sri Lanka—she sought out the continuities between her somewhat idealised notions of British literary Augustanism and Australian literary life. Australia held the hope of civilisation. The image of A D Hope was a lodestar. The clash between these high literary expectations and the reality of living and working in Australia is rendered as high (and sometimes low) comedy of manners in *A Change of Skies*; and a gradual recognition of Australia's compensating multicultural possibilities is confronted by a residual, recidivist racialism.

Several stories in *Masterpiece* recreate the privileged but narrowly prescribed milieu of 1940s and '50s Ceylon. Gooneratne comically and affectionately recalls this period of protection and prudery for young women and the perils of romance that transgressed from time to time the boundaries of race, colour and creed. A mixture of

Jane Austen-style comedy and pathos informs her story called
'Waste' about a truncated romance across Sinhala and Tamil lines
which reverberates throughout a woman's life.[9]

The clash of traditional ways of living with Western modernity
is continually re-enacted in Gooneratne's stories—often memorably
in her campus narratives. In 'Masterpiece',[10] the title story to her
collection, Gooneratne introduces an Australian interlocutor into a
literature seminar at a university in a small village between Delhi and
Hyderabad. The Indian story teller's topic is a masterpiece from this
village, the *Gita Govinda*, or 'The Song of the Shepherd' from
twelfth century Sanskrit. The narrator describes the deep
identification of villagers with the Gita's protagonists: 'Lord
Krishna, with his beautiful body and strong shoulders, is every
villager's son. Radha, of the long, lustrous eyes and shy smile is
every village woman's daughter'.[11] The seminar audience is told
about the putative author of the poem, Sri Jayadera—a 'man of
settled habits' whose wife served his every need, believing him to be
a genius, as the villagers also think. The Australian interventionist in
this seminar takes strong exception to the notion of genius and
questions the woman's role as handmaid. When the poet finds his
inspiration has mysteriously disappeared and he can no longer write
his great poem, he is amazed to find that it has been completed
nevertheless. The villagers believe that Lord Krishna has 'descended
in glory from his lotus throne in the temple, and climbed the hill to
a poet's house in order to complete a classic poem'.[12] But the
Australian will have none of that. The poet has suffered 'writer's
block', he declares, and the poet's wife has completed the poem for
him. The Indian storyteller ends with some gentle advice to the
Australian, who has recently moved to Delhi to teach, about 'the art
of interruption':

> It is not that we do not welcome interruption. We do. But it must
> be constructive interruption. A person may say 'Yes?' Or he may
> say, 'And so, what happened next?' Such interruptions allow the
> story to move smoothly onwards, to a proper conclusion'.[13]

It is a nicely timed deflation of the postmodern Australian's literal
and sceptical take on the truths of a story, as well as a reminder of
the continuing traditionalism of rural India.

Gooneratne takes campus life to the sky in 'A Postcolonial Love
Story',[14] with its echoes of Erica Jong's 'mile high club' in her

notorious 1970s feminist novel *Fear of Flying*. In this story, Gooneratne effectively deploys an American male academic as first-person narrator of a story about his mid-air sexual encounter with a former student from Singapore, Leila Tan, who has become a successful professor teaching Asian Studies at an American university. In a scene depicting this apparently ultimate experience of liberation and release, Gooneratne cleverly parodies in her pompous male professor the changing discourses of enterprise and colonisation:

> The rewards of enterprise were immediate and overwhelming. The brave explorer I dispatched to take possession (growing, as I remember well, stouter and more adventurous by the second) signalled a smooth passage, a triumphant progress. '*O my America!*' I heard myself saying, to my own astonishment. '*My new-found-land!*' And then, over and over again, her name. 'Leila', I whispered, my face buried in her hair. 'Leila'.[15]

But Gooneratne's postcolonial Singaporean professor has the last word. She leaves her aircraft lover with a small package containing her tights gift-wrapped with a pink silk bow, as a gift for his wife, with the instruction to tell her that he got them 'from the Duty Free'.[16] However, Gooneratne's post-colonial 'freedoms' are never transformative experiences in the long-term. She has learnt the ironies of a mixed economy of emotions and experience: even in mid-air interludes, she suggests, we can never break entirely free of 'home'—of the attitudes that bind us—and its antithesis 'away'.

Safina Uberoi's film *My Mother India*[17] has won a number of awards including the Australian Film Critics' Circle ATOM award for best documentary, the New South Wales Premier's Literary Award for best screenplay and the Hawaii Film Festival's Special Jury Award. The film commenced showing in Australian cities in late 2002, and was followed up by showings in Britain and India and on SBS television in Australia.

The voice-over narrator in *My Mother India* is Safina Uberoi, its director and writer of the screenplay. The film's principal character and major point of view is Uberoi's Australian mother, Patricia, who, after moving to Delhi with the Sikh husband she met at the Australian National University in Canberra, chooses to stay on in India, despite the effects of partition, continuing anti-Sikh violence and having to forego her Australian citizenship. Uberoi tells us that

the film is her tribute to her mother but that it is also the mother's
gift to the daughter. In these ways, the film partakes of, and
contributes to the burgeoning genre of biography. While the film
expresses sentiments and strong emotions it avoids sentimentality in
its depictions of family life in India.

Safina Uberoi was living in Sydney but commuting regularly to
India, which provides the principal inspiration for her films. While
she fully acknowledges her dual inheritance to India and Australia
(more to India than Australia in this film), she avoids the free-
floating postmodern scepticism satirised by Gooneratne in her
'Postcolonial Love Story'. Like Gooneratne's, Uberoi's work
depends on a relatively in-depth bilateralism of outlook rather than
the multiplications of a theoretical postmodernism. It approaches
what might be called a 'critical regionalism' that includes both India
and Australia.

The opening sequences of *My Mother India* take us back to the
kind of public prudery dramatised in 1950s Sri Lanka in
Gooneratne's stories. Uberoi humorously and mockingly evokes the
Indian grandmother's and the neighbourhood's shock at her
Australian mother's panties and bra flagrantly drying on a backyard
clothesline, for all to see. Patricia's parents, Safina's Canberra-based
Australian grandparents, never visit their daughter in India; they
retain an Anglo-Australian stereotype of their daughter's fate as 'a
terrible jump into the black hole of Calcutta'.[18]

My Mother India commences with social comedy and domestic
drama, but it sets these people and their situation against graphic,
documentary renderings of modern Indian history, from partition
in 1947 to the racial conflicts of the early 1980s and beyond. As
Patricia nurses her father-in-law, a former poet and guru, through
the dementia of his dying, she watches him re-live his past. His
madness seems to be echoed in Indira Gandhi's decision to storm
the Golden Temple in Amritsar in 1984 and the various retributions
against Sikhs which followed. While the Anglo-Australian Patricia's
perspective dominates the film, we are also shown the father's
necessary disguises to prevent him from being recognised as a Sikh
after he and his family are saved by a friendly Hindu family, and
something of the shame of those subterfuges. He and his family
know what it is like to lose both his religious identity and his home.
His subsequent return to a Sikh identity influences his daughter's

choice to reinscribe his religion and she proudly proclaims that she has never cut her hair.

Although Safina Uberoi's Australian mother, Patricia, chooses to become an Indian citizen, and to stay in India, she recalls doing so with deeply divided emotions and she sends a younger son and later a younger daughter to Australia for their safety and education. The son, who is sent secretly by his mother to stay with her parents in Canberra when anti-Sikh violence is at its height in India, has a small part in the film and appears curiously uni-dimensional as he describes, in a broad Australian accent, his apparent assimilation. Safina's view is that her brother missed out on the healing process that took place in India, when, in her view, the whole community came together to help those who survived.[19]

Questions of home, belonging and identity are posed implicitly and explicitly throughout *My Mother India*. Safina Uberoi feels that she belongs to two places, she says, and therefore never totally to one. This, she believes, carries its problems of being always sympathetic to both sides but it is also a privileged position for an artist, whose bifocal vision can test the real internal dynamics of hybridity.[20] Like Gooneratne—but unlike some of the refugee women interviewed for *Weaving a Double Cloth*—Uberoi speaks English impeccably, with a sense of its performative power and its nuances. Safina's mother's teaching and her school, university and acting experience in Delhi contributed to an articulacy that is enriched, like Gooneratne's, by the accents of the homeland, lending it an exotic quality for Australians which is not shared by immigrants whose English is less accomplished.

Although Indonesia is geographically closer to Australia than India and Sri Lanka, its relationship with Australia is more fraught with tensions and misunderstandings, as demonstrated in East Timor and the Bali bombings. This is what makes Dewi Anggraeni's writings such an important part of late twentieth and early twenty-first century Australian literature. Hers is the only written essay in response to the questions of identity, belonging and 'home' raised in *Weaving a Double Cloth*.[21] The development of high-level skills in speaking and especially in writing in English provide her with a powerful vehicle for making her distinctive mark on contemporary Australian culture.

Dewi Anggraeni was born into what she describes as 'an ordinary middle-class family in what was then Batavia (now Jakarta), just before the declaration of independence in Indonesia in 1945'.[22] Dewi's mother was Sundanese from West Java and she grew up in Cianjur in the mountains between Jakarta and Bandung. Of part-Chinese descent, she changed her Chinese name after graduating from the Universitas Indonesia. Despite political pressures, she says:

> I dropped my Chinese name voluntarily, with no sense of guilt. I was brought up as an Indonesian, went to Indonesian schools and university, and my friends were mostly Indonesian, either racially or emotionally. I knew how to behave in Indonesian culture and felt completely at ease with it. Psychologically and emotionally, I was Indonesian.[23]

This identification by a person of Chinese descent with the emergent Indonesian nation is remarkably similar to cultural critic Ien Ang's in her book *On Not Speaking Chinese*, where she writes of 'the prison-house of Chineseness' and describes herself as a 'migrant' rather than a 'diasporic' intellectual, because the latter terminology too strongly stresses 'roots' and a narrowing of identity to 'blood and race'.[24] Dewi Anggraeni has similarly seen herself in international terms and her learning of French, English and Mandarin as well as Bahasa Indonesian were major factors in earning her this role.

Dewi Anggraeni migrated to Australia in 1972 after having spent a period in this country in 1970. Her summary description of her move to Australia is romantic: 'I fell in love with Melbourne and decided to live the rest of my life in this beautiful city'.[25] The romance is at least partially linked to her relationship with her Australian husband, publisher and environmentalist Ian Fraser. Her Melbourne begins and ends with Eltham, where she and Fraser chose to live. Another major factor in Anggraeni's writing life is her experience as a journalist, which has taken her to many parts of the world and which she views as a significant contributor to her fiction writing, enabling her, for example, to research aspects of novels and stories she wishes to write. Having taught in schools, then adult migrant education, she worked on a freelance, then part-time basis with *Tempo*, the Indonesian weekly magazine before becoming a full-time journalist there in 1991, before the magazine was banned by the Soeharto government from 1994 to 1998. After that hiatus, Anggraeni has continued to write for *Tempo* as well as *Jakarta Post*, the *Age* in Melbourne, and elsewhere.

Dewi Anggraeni's journalism as well as her fiction is a major contribution to the understanding of Indonesian society at a deep level. Journalism, she says, taught her to be more outgoing and assertive: 'The fiction writer side of me', she says, 'watched this transformation with interest':

> Not only did I observe the change in me, I also studied how others interacted with me as my more assertive self—how they took me more seriously. Unconsciously I actually moved further into Australian mores. Curiously, as I widened my cultural space, I also rediscovered my Indonesian psyche.[26]

It is difficult to think of an Australian-based writer who better exhibits emotional intelligence in her writing than Anggraeni; this may have something to do with her dual Indonesian and Australian inheritances. In Indonesia, she says, people tend to operate more than Australians at 'an intuitive level'[27] and she finds this appealing, as she does the Australian freedom to step forward and ask difficult questions. She describes an earlier phase of 'feeling Indonesian in Australia and Australian in Indonesia', but has now entered 'a subsequent phase of feeling Indonesian and Australian in respective countries, which is more at peace with myself'.[28] Home, she says, will always be her 'beloved Melbourne', but her 'cultural residence, ... deep down in [her] psyche, [is] a place that overlaps both cultures'.[29]

Towards the end of her fertile study *The Politics of Home*, Rosemary Marangoly George reflects on some of the consequences of immigration in an era of postcolonialism and postmodernist ideas:

> Immigration and the fictions it engenders teach a certain detachment about 'home'. In these texts identity is linked only hypothetically (and through hyphenation) to a specific geographical place on the map. And yet, wandering on the margins of another's culture does not necessarily mean that one is marginal. Home in the immigrant genre is a fiction that one can move beyond or recreate at will. The association between an adequate self and a place to call home is held up to scrutiny and then let go. As postmodern and postcolonial subjects, we surprise ourselves with our detachment to the things we were taught to be attached to.[30]

Dewi Anggraeni's experience as an immigrant in Australia would support aspects of this statement, especially the capacity for a relative detachment. Yet for Anggraeni, this capacity has changed in different phases of the life-cycle. In the first phase, certain things and places remind her of the homeland. Then, visiting the homeland, she finds herself reminded of the adoptive country. Thereafter, she becomes increasingly bicultural and more at peace with herself, interspersed with occasional problems and crises. In the latter phase, she is able to transfer at will between her two now familiar cultures. But like Piagetian or Freudian stages, the two cultures offer no simple upward gradient towards maturity or wisdom. There are regressions, substitutions, transferences, failures of nerve in both countries.

Anggraeni's fiction avoids simplistic theorising in its cross-cultural representations, especially where these involve gender and power relations. In her long story 'Uncertain Step' in *Stories of Indian Pacific*[31] Anggraeni reveals the tensions, crises and misunderstandings of an Indonesian woman who comes to Australia to renew a relationship with an Australian man who has proposed to her in Indonesia. Anggraeni's alter ego in the story, Aryani, flies to Kalgoorlie to meet Steve and drives across the Nullarbor with him to Adelaide. She feels foreign and vulnerable and her perception of the landscape interacts surrealistically with her sense of self:

> Aryani looks incredulously at the straight road, dividing a carpet of saltbush, sheoak, eucalypt and acacia. Dwarfed by the immense space, these trees look like vegetables in a gigantic vegetable patch. She gains the sensation of travelling through time, the landscape so unchanging and the passage almost physically still.[32]

Aryani is often mistaken for a 'mail-order bride' and has to deal with the consequent social constraints. Indeed, the story depends on an Australian reader's prior knowledge of this sort of stereotypical relationship. Anggraeni works to counter these expectations by showing that cross-cultural marriage can be much more than mail-order relationships.

A fascinating glimpse of cross-cultural gender differences is offered in a scene in 'Uncertain Step' in which Steve and Aryani go out to dinner with friends in Melbourne, where they are entertained by a belly dancer. Aryani notices a difference between Steve's discomfort when he is approached by the woman and the Arab men's obvious involvement in the sexuality of the dance. She herself feels drawn to the woman, who winks at her complicity, leaving her with an inner warmth. Aryani laughs at Steve's embarrassment, remarking on his 'uptight' and 'English' behaviour, 'scared of being overpowered by [the] woman's sexuality'.[33] Yet she knows that this Anglo-Celtic man would have behaved quite unrestrainedly behind closed doors, and she relates this to his present attitude which is so similar to that of secretive Javanese and Sundanese men. Back in their motel room, the two banter seriously about the incident. Steve is puzzled that Aryani didn't seem upset that the woman had teased him in such a 'blatantly physical' way. No, she wasn't upset, Aryani explains, because she felt that the woman wasn't trying to snatch him away from her; rather, the dancer was inviting her to 'join in the fun'.[34] The episode is a typically acute reading of the dynamics of cross-cultural emotions—in this case, of 'a sensitive new age guy' learning about the theatrics of desire. And it has the sense of immediacy that arises from close observation, perhaps enabled by the fact that Dewi Anggraeni's university graduate daughter has worked as a belly dancer in Melbourne. But the point here is that writing about cross-cultural human relationships at this depth of intuitive insight and understanding is a remarkable achievement. Mixed signals, desire, confusion, and sexual jealousy—these are notoriously difficult topics to write about. But what fertile territory they are in contemporary Australia, and the world at large.

An oversimplifying tendency is sometimes to be found in postcolonial theorising, whereby a focus on sexuality in 'Western' texts about 'Oriental' societies somehow renders the West as 'Orientalist' and exploitative. This kind of 'Orientalism' is not apparent in Blanche d'Alpuget's novel *Monkeys in the Dark*;[35] for instance, in her depiction of the love affair between Alexandra Wheatfield and the Sumatran intellectual, poet and political activist, Maruli Hutabarat. Or in Alex's enjoyment in this novel of 'the way the city masses flirted'. Alex observes—good journalist that she is, intuiting the atmosphere and feeling of a place—that 'Sex was in the air, like the clove-fragrant smell of *kretek* smoke'.[36] D'Alpuget commented also in an interview on the 'smell of sex in the air' when she had lived in Jakarta in 1965 at the age of 22:

> It's natural. It's what we poor injured Christians don't have: it's a lack in the Judaeo-Christian tradition, which is dominated by fear and loathing of sexuality. But in the Hindu Buddhist tradition (the

Islamic thing is different ...) that was the norm ... When a group of
Indonesian women got together, all we'd talk about would be sex.
More and better tricks.[37]

D'Alpuget is a very different writer from Dewi Anggraeni, but she
has crossed the gap between Australia and Indonesia and charted
also the swirling waters of sexuality. No mature, 'family closeness'
across cultures can be achieved without such explorers.

In the third of her *Stories of Indian Pacific*, 'Crossroads',[38] Dewi
Anggraeni explores both the problematic nature of sexuality across
cultures and the possibilities of friendship. When Australian rock
star Justin visits Bali he is quickly entranced by a young woman
Wayan who works in a street stall but is a poet manqué. She
introduces him to Nyoman Sumadri, a poet, playwright, public
performer and left-wing activist, based on the famous W S Rendra.
(The story is dedicated to Rendra.) The friendship that develops
between the Australian rock star and the Indonesian poet is
intriguing, with most of the lessons needing to be learnt by the
Australian and the moral authority lying chiefly with the Indonesian.
Across the space of years and several visits, Justin learns of Wayan's
death (and meets her son) and seeks out Nyoman, who has been
jailed for his outspoken views. Each learns something about the
perils of fame and its responsibilities. As Nyoman pronounces,
poetically, their friendship strengthens his faith in the future, though
the two meet only once in a while, 'at the crossroads'.[39]

This is not the first time that the image of 'crossroads' has been
used to typify Australians' relationship to Asia, or a part of what we
call Asia. Its originality in Anggraeni's hands lies in its application to
a kind of international mateship between men, in the popular and
contemporary arts, and to men and women in their personal and
familial relations. Politics is intertwined in this—and Anggraeni is a
sufficient realist to recognise and incorporate something of this in
her stories—but the focus is on the problematics of human and
intuitive relationships in which fears, desires and dreams play their
part.

In *Neighbourhood Tales: A Bilingual Collection of Short Stories*[40]
Anggraeni focuses on cross-cultural conflicts or misunderstandings
ranging from manners and appearance to differences of food,
sexual mores or historical and political legacies. Most are first-
person narratives, usually from an Indonesian Australian woman's

point of view. An interest in dreams or visions recurs. Intuition, and even extra-sensory perception or synesthesia disrupt the surface of 'civilised' behaviour. Music can also lead one into a third realm of being. In 'Eleven Year Slip',[41] Anggraeni's character Letty's impulsive decision to sleep with an old flame when he visits from Indonesia evokes not only the mixed emotional reactions of Letty but also of her Australian husband. The story's twist is to reveal the emotional bankruptcy of a German Australian psychoanalyst's analysis of the marriage and the meaning of Letty's infidelity. An enigma remains about the power of desire and impulse.

In summary, some recent works by Gooneratne, Uberoi and Anggraeni have a remarkable capacity to cross the gap hypothesised by Christopher Koch towards a kind of 'family closeness' between Australia, India and Indonesia, though not in the ways he predicted. In the vanguard of any such relationship, it seems, are intelligent, artistic women who communicate at a high level of skill and artistry in English. But each of them also reveals the value of a multi-lingual upbringing. There are indications that a 'special closeness' may be developing in the Indo-Asia–Pacific region that has been the focus here.

All these works were conceived and produced before 11 September 2001, the Bali bombings of 12 October 2002 and the 'war on terror'. Nevertheless, the Tamil uprisings in Sri Lanka, anti-Sikh violence in India and volatile conditions in Indonesia lie behind their depictions of individuals and relationships. It is to be hoped that currently security-obsessed Australian policies do not prevent Australians, Indians and Indonesians from learning to interact freely and flexibly towards expanded notions of self and nation.

Crossing Cultures: Australia and the Asia–Pacific

Maps are presented as objective guides, but they have their basis in the notoriously subjective human activities of looking and seeing. Viewers of Australia and its place in the world seem to have been particularly aware of the difficulty of mapping the vast continent and its relationship to elsewhere. Thus Simon Ryan's book *The Cartographic Eye*, deliberately puns on the word 'eye' as it sets out to deconstruct early explorers' representations of Australia.[1] The figure of the father in Peter Carey's disturbing story 'Do You Love Me?'[2] is a self-confident and dominating cartographer whose vocation confirms the substantiality of the physical world and its outlines; eerily, at the end of the story, however, the son watches his mapmaking father dematerialise. He and his maps turn out to be not so substantial or enduring after all.

Australians may be especially aware of the subjectivity involved in the making and publishing of maps. Eurocentric maps of the world have traditionally placed what was once called The Great South Land at the bottom of the world, where you might wipe your feet on it, or do something more obscene.

The Antipodes (from the Greek word meaning 'having the feet opposite') were a place diametrically opposite to the defining, European party, and Antipodeans—the inhabitants of the Antipodes—as Bernard Smith showed in *European Vision and the South Pacific*,[3] were strange, distorted creatures. The perceiving eye of the northern hemisphere explorer and mapmaker was necessarily influenced by the ideology of the maps he followed; even more so the artists who followed sketches of Aboriginal people (those on Cook's voyages to the Pacific, for example), which often seem based not just on raw perception but also on European notions of warrior peoples, noble savages or colonial clowns.[4] Expectations of topsy-turvydom in the antipodes were reflected in the late nineteenth century by Mark Twain in *Following the Equator*, when he said he was led to expect, and found in the country Down Under, that 'real life' was 'like the most beautiful Lies ... full of surprises, and adventures, and incongruities and contradictions, and incredibilities ...'[5]

Because Australia was settled (or invaded) by British Europeans in the late eighteenth century—many of whom, the convicts especially, did not want to be there—the seeing eye has recorded many strange visions. Indeed, the image of the visionary, or prophet emerging from across the seas or from the desert, has been a persistent aspect of white Australian wish-fulfilment fantasy. Australian poets of the mid-twentieth century have been especially prone to it. James McAuley's epic poem *Captain Quiros*[6] exemplifies the visionary explorer on the high seas. A D Hope's earlier poem 'Australia' is savagely critical of his home country where 'second-hand Europeans pullulate/timidly on the edge of alien shores', but he finally places his faith in visionaries from the desert, Australia's core:

> Hoping, if still from the deserts the prophets come,
> Such savage and scarlet as no green hills dare
> Springs in that waste, some spirit which escapes
> The learned doubt, the chatter of cultured apes
> Which is called civilization over there.[7]

Hope's ambivalence in this poem is directed towards both Europe—the traditional source of civilisation—and Australia his native culture, which seems, at this point, on the eve of the second world war, so thin. Asia, or the Pacific Islands, do not register. This ambivalence about the sources of civilisation is also evident with a somewhat different slant, in Judith Wright's poem 'Bullocky', which was so often read by teachers and students as a celebration of the myth of the visionary and heroic white pioneer settler that the poet (who wanted the bullock driver to be seen as 'mad')[8] threatened to withdraw rights for the poem to appear in school anthologies. The 'double tree' that Wright discerned in her inheritance was a British and Australian hybrid, but she was aware of the harm to the land and to the original inhabitants, the Aborigines, that these new settlers had done.

In this context of a colonial and post-colonial culture in Australia, radically uncertain of its own place in the world—how have Asia and the Pacific been perceived and mapped? Let us consider the Pacific islands first. In his book *Representing the South Pacific*, Rod Edmond makes the important point that 'The attempt to describe another culture is never simply an act of appropriation, nor are images of the other merely versions of the self-image of the observer'.[9] Some colonial accounts of New Guinea would support this view, as do some of the contributions to Nigel Krauth's anthology *New Guinea Images in Australian Literature*.[10] For example, E W Cole's 'Account of a Race of Human Beings with Tails' (c. 1873), in Krauth's anthology, is not a piece of gratuitous and condescending groesquerie: it is a clever satire turned back on readers which ridicules their ignorance of their nearest island neighbour—later to become Australia's first and only colony (or rather, quasi- or proxy colony).[11] New Guinea is the core culture of Melanesia, and Australian visitors or expatriates have written exotic adventure tales, action stories of fighting the Japanese there during the second world war, and stories and verse about the independence of PNG, and its aftermath.

One major Australian novel, Randolph Stow's *Visitants*,[12] is set in the Trobriand Islands (off eastern New Guinea and part of the nation of Papua New Guinea). The novel shows a confrontation of two civilisations during an official enquiry on the island of Kailuanan. As Tony Hassall has observed, 'the white characters occupy a position of uneasy colonial authority over a Melanesian people only a few years away from independence'.[13] The novel is sensitive, subtle and compelling. Other notable fiction about Papua New Guinea has been written by Trevor Shearston and Jean Bedford.

A colonialist perspective characterises much Australian writing about the Pacific before the first world war. The title of Robert Dixon's book *Writing the Colonial Adventure*,[14] which covers the period 1875 to 1914, suggests this perspective and the genre that supported colonial adventuring. Louis Becke's stories bear the marks of this genre too, but his prevailing perspective is that of the trader between islands. Indeed, as shown in Essay 14, Becke steered an interesting course between the missionaries' view of Oceania as a world to convert and the colonialist view of necessary Western dominance; and he revealed a mixed economy between 'outsiders' and 'insiders' in the Pacific, showing how, despite the often destructive influence of Europeans and Americans in the Pacific, the people of the islands could now and then turn the tables on the white interlopers and survive, and sometimes thrive, by adhering to traditional values and loyalty to place, region and community.

Because of the relatively small populations and economies of the Pacific islands, and their scattering across a vast ocean, they have seldom caused great anxiety or fear in the Australian public mind—except perhaps when nuclear testing has been carried out there. However, the coups in Fiji in 1987 and 1991 occasioned enormous interest and concern in the public media. Whereas Albert Wendt, the Samoan novelist, short-story writer and essayist from New Zealand, wrote from the perspective of an indigenous Pacific islander,[15] the most powerful literary witnesses to the Fijian troubles have not been indigenes but have generally been Indo-Fijian. The most engaging and persuasive of these Australian-based writers is Satendra Nandan, whose semi-autobiographical novel *The Wounded Sea*,[16] is framed by his experience of imprisonment, cruelty and humiliation, as a Labour minister in Dr Timoci Bavadra's coalition cabinet, during the two Fijian coups in 1987. Sudesh Mishra has astutely observed that the novel is woven around the notion of *maya*, or deception; its triumph, Mishra suggests, may be in Nandan's attempts 'to find a way out of the morass of personal, communal and national deceit'.[17]

Nandan's three books of poetry, *Faces in a Village* (1976), *Voices in the River* (1985) and *Lines Across Black Water* (1998) reveal a Romantic temperament with a strong sense of the poetry of place, especially the semi-paradisal Fiji of his childhood. Educated in Fiji, India, Britain and Australia, Nandan is a distinguished man of letters in his adoptive country Australia, with a strong belief in universal human rights, an earthy sense of humour and a canny understanding of politics. His book of essays *Fiji: Paradise in Pieces*[18] and his memoir, *Requiem for a Rainbow*[19] contribute to the *roman fleuve* of this grandson of indentured Indian labourers whose rights to a free and fulfilled life in Fiji, like those of so many of his countrymen and women, were flagrantly violated. From an Australian point of view, one of the grim ironies of the Fiji coups of 1987 is that their leader, Colonel Sitiveni Rabuka, was trained at Duntroon Military College in Canberra.

Introducing a book of wide-ranging essays and commentaries on the most recent coups in Fiji, another Indian Fijian academic in Australia, Brij Lal, observes:

> In the Eighteenth Brumaire of Louis Napoleon, Marx remarks that history repeats itself, so to speak, twice: the first time as tragedy, the second as farce. The events in Fiji of May–July 2000 would tend to exemplify this dictum. One coup is bad enough, but three in thirteen staggers the imagination.[20]

Fiji, then, together with Bougainville, the Solomon Islands and other parts of the Pacific contributes to what military strategists call an 'arc of instability' in the region to which Australia, in economic, geopolitical and, increasingly, cultural terms, belongs.

If fear does not play a significant part in Australian reports and imaginings about the Pacific Islands, this emotion has been a major element in responses to 'Asia'. It is difficult for many present-day Australians to place themselves back in the mindset of federationist Australians who believed in the 'White Australia policy' as an article of faith. Yet it was only in the 1967 referendum that all Aboriginal Australians were granted full citizenship and voting rights. And Australians were still debating anti-Asian immigration policies in the mid-1980s.

In the early twenty-first century, official responses to asylum seekers from Afghanistan, Iraq and elsewhere, who had sought to enter Australia in leaky boats from Indonesia seemed to reignite historic fears of invasion.

On the other hand, the post–second world war inauguration in 1950 of the Colombo Plan for technical and educational aid to South-East Asia set a pattern for positive educational and cultural interaction in the region, though this occurred against the background of accelerated European immigration into Australia and a continuing fear and suspicion of the countries of Asia, especially of Japan and China. India was perhaps the exception to this generalised fear and suspicion of 'Asia', because a certain amount of cultural interaction had occurred between these outposts of empire—countries which shared some of the economic benefits, literature and biased outlooks of the British Raj.

Australians had long been fed the line—in newspapers, magazines, cartoons, plays and films—that China and Japan were the countries to fear. More recently, in some hands, Indonesia has played that role (e.g. in children's books by John Marsden such as *Tomorrow When the World Begins*). To some extent, the fear of China and Chinese people began during the mid-nineteenth century goldrushes when Chinese outnumbered, and outworked, Anglo-Australians on some of the goldfields, and were ridiculed and had their rights reduced accordingly. The invasion scare novels of the early twentieth century arose from such embedded stereotypes and a sense of European isolation at the bottom of the world. Randolph Bedford's *White Australia: or, the Empty North*[21] is a melodrama about Australia's invasion by Japan—a long-term prophecy indeed, since the Japanese bombing of Darwin and submarines in Sydney Harbour did not occur until 1942. Other works in this genre include *The Coloured Conquest* (1904) by 'Rata' (Thomas Roydhouse) and *White or Yellow: The Story of the Race War of AD 1908*. In Erle Cox's *Out of the Silence*, the sole survivor of a prehistoric civilisation proposes to turn the world into a Utopia by wiping out every last member of the 'coloured races'. With the benefit of hindsight, it is clear that these were paranoid responses.

David Walker's important book *Anxious Nation: Australia and the Rise of Asia 1850–1939*[22] highlights three major elements in the cultural dynamics that underlie such writings. First, Asia was commonly depicted as 'a world of huge populations "teeming" with a terrible energy', while Australia was 'empty'; second, that 'imagined encounters were deeply implicated in the gendering process', while masculinity was endangered by the female principle; and third, there was in some minds an apprehension that 'in some way rampant "Asia" might "Aboriginalise" the Australian people'. Beside these anxieties was a competing suspicion that 'proximity to Asia might bring considerable trade benefits'. By the 1980s and '90s, this now consciously and publicly recognised benefit led to a re-mapping of Australia in relation to a region called 'the Asia–Pacific', which principally meant potentially enhanced trading opportunities with East Asia—China, Japan and Korea—together with the 'tiger economies' of Southeast Asia. Walker is not the only cultural analyst to have observed a continuing underlying ambivalence in Australian attitudes towards Asia. In Australian films and other popular culture forms, anthropologist and comparative sociologist, Annette

Hamilton, proposed a notion of the 'National Imaginary', drawing on Durkheim and Lacan, which enabled her to show that Australian cultural representations of two groups, Aborigines and Asians, stem from their positions respectively at the 'empty heart' and 'fragile boundaries' of the Australian consciousness.[23] Hamilton demonstrates a deep ambivalence in the majority white Australians' attitudes to these two groups in her analysis of selected films in which Aborigines and Asians are major subjects.

Essays and novels by leading Australian writers such as Christopher Koch, Nicholas Jose and Brian Castro take deep soundings of the real relations between Australians and Asians. The title essay in Koch's volume *Crossing the Gap*[24] describes his participation in the last phase of a historical moment—the end of P & O, Shaw Savill and Lloyd Triestino passenger ships which transported generations of Australians born before 1945 past Asia to England and Europe. Along the way, Koch and a friend broke with tradition and took a detour in India—a detour that found its way into Koch's second novel, *Across the Sea Wall*.[25] What he learnt—from the experience on trains, talking with Indians and living there for a time—was that 'it was the Indians who were our brothers under the skin—not the British'.[26]

The first port of call in Koch's formative sea voyage was Jakarta—a city to which he returned later in his best-known novel *The Year of Living Dangerously*.[27] Koch's Australian journalist-protagonist in this novel, Guy Hamilton, gets more involved than he intends to in the intrigue and turmoil that led to Sukarno's fall from power in 1965. Characteristically, Koch's protagonist gets injured, though not fatally. In his later Miles Franklin award-winning novel *Highways to a War*,[28] Koch's cameraman-hero, Mike Langford, gets more deeply involved in the wars in Vietnam and Cambodia, and is killed. All three of Koch's protagonists have deep attachments to the places of their Australian upbringing, and his novels show a progressive deepening of involvement in Asia, from tourism in *Across the Sea Wall* to professional engagement and injury in *The Year of Living Dangerously*, and the crucifixion of the protagonist in Cambodia by the Khmer Rouge in *Highways to a War*. Like many Australians who took part in the wars in Indo-China, Koch sees their experience as a definitive end of innocence, and sometimes of their lives. Yet he remains deeply attracted to the region.

Tasmania is Koch's islanded world of childhood, sensuous experience and Anglo-Australian culture. Crossing the gap between island and mainland and from the Australian mainland to Asia is a recurrent pattern of questing inscribed in much of Koch's work. There are many ways of making the cultural crossing, including the way suggested by Australian poet Les Murray. Koch quotes from Les Murray's poem 'Sanskrit'—the first of Murray's Hindu-inspired poems in his *Walking to the Cattle Place*[29] sequence—to demonstrate the kind of cross-fertilisation of artistic minds that can occur in the transmission of myth.

An alternative slant on large-scale Asia from an Australian viewpoint is provided by Nicholas Jose. Born in London in 1952, and raised in Adelaide, Jose is twenty years younger than Tasmanian-born Koch. Jose's grandfather was born in China and his great-grandfather worked there as a missionary in the 1890s. After completing a DPhil in English at Oxford University, Jose taught in the English Department at the Australian National University, before taking the adventurous step of teaching and writing in China in 1986–87, at the Beijing Foreign Studies University and the East China Teachers' University in Shanghai. These studies led to his appointment as cultural counsellor at the Australian embassy in Beijing from 1987–90.

Jose's best-known novel is *Avenue of Eternal Peace*,[30] which predicted the brave but futile Tiananmen Square demonstrations in May–June 1989 (the manuscript of the novel was completed in 1987). The novel was subsequently filmed. Jose's protagonist in the novel is Wally Frith, an Australian doctor on sabbatical leave in China. Frith is an expert on cancer, whose wife has died of the disease and he goes to China partly to make contact with a doctor whose published work suggests a 'Chinese' approach to medicine. Jose's novel is often buoyant and humorous in its treatment of cross-cultural perceptions, such as a typical Chinese view of Westerners:

> Chinese thought foreigners looked funny, and foreigners on long-term residence in China lived up to their perception, their hair ill-cropped, their expressions hunted, their eyes sunken, their noses growing longer by the day.[31]

A critical irony is directed more at Westerners than at the Chinese. Dulcia, an energetic American 'liberated woman', for example, has an exalted view of her own importance, despite her limited outlook:

> She had clear moral convictions. Wilhelm Reich and Tina Turner stood beside Abe Lincoln in her pantheon. She was an agent of liberation waging a personal campaign to help China.[32]

Jose is prudently sceptical about the capacity of the West to change China, but his concerns about Chinese restrictions on human freedoms, including homosexual expression, emerge through vividly realised scenes showing cross-cultural differences and occasional clashes.

Jose's interest in China has been long-term and deep. His novel *The Rose Crossing*[33] extends the author's imaginative reach from the present, backwards to an imagined seventeenth-century 'crossing' between representative Chinese and European cultures. This occurs when a naturalist, Edward Popple, and his daughter, Rosamund, find refuge on an uncharted island in the Indian Ocean (there are shades here of *The Tempest*). There they encounter Lou Lu, a Chinese eunuch, and an apparently impotent young prince, who are lost on their way to Rome to petition the Pope. Notions of hybridity are explored in the novel through the sexual attraction of the Chinese and European youngsters and in images of the cross-breeding of roses. Jose's knowledge of seventeenth-century English and attitudes of the time enables him to build a fabulous illusion of reality, and beyond that, an allegory of cross-cultural fertilising possibilities.

In his book of essays and occasional papers, *Chinese Whispers*,[34] Nicholas Jose attempts a quite sophisticated exposition of Australia's internalised relationship to China:

> Australia has a relationship with China that goes back before white invasion and has gone on ever since, with different elements of the relationship made visible, or invisible, at different times. China in that sense, is part of what Australia is, as Australia is part of a world that includes mainland China, Taiwan, Hong Kong, Singapore and the Chinese diaspora, especially in Southeast Asia, as well as the Chinese in Australia. The story of China in Australia differs from the story of China in Britain or the United States, or in Malaysia or Indonesia, although all those stories are sometimes strands in the Australian story. And to talk of the Chinese people in Australia

requires fine differentiation according to where people have come
from, how long they have been here, what languages they speak,
and what cultures they identify with. There are many Australians of
partial Chinese ancestry, which only at a certain point becomes
meaningless or irrelevant to them—and then seldom finally. And
there are all those non-Chinese Australians whose lives or whose
ancestors' lives have been affected by China.[35]

Jose is critical of the broad-brush use of Said's Orientalism to such
relationships, because it inevitably oversimplifies in a reductionist
way the actual complexities of different people with different
histories. The relations between Australian and Chinese polities are
crucial to the self-understanding of Australians, as Jose remarks:

> Although far from our nearest neighbour, China has been especially
> significant in the Australian experience of Asia. China and the
> Chinese have weighed heavily in policy decisions about White
> Australia, the Vietnam War and other 'Asian' issues. It is only in
> exceptional circumstances, such as the second world war, that we
> distinguish sharply between Chinese and other Asians. Likewise
> Japan's pre-eminence in recent times, in contradistinction to China,
> has forced a refinement of our understanding of Asia as a whole.
>
> Inasmuch as Australia's identity has been formed through a
> dialectic (often silent) with what is perceived and feared as non-
> Australian, the relationships with the Chinese world reflect some of
> the not always articulated tendencies of Australian society and
> culture.[36]

Since Jose published his views in *Chinese Whispers* in 1995, a number
of important scholarly projects and publications have made the
silent dialectic about which he wrote more public. Chief among
these, perhaps, is a special joint issue of the *Journal of Australian
Studies* and *Australian Cultural History* in 2000, edited by Helen
Gilbert, Tseen Khoo and Jacqueline Lo called *Diaspora: Negotiating
Asian-Australia*.[37] In their introductory essay, the editors make a
case for the use of a hyphen in 'Asian-Australian' as a claim on the
hybridity or 'third space' theorised by Homi Bhabha:

> The position of inbetweenness—of being both Asian and
> Australian—unsettles dominant expectations of the unproblematic
> homology between cultural, racial and national identity. However,
> this reconfiguration of Asian-Australianness should not be
> mistaken for a teleology of progress towards stability and
> belonging. Rather, the emerging discourse of Asian-Australia is a

response to the exlusionary identity politics that characterise hegemonic multiculturalism and the new racism. As a provisional category of identification to be mobilised strategically in the face of racist politics, 'Asian-Australia' is a portmanteau term that unites peoples of various 'Asian' ethnicities, enabling a degree of political solidarity and critical purchase.[38]

While the editors make a claim here for solidarity across various 'Asian' ethnicities, two of them have Chinese-Australian heritages (via Malaysia in Jacqueline Lo's case) and a large number of contributions to the volume confirm Nicholas Jose's view that people of Chinese heritage (however far back) tend to dominate Australian notions of Asianness. This view is counterbalanced to some extent by new players such as Filipino-Australian Merlinda Bobis's book of stories *White Turtle*,[39] Bangladeshi Australian Adib Khan's novels and stories[40] and the novels of Indonesian Australian Dewi Anggraeni.[41]

Further indications of important scholarly activity in Asian-Australian studies are provided by two books which illuminate the Chinese connection from a close-in perspective: Shen Yuanfeng's study of Chinese-Australian autobiographies, *Dragon Seed in the Antipodes*[42] and Wenche Ommundsen's edited collection of essays on Chinese-Australian writing, *Bastard Moon*.[43] Ommundsen's essays explore 'the rich variety of writings by Chinese Australians, from the earliest petitions in which Chinese appealed against discrimination on the goldfields to the latest blossoming of creative output from the "Tiananmen Square" generation of immigrants'.[44]

The single writer who has perhaps most radically challenged Australian thinking about Australian-Asian cultural relations is novelist and essayist Brian Castro. Castro was born in Hong Kong in 1950 of an English and Chinese mother and a Portuguese father from Shanghai. After migrating to Australia he worked as a teacher of English and French in Australia and France from 1972 to 1979, before becoming a full-time writer. His prize-winning first novel, *Birds of Passage*,[45] indicates in its title the perspective of the migrant traveller, and the problematics of assigning any kind of fixed identity based on location or ethnicity. The novel's dual narratives— of Shan, a Chinese who takes part in the mid-nineteenth century Australian goldrushes, and Seamus, his mixed race descendant— together reveal the absurdity of conventional, fixed myths about Australian identity.

A postmodern, deconstructive approach to myth, culture and society characterises Castro's fiction and essay writing. His book of essays *Looking for Estrellita*[46] is full of witty, epigrammatic and often insightful comments which are designed to upset applecarts. Two of the pieces in this volume, 'Writing Asia' and 'Auto/biography' had their origins in lectures given by Castro in 1995, when he was Writing Fellow at Canberra's universities. In 'Auto/biography', Castro performs as a kind of trickster in order to break down genres, categories and classifications: his purpose is to show that 'faking' or reinventing a life is what many do to survive in a rapidly changing world. Scepticism is the most important virtue. Castro writes, he says, because he wants to write himself out of 'an artificially imposed corner', and uses critical theory to 'subvert genres'. What he brings to writing is 'a mixture of forms, a mixture of character types, a mixture of ethnicities'. Hybridity, he believes, is 'a powerfully transgressive quality' and that is the sign under which he prefers to operate rather than endorsing the 'truth-claims' of science, literature or history. 'Cross-genres', Castro asserts, 'relieve the schizophrenic pressures upon the dichotomy of authenticity and inauthenticity. If you cross borders regularly you do not really have to defend them'. If not exactly Everyman, Castro's preferred protagonist is trans-national man or woman (or woman/man), forever in flux.

Castro's lecture 'Writing Asia'[47] is similarly challenging. On the cusp of a new century, he asserts, 'nothing counts except images; images of the way we project ourselves; images of others'. It is the age of self-promotion and an age of considerable 'anxiety'. The age is characterised by a rage for 'authenticity'—a term about which Castro expresses scepticism bordering on scorn. Wondering why he seems to be attracted, in his fiction writing, to 'hybrid forms and strange juxtapositions', Castro observes that most of his novels 'deal with two or three "voices" and move through several different spaces, rather in the manner of a hologram'. He is concerned that his abandonment of 'a fixed, two-dimensional reality' in favour of a hybridity of forms and meanings tends to cause 'embarrassment or puzzlement'. Paradoxically, however, Castro's attempted abandonment of the criterion of 'authenticity' seems to require its endorsement when he describes being born 'between states, on a steam ferry between Macau and Hong Kong'. His achievement is to raise questions about the interplay of words and experience in representations of self, origins and country. Castro advocates better understanding of language—or rather languages, since he believes that polyglots are freer than monoglots. The better our grasp of language, and especially Asian languages—the better is our chance, as Australians, of participating in Asia.

As a writer, Brian Castro felt constrained by the so-called 'Asian immigration debate of 1984', following Geoffrey Blainey's Warrnambool lecture and his subsequent book *All for Australia*.[48] Some Asian-Australian writers and artists have felt similarly angry, or constrained, by subsequent 'anti-Asian' sentiment in media reports, talk-back radio programs or letters to editors about immigration, refugees or other media-induced, if not media-produced crises. These constraints may be easing. But Brian Castro's challenge remains:

> ... Australia ... has written off Asia for almost 200 years; written off the countries of Asia, with various cultural traditions of thousands of years. Perhaps it is time to write 'Asia', to write within it and of it, rather than just about it. The word Asia is found, after all, in the word Australia. If Australia wants to refigure itself in its relationship to the countries of Asia, to become part of Asia, as it were, then Asia must also be part of Australia.[49]

Such a bold change would involve a reconfiguration of the known and previously trusted maps. It might be work for visionaries. But strange things have happened, and continue to happen in Australia. We will continue to be influenced by Europe and America, the traditional sources of majority Australian culture. But enhanced interaction with Indo-Asia–Pacific countries is already generating, and will generate further beneficial changes to Australian culture and society.

The Unsettled 1970s—Moorhouse, Wilding, Viidikas

The decade of the 1970s in Australia was dubbed by its leader in short fiction, Frank Moorhouse, as the 'Days of Wine and Rage'. Two authors who appear in Moorhouse's anthology with that title, Michael Wilding and Vicki Viidikas, contributed, along with Moorhouse, to the reimagining of land and cityscape, and of home and away, that occurred at this time in short fiction, and presented themselves as barometers of changing lifestyles and expectations. *Days of Wine and Rage* presented the city of Sydney, and especially the suburb of Balmain—Frenchified by Moorhouse as 'Le Ghetto de Balmain'—as the social laboratory of modernity in Australia. In 1970, Moorhouse was 32 years old, Wilding was 28 and Viidikas 22.

Those against 'Balmain regional writing', as it was sometimes called in self-defence by writers and critics elsewhere, were typecast by Balmain advocates as hostile to 'the new writing, especially young writing, sexual explicitness, experiment'.[1] Moorhouse was by origin a country boy from the small town of Nowra in south-coast New South Wales. Balmain—the main homeplace of Moorhouse, Wilding and Viidikas in the 1970s—was to some extent a triumph for its publicists and promoters because it provided not only living quarters but a launching pad for writers and film makers.

Moorhouse's 'discontinuous fictions' interweave in the 1970s and '80s with his journalistic writings, conference papers and other forms of commentary and analysis. In a conference paper called

'The Bush against the Laundromat' in Canberra in 1973 Moorhouse remarked:

> Our society lives out the city/country polarity both ritualistically and earnestly. At its strongest we have Thoreaus in the outskirts of our cities and in the bush—hermits whom as a child in the country I remember watching and persecuting. I remember with others stoning their camps and it remains a humiliating guilt. I guess we were instruments of the town's own restrained fear of deviation.
>
> Again, at its strongest we have the current phenomenon of rural communalism and the flight from the city. At its weakest, mildest, we have the symbolic return to nature—the weekend drive, the Sunday driver, drinking a thermos of tea around a drum of rubbish at a roadside rest stop.[2]

As a discerning, and suitably ironic, chronicler of his times, whether in conference papers or in short fiction, Moorhouse has nevertheless displayed his own value judgements; for example, in the attitude he took against what he called the 'mystical' element in communalism:

> There is mysticism in the movement. It goes from the formalised mysticism of Hare Krishna and Meher Baba to a low-key non-doctrinaire form of Australian transcendentalism ... But there is a recoil from the 'artficiality' of city life, a stress on the primary intuitions, and a belief in beneficial psychological changes from being close to plants and animals. There are traces of pantheism, belief in illimitable human potential, and anti-materialism. And basic anti-city emotion.[3]

Moorhouse's dialogues between city and country are exemplified in some of his strongest short stories. In 'The Commune Does Not Want You',[4] for example, Moorhouse's first-person narrator describes his attempt to pursue the object of his jilted desire, Milton (based on his notion of Michael Wilding) to the communal inner-Sydney house where Milton lives, which had advertised for a lodger. The Moorhouse persona wears a bow tie and tries to present himself as middle-class and rational when he knocks and is allowed into the dark interior:

> I groped my way into the commune.
>   There appeared in the dim light, amid the raga music, to be a person in every room or the shape of a person. Were they the residents or were they the callers? Or were they too answering the

advertisement for the room? In a commune there is always this group sitting around the kitchen table reading or picking at themselves, toes or noses, drinking tea, and you don't know if any of them live there or whether you can sit in that chair or is that Big Paddy's chair or is that where Papa Milton sits.[5]

Going further into the darkened depths of the house, the speaker steps on a pig which squeals. He learns its name is Pushkin. This is a version of the country brought to town—softened by the raga which adds a touch of India to the scene (an essential element of the exotic at this time). The story has some humorous dialogic encounters. Moorhouse's narrator asks one of the inhabitants, a young woman, how the commune is coming along and she replies: 'Look man, this is a house we all share, if you want to call it a commune you call it a commune, but for us it is a simple experiment in shared living with a poly-functional endospace'.[6]

The narrative is structured, like many of Moorhouse's at this time, to show the narrator's defeat: his mission or purpose is rejected, because in this case he never sees Milton. As he is moved towards the door, in this story with Kafkaesque overtones, he manages a last Socratic question: 'Is there a commune for people who do not fit very well into communes?' But his guide says with allegorical firmness: 'I was instructed not to talk with you any further. You must go now'.[7]

As mentioned earlier, Moorhouse is a country boy by origin and some of the sceptical wit in his ironic and humorous stories derives from this source. Moorhouse's sympathetic interest in small-time farmers and their tribulations was reawakened when he edited *A Steele Rudd Selection* in 1986. It is doubly ironic that Moorhouse, the averred spokesman for inner city living—the chief apologist for, and commentator on, the Sydney Push—should in some respects be its most trenchant critic. Milton's commune, for example, where the country is brought to the city, turns out to be authoritarian and predictable—not able to cope with the anarchistic libertarianism to which Moorhouse and others tried to give credence at this time. In some of his stories of the 1980s, Moorhouse returned to the bush, but he did so in an assimilated urbanite's way—by then it was an 'away' zone that was also close to his former 'home'. Moorhouse's story 'From a Bush Log Book I'[8] presents the semi-autobiographical narrator returning to the Budawang Ranges with his girlfriend Belle while he turns forty. They have, he says, 'debauched' in motel rooms and restaurants along the coast and the move to the country's interior parallels his restless interiorisation of a sense of lost youth: 'he was trying to solve the loss of his young girl-friend who was overseas and "in love"'.[9] But another pressure works on him too:

> He also had some home-yearnings which came on at Christmas. His family was not in town for this Christmas, but anyhow his home-yearnings had been displaced over the years away from his family in the town to the bush about fifty kilometres away from, but behind, the coastal town where he had grown up—the Sassafras bush in the Budawang Ranges.[10]

Moorhouse has remarked in an interview that 'all relationships have their own environment, and become very fragile when they're moved out of it'.[11] Expanding on this, he observed that '[the bush is] just the wrong place for some people to be'. Moorhouse himself, though, had 'almost consciously reclaimed' that part of himself. Brought up as a cub, a scout, and an army cadet with brothers who were backpackers and canoeists, and then spending three years in the army, Moorhouse had lived in 'an outdoor family', on which he had turned his back after leaving school. But in his thirties he made a 'tentative re-entry to the bush', gradually found he had a taste for it, and then found it an addiction. At times, he has said, he feels he belongs in the virgin bush of the Budawang Ranges, and that he ought to become 'a hermit'.[12] In the general mobility of Moorhouse's moods and assertions throughout his short fiction, interviews and autobiographical commentary, the idea of the bush, his bush, represents a stabilising influence. Against this is posed the travelling self, typified in the figure of Francois Blase, 'cultural ambassador', who sees the world comically from the refuge of Hilton hotels.[13] The apogee of this traveller and cultural diplomat appears in Moorhouse's two great novels of the League of Nations, *Grand Days* and *Dark Palace*.[14]

Michael Wilding's representations of cities and their alternatives have a different focus and emphasis from Moorhouse's. Wilding's perspective might be summed up in the title of his story 'Outline for Urban Fantasies' in his eighth volume of stories *This is for You* (1994), in which various alternatives to a dystopian present are produced in a style reminiscent of Beckett. One of them is a fleeting, parodic recollection in Australia of an olde England that never existed—quite unlike his graphic realisations of the English Midlands of Wilding's youth in *The West Midland Underground* (1975):

> At certain times bells ring, chimes, sirens, to remind us of available services, like the street cries of old England, the plangent electronic perpetuation of Greensleeves through the suburban afternoon, ice cream, or a brief peal or so, divine service, that was how the streets used to be.[15]

Wilding's narrative persona, having tried various escape hatches in previous volumes such as Sydney's pubs, beaches, sex, beer, marijuana and air travel, mordantly enters a recurrent urban fantasy—that of space:

> A spaceship and we suspect the captain has bailed out. Or whatever they do. We don't know what they do. Maybe he rematerialises here once in a while just to deceive us. The dead hand. Opening the porthole. From outside. Crawling up from the vine-cloning experiments below. And the punkas hang there silent, still, the punka wallahs all gone.[16]

This last sentence is a finely tuned mock lament for colonial times past, recalling a graphic image from Forster's *A Passage to India*. It serves as a reminder of the bold, post-colonial spirit which led Wilding in the 1970s to read widely in Australian and other literatures and to edit the Asian and Pacific Writing series for the University of Queensland Press.

In Wilding's first volume, *Aspects of the Dying Process* (1972), the exotic 'away' country of Australia is imaged through the eyes of a tentative young man fresh from England who encounters Sydney's beaches and their hedonistic young women—'sybaritic' is his word for their easygoing way of life. As Robert Drewe would demonstrate in *Bodysurfers*, and in his *Picador Book of the Beach*, for city-dwelling young Australians the beaches offered a contemporary version of wilderness.

But the fears and anxieties of the European consciousness when confronted by 'the wild'—wherever this is encountered—is Wilding's principal subject. His story 'As Boys to Wanton Flies' demonstrates with saturnine humour the European horror of Australian wildlife, even in the suburbs: indeed, in this story the suburbs seem to breed the conditions for a mother-induced phobia about Australian insects. When the maid Erika tricks the middle-class boy by filling his bed with insects and coaxing him to climb in, he screams with all the abject terror of Munch's archetypal mouth:

> [He] ran screaming, howling, naked through the house, the garden, the street, screaming one single high note as he ran, smeared over with slime and crushed paste and pulsing dying living insects, being eaten and stung and torn as he ran ... [He] ran, impelled on his single ceaseless note of terror, and he would never come back.[17]

We generally see nature in Wilding's short fiction through the filter of a literary consciousness which expresses the anxieties, fears and desires of that person (in the above case comically and hyperbolically) rather than any naturalistic account of place or region.

Wilding's interest in 'nature', away from his native West Midlands, may be tested in his fictional use of trees. His story 'For Trees'[18] was written after Wilding visited Oregon in the early 1990s, and is based partly on a newspaper report. Wilding's story depicts the autobiographical narrator as being in that 'half-away' state that perhaps characterises academic travellers giving papers at foreign universities:

> living suspended in this capsule of otherness, flown in from somewhere no more rooted, no more alienated than this sense of suspension, wondering is this the life, advance purchase bargain discount stay over Saturday night required jetsetting, what grand design can this scratchy itinerary fulfil?[19]

The campus he is visiting is in logging country in America's North-West and the reveries that recur for this narrator have to do with a sense of his own transience and the apparent rootedness—in the tree sense—of other people. The town visited by Wilding's narrator, together with its problematic economy, the flowering street trees and its little timber houses is based on Eugene, Oregon. The central incident is the visit of a tree feller to his host's house, to rid the block of a tree so that another room can be built on to his little timber house. The narrator's reverie provides a running commentary:

> It was not my tree, not my house, not my business, this was logging country, thousands of trees were felled every day and sawn into

timber for housing and pulped into paper for newsprint, books, notepads, where would I be without wood pulp, back to plague rags again?[20]

This semi-naturalistic, mordant commentary is interrupted by the tree feller's story of his work partner who he says is 'sick, in hospital'. Rapidly (and typically) Wilding's story lurches from an apparently normal suburban situation to the strange and abnormal when the tree feller explains that his workmate will not be let out of hospital in a hurry:

> You must have read about it [he explains.] It was in the papers. He got this belief the people next door were sperm banks for aliens. So he went in there and hacked them to pieces.[21]

Violence and horror lurk everywhere in apparently 'normal and natural' situations in Wilding's fiction. In this story, the narrator dreams of trees that talk to him, and Wilding uses the fantasia to good thematic effect:

> The trees leaned over and whispered.
> 'He was right, you know', they said. They were aliens. So are you, an alien. You are all aliens. But you can be open to us too. The spirit of the hamadryads can enter you and help us. Before the alien human came this was all forest. Everything you see was living timber. No Highway 99. No Best Western Motel. No campus cleared for doubtful learning. This was the still soft land of the tree spirits and we lived here in peace. We hurt no-one. Whoever heard of trees killing anyone till they started logging? Unless we were blown over in a gale and ourselves killed too, but that wasn't us, that was the windy elements'.[22]

The spirit of the place enters insinuatingly into Wilding's persona:

> The newspaper lay on the wooden table. The wooden walls kept out the wind. The spirits spoke through the dead timber as if through a sounding box, like music through a flute or violin.
> 'Taking possession was not a good way', they said. 'Taking possession never is. This is what we are trying to tell you. We do not want to chop up aliens. We do not want aliens to come and chop us up. It might have been a dramatic way of making our case. Timber terrorism. But we regret it. As we regret the daily felling of our fellow trees. So you can speak for us now. You can take our

message. The airwaves would be preferable to paper and print. Readings. Even just speaking, talking. We have a case. We entrust it to you'.[23]

Wilding's story cross-cuts to a concluding scene of apparent normality. The tree at his friendly host's house has been felled, his host saws it into lengths to fit into the potbellied stove. The apparent security of this domestic scene counterpoints in lower key his vivid dreams of the night before. The author does not become a propagandist for trees, but their intervention in his dream-life has thrown routine normality into disarray.

Having striven to overcome what he felt to be the restrictive conventions of Australian bush realism via Lawson and Rudd in the 1960s and '70s, Wilding used postmodernist fictional techniques to represent the disjunctions of contemporary living in the Vietnam and post-Vietnam era. It was later, with *The Paraguayan Experiment*, in 1985, that he rediscovered the strength of realist conventions and the power of narrative. Wilding has generally written with a strong sense of narrative styles, frames and conventions, even when he flouts them. One such generic frame is the pastoral, which has been recurrently present in Wilding's writing, reinforced by his understanding from Milton's *Paradise Lost*, on which he wrote a monograph in 1969, of the emotions associated with exile from a state of grace.

Bruce Clunies Ross has written interestingly on the pastoral aspects of Wilding's fiction, suggesting that:

> Wilding did not become an exile writing about 'home', but exploited his background to create a distinctive response to his new [Australian] environment. 'Home' was transformed in a manner typical for exiles. Its formative images were lodged in memory and the West Midlands became a mental landscape which generated associations, legends and associations ... There is, perhaps, a mysterious underground leading from the [English] West Midlands to pastoral Australia.[24]

Beside Clunies Ross's commentary may be placed Wilding's own observations in a 1994 interview that, although he grew up in the English countryside and learned a love of nature from his parents, he had experienced a childhood 'far from the coast, in the classic English climate':

The beaches and sea and the sun of Australia were strikingly new to me and made their own distinct impact. Australia is a very beautiful country and I responded to it readily and still do. Though I might add that the natural settings in my fiction usually have an emotional or metaphoric or symbolic significance; realistic observation is part of it, but there is also the purpose of establishing an emotional mood, for support or contrast, to the events.[25]

We have seen Wilding's incorporation of the idea of nature into a literary form that enables trees to speak in the story 'For Trees', and it is even more evident in the surreal imagery of an Australian story 'The Phallic Forest' and the novel *Pacific Highway* (1982). What Wilding saw as the 'much more sensual' Australian society was reflected in stories of conflict between the 'older repressive values and the new emerging sexual openness [of the 1970s]'.[26] The overcoming of personal and societal puritanism and political conservatism gives Wilding's fiction of this period a buoyancy which his later story 'Under Saturn' (1988) presents in much darker tones. The gloomy dystopias of this and other later stories reflect a recognition by Wilding that the liberations sought in youth were insufficiently informed by an understanding of political and social forces; once that understanding is more fully reached, the sign of Saturn, of coldness, withdrawal and gloominess, prevails. The revivification of the species through beach or forest life seems increasingly remote, and 'home' a more distant prospect than ever. The mythic force of paradise lost reasserts itself.

The third member of this trio of experimental short fictionists of the 1970s, Vicki Viidikas, had less support structures beyond the Push than her male counterparts. While expressing her periodic intoxication with a cocktail of drugs, sex and rock 'n' roll, Viidikas's writing reflects a sense that she sailed closer to the abyss than her friends Moorhouse and Wilding. Her death in isolated circumstances in Sydney on 27 November 1998 retrospectively highlights the fragmentary quality of her stories and prose pieces in the volumes *Wrappings* (1974) and *India Ink* (1984), in which she strove above all for naturalness and authenticity.[27] Viidikas's settings were principally inner-city Balmain and East Sydney and the 'alternative' settlements of the north and south coasts of New South Wales. The poetic intensity in much of her writing sets her apart from Moorhouse and Wilding: in an obituary, Wilding described this daughter of an Estonian violin-maker father and an Australian mother who claimed descent from Ned Kelly's family, as 'a striking, effervescent figure around the pubs, the parties and the waterfront readings [of the late 1960s and early '70s]'.

For Viidikas, glimpses of natural surroundings appear in her writings as lyrical relief and solace from the emotional confusions, intensities and debilities of urban living, as in 'Love an Apple':

> The grass lay flat along the hill, under the wind, the silence thickening along the ridge by the sea. With every chance of nothing more than the trees rooting and uprooting and growing and dying, plants breaking out in new leaves, splintering and curling back into the earth, the constant, the constant hush and lull.[28]

Or in 'Trying to Catch the Voice': 'Maybe it was the trees I imagined had ears, putting my arms around their knobbly trunks, laying my face against their skin as they stood there tall messengers.'[29]

Occasionally, Viidikas leaves the rancid backyards of working-class (though incipiently gentrified) Balmain for escapades with rich criminals from the North Shore, as in 'The Snowman in the Dutch Masterpiece'.[30]

In the search for 'authentic' experience, Viidikas gave herself up more than her male counterparts to the extreme, and in the end, destructive urban life of her generation. Her writings are redolent of the popular music of Jimi Hendrix, the Rolling Stones, Jefferson Airplane and others she quotes in her writings. Her importance in the triptych which also contains Moorhouse and Wilding is that she was less cautious, a greater extremist. Moreover she immersed herself in an India which Moorhouse and Wilding saw principally from a distance. What drew her there was not just drugs, but a sense of living on the edge. She concludes a short prose piece 'Weekend in Bombay' in her collection *India Ink*, with these lines:

> There's too much room to be alone in, too much time to further drown in. Oh Age of Disenchantment, we're singing as we cut down our families, we're composing a sonata to war and greed, jazz for the tribe with its pride and anger. We sleep now in a treeless world.[31]

Viidikas's voice of the neo-romantic adventurer and lyricist is more intense than that of her ironic male contemporaries. India, which Viidikas was writing about in prose and verse in *Westerly* and other magazines in the early 1970s, was in some respects an escape from the 'treeless world' to the hippy trails of the Himalayas and elsewhere. The flavour of the genre can be tasted in her story called 'The Clothesline in the Himalayas' in which the narrator's male companion, Bear, shares his ingenuity with her:

> Bear was making his 90th chillum for the day and hunting round for some string to make a gooley out of. The only string left was the clothesline. 'Don't smoke the clothesline', I said feeling sorry for myself. 'There's nothing else to use', he grunted, undoing one end of the line, cutting and winding a piece of it artistically into a ball. He then stuck it on the end of a bent nail (his gooley nail) and set the ball alight till it was a perfect glowing coal. As he dropped it into the chillum I smiled—who wouldn't smoke the clothesline when it was such magnificent grass?[32]

Desecration of the domestic icon of the clothesline is rendered humorously here but the gothic and exotic elements of landscape are part of Viidikas's trip too:

> Bear and I spent mornings stumbling down mountain sides sloping into the cheeks of monsters—earth monsters humped and riddled with dried trees' roots, petrified bushes and the ghosts of Tibetans' bones (the bodies of the dead are smashed up and their bones thrown in the snow). The air in these mountains is so dense and mauve like an ocean you can wade into, veil upon mysterious veil. And the sweet smell of tea bushes floats up from the estates—you can see women picking the leaf tips and throwing them over their shoulders into baskets tied on their backs. They move silently down rows of bushes swinging their long black plaits, ornate gold rings hanging from the centre of their noses.[33]

But Viidikas's exotic India, here perceived from a distance, was also found in the grime and poverty of cities such as Calcutta, as in her story 'The Silk Trousers', where a young Australian woman observes with fascinated horror a man with a monkey, and fantasises about him, before experiencing a nihilistic vision of self-exposure:

> She would run before he devoured her. That man retained a power from thousands of years of spiritual birthright—he had tiger and elephant gods to advise him, and she had culturally nothing. A twisted image of a son of God impaled on a wooden cross, a pale corpse who made her a sinner before she was even born. Two

thousand years of guilt to absolve—no time for dancing or feasting or love-making. Her heritage was ashes, penance, and self-absolution through repression.[34]

This, then, is the escape which Viidikas sought in her India—the romance of living without inherited guilt and an accompanying sense of impending punishment. More than Nimbin, or other Australian retreats, India gave her the impetus to express the wildest of dreams, unhedged by the frames and ironies of 'civilised' expectations. It is difficult to imagine Viikidas, in her downward spiral to a lonely death, ever reaching even the provisional sense of belonging expressed in the writings of Moorhouse or Wilding.

From the perspective of the twenty-first century, the shock tactics of late 1960s and '70s avant garde writers such as Moorhouse, Wilding and Viidikas may seem less than shocking. But as Moorhouse observed with some exaggeration in 2000, 'Australia was the most censored country in the English language, we had to write in a fugitive way'.[35] It is arguable that the conservatism of an older Australian generation was in part a colonial legacy, and writers such as these three were 'post-colonial' in their attempts at sexual liberation, revolutionary politics and anti-censorship tactics. However, in retrospect, their main contribution in the 1970s may have been their imagined alternatives to what they saw as the settled suburbanism and small country-town outlook of older Australians. The spaces and modes of living they envisaged in their fiction—urban, suburban, rural and international—expressed a rapidly increasing mobility in the Australian population at large, and gave warning that Australians would never again feel 'settled' or 'at home' in the ways proposed by the previous generation of post–second world war reconstructionists.

20

A West-Side Story

When I moved to Canberra from Perth in 1993 it was for a job—
not for a change of air or landscape. The latter were accessories
after the fact, but they have sustained and strengthened my
appreciation of the 'new place' in my life. The vertical perspective
of hills and mountains is a significant shift. The Darling Range east
of Perth where bushrangers discovered their hidden valley and
trains later struggled up the hills has now been flattened out by
highways leading inland—and Multanova cameras flash on unwary
motorists who have failed to check in local newspaper or radio
reports where they are hidden. By contrast, as I write this winter
morning, I look west towards the high Brindabella Range at the
snow-covered mountains scarred by recent bushfires but largely
unmarked as yet by roads or railways. One person's vision of
sublimity is of course another's joke. A friend from Perth remarked
of this view that the white sand dunes out there remind him of
home.

The more we retreat to the virtual reality of books, television and
the Internet, the more we seem to need a clear and present sense of
place. But such a sense is always infused with memories of former
places, which jostle with new and as yet unseen places of the mind.
Yearning for other cities of the mind that I might inhabit in early
1960s Perth, I wrote my BA honours dissertation in afternoons and
evenings at the University of Western Australia library—a building
now inhabited by the managers and administrators of the university.
The thesis topic I chose was 'Images of the City in the Poetry of
T S Eliot and Baudelaire'. In the mornings, I taught life-saving
classes on the Swan River and saw the world through sunglasses

across a zinc-creamed nose. In the afternoons and evenings, I was able to indulge in dreams of foggy London and Paris. In T-shirt, shorts and thongs, I identified with Baudelaire's *flaneur* chasing the phantasms of fallen women through Paris's gas-lit boulevards. I was a mind-traveller. To this point, my actual overseas travel had been restricted to Rottnest Island, 18 km west of Fremantle. By my early twenties, I had also ventured eastward by train across the vast Nullarbor Plain to Adelaide, where I played football for my teachers' college team. If I succeeded in fulfilling a seductive dream of 'neck neck necking on the Nullarbor' I have long forgotten it. As for lessons of the earth, I learnt in Adelaide that not all soil is coastal sandplain, that you have to learn to run, turn and twist differently on damp clayey surfaces where the oval ball can skid and grubber instead of bouncing fast and high as it does on compacted sandy surfaces. These were my deeply limited lessons of the earth.

If the pleasure of living in Canberra is one of Australia's best-kept secrets (which I won't divulge here), another less underground recognition is the quality of life that is possible in Australia's West. I have often thought of Blainey's 'tyranny of distance' as a curse for him as a Victorian but something of a blessing for West Australians enabling us to develop a separate sense of community if we have the wit to do so. I began to see these possibilities from a distance when, as a Rhodes scholar in Oxford in the mid to late 1960s, I began to read the literature of my home country and my home state. On my return, editing the quarterly literary magazine *Westerly* from the early 1970s until my departure for Canberra two decades later, and writing and editing a string of books on Western Australian literature, I set out to build an imaginative picture of 'my' home state. Among the major writers who helped me to form a sense of place that required imaginative renewal were Randolph Stow, Dorothy Hewett, Peter Cowan, Robert Drewe and Tim Winton.

When poet and teacher Bill Grono and I put together the anthology *Wide Domain: Western Australian Themes and Images*,[1] we chose an anonymous poem from the Perth *Sunday Times* in 1899 as an opening salvo to the volume:

> Land of Forests, Fleas and Flies,
> Blighted hopes and blighted eyes,
> Art thou hell in Earth's disguise,
>   Westralia?

The poem's concluding stanzas carry more than a hint of prophetic relevance:

> Home of brokers, bummers, sharks,
> Nest of sharpers, mining sharks,
> Dried up lakes and desert parks,
>   Westralia!
>
> Land of humpies, brothels, inns,
> Old bag huts and empty tins,
> Land of blackest, grievous sins,
>   Westralia.

Anger and criticism can be a sign of love. Randolph Stow's alter ego, Rick, in *The Merry-go-round in the Sea*[2] explodes to his young cousin, Rob, about the 'shoddiness and wowserism' he finds in postwar Western Australia and the 'unspeakable bloody boredom of belonging to a country that keeps up a sort of chorus: "Relax, mate, relax, don't make the pace too hot"'. Rick, like Stow, becomes an Australian expatriate, but Rob remains in his native land.

Taking a lead from Stow, Dorothy Hewett wrote of the 'brutal innocence'[3] of her fellow West Australians and moved to Sydney in 1974. She kept returning, however, to her 'garden state' to explore the sources of her inspiration as a writer, as did Robert Drewe.

Coming from a place whose major writers both hate and love it so vigorously, I found myself towards the end of my first year in Canberra introducing Tim Winton to a packed audience at University House at the ANU. Tim had recently visited Europe and had written a meditative essay accompanied by photographs, *Land's Edge*.[4] We talked at the top table, surrounded by Leonard French's magnificent stained glass windows, of fishing, football and writing books. His talk and reading were warm, celebratory and humorous, evoking a sense of need for community and belonging to Australia's land and seascapes. My stomach flipped as I heard these lines from *Land's Edge*:

> There is nowhere else I'd rather be, nothing else I would prefer to be doing. I am at the beach looking west with the continent behind me as the sun tracks down to the sea. I have my bearings.

Gaining one's bearings, physically and emotionally, in Australia has been a major preoccupation of many of our writers, artists and thinkers. The changing dramas of attachment, detachment, reattachment to place, community and nation are often seen to have their roots in the personal histories of childhood. Why is the little noun 'home' so resonant in contemporary ears? Have the new technologies of travel and communication eroded our capacity to belong—or more importantly, perhaps, to feel we belong? The turn towards biography and autobiography in the late twentieth and early twenty-first century, along with a cooling of postmodernist theory, may testify to a growing intellectual awareness of the need to explore the human dimensions of belonging.

The search often begins with parents. Mine both lived their last years and died in Western Australia after I had moved to Canberra. I returned to Perth to mourn over each of their bodies, to cremate them and to remember and celebrate their lives with other family members. They remain as voices in my head. The nodal point in my parents' fortunes was a particular place—the eastern goldfields town of Kalgoorlie, whence my father's father, Harry Bennett senior, had migrated from Liverpool in 1897, during a late phase of the goldrushes, to work on the railways. My grandfather shared a tent with the Mining Warden for a time, and took out a miner's right, but his occasional efforts as a prospector never paid off. Wealth from gambling in its various forms has never been part of my family's inheritance. My grandfather on my mother's side is said to have been banned from every race-course in Western Australia and he may have committed suicide. It is not surprising that my mother frowned—with a deeply furrowed brow—on gambling and 'strong drink'. She adopted a traditional role of Australian mothers of her time as a benign member of God's police. Her job, as she saw it, was to 'civilise' her three sons, to keep her husband on the straight and narrow, and to inculcate moral values. As one consequence, girls remained to her sons a mysterious, foreign species. But that is to leap ahead.

Places as well as genes make people. My father was born in Kalgoorlie and his relationship with my mother was celebrated there by a day out at the Kalgoorlie Cup. As a melting pot of t'othersiders and locals—of eastern states refugees and westerners—Kalgoorlie in the 1930s was a lively place for courting. Open-air brass band performances, dances, amateur repertory productions, vaudeville, magicians, motor cycle races, football carnivals, horse-racing were some of the attractions. A vigorous journalism reinforced the Bulletin-style 'manly culture' of the goldfields. The jokes, stories, cartoons and verse of these papers together with *Smith's Weekly* entered family folklore.

Harry Bennett senior loved music and acting. In Kalgoorlie, Bunbury and Geraldton, wherever he was posted with the railways, he conducted at charity concerts, and was stage manager and producer of amateur repertory plays. His son, Harry junior, my father, inherited a taste for popular music, drama, storytelling and jokes, at which he would usually laugh long and loud ahead of his audience. In his own wanderings through country Western Australia, in a variety of bank jobs, he also developed skills as a cartoonist and was sometimes rewarded with publication in local newspapers. His was a largely verbal and visual culture. Unlike my mother, he did not read much, but was an avid listener to radio favourites such as Roy Rene ('Mo'), George Wallace and programs such as 'Much Binding in the Marsh' and 'Take it from Here' (with Ron and Eth), which he preferred to the Goons. As with many of their generation, my parents' education did not extend beyond primary schooling. In the early postwar years, they saw in their sons the opportunity for an education beyond their own and the three sons all benefited from this.

Little is written about the influence of siblings. In my case, my two younger brothers and I shared almost everything. The space we inhabited was a louvre-windowed asbestos sleepout tacked onto the back of a 1930s brick and tile house in suburban Wembley. The house overlooked a string of corrugated iron factories which produced pipes and stoves, where a siren sounded and hammering began at seven in the morning. In our sleepout, we snored, farted, languished and laughed most nights of every week from boyhood to puberty and early manhood between 1948 and the early 1960s. We shared that sleepout over fourteen years of our lives for some forty thousand hours. What remains is an indelible thread of connection across oceans and continents between these boys. But what did they know of each other? We told each other a lot, in joking, bantering ways, about our sporting exploits and disasters, our adventures at school, and a strictly limited selection of our worst nightmares. We kept many of our fears and uncertainties at bay like this. We kept busy at sport, study, the local Anglican church and later, parties. I sensed a deep melancholy in my mother, with which I identified, but this was balanced by my father's capacity to turn doom and disaster into a well-turned anecdote or joke.

The inner spaces of my childhood home held few of the
seductive mysteries of furniture, objects or spaces evoked so finely
by David Malouf in his story/essay *12 Edmonstone Street*.[5] The
backyard and the street were where the Bennett boys' daytime
dramas were played out. High-marking duels punctuated the winter
months and fuelled dreams of the 'screamer' each of us would take
in front of a packed grandstand at Subiaco Oval—the leap, ride and
lift-off to a footballer's heaven. In summer months a broken-
slabbed concrete path served as pitch for Test matches with school
friends where phenomenal catches were matched by stupendous
appeals that rattled neighbours' windows. Our mother would appear
periodically and attempt to calm the players down with a glass of
'cordial' and warn against further broken windows and crushed rose
bushes. We were seldom still. I have read some desperate
contemporary experts on obesity recommending the return of
backyard Test cricket, but backyards have shrunk.

I grew up in a house with no car. The bike was our usual mode
of transport to school, beach, football, cricket or athletics training.
Punctures, twisted chains and faulty brakes provided regular work
for Mr Latham, several streets away, who also did a solid trade in
recycled bikes. Ours were all comprised of reconstituted bicycle
parts. The best of a series of summer jobs to earn pocket money
was that of a bike-riding postie. The challenge was to keep the
ankles clear of barking dogs and to charm the occasional mothers
(never unfortunately their daughters) who would emerge at the
sound of the postie's whistle with a glass of lemon or lime cordial.
The great advantage of the postie's job was that you could start early
in the morning and finish in early afternoon in time to ride to the
beach. Without hat or suncream, except for the compulsory zinc-
creamed nose, you could sunbake or surf, casting about through
squinting eyes for 'talent'. We were all then 'bodysurfers', in Robert
Drewe's suggestive use of the term[6]—superior in our way to those
who relied on the effete technology of the surfboard.

On a clear day, in the middle distance, you could see the holiday
island of Rottnest with its two lighthouses. Riding the small waves,
you would chiack fellow surfers about the big one 'out the back' that
would soon propel you in speedy triumph to the shore. Danger and
excitement were represented too by the threat of sharks. Lifesavers
with binoculars kept a lookout from towers at the end of rocky
groynes or watched from their large-hulled rowboats as they swept

along the coast, oars flashing. Overhead, light aircraft would double up on their role as advertisers to display their public interest by reporting the shapes of suspected sharks lurking out beyond the breakers. Imagination prefigures experience. I knew all about grey nurses, tigers and hammerheads but I never saw a live shark. Years later, after experiencing and rejecting the cobblestones and deckchairs of British beaches, I brought my English bride to my Western homeland to be greeted by the *Daily News* headline of a shark attack. The victim was a next-door neighbour of my uncle. The sharks were getting closer.

I am attracted to a West Coast myth of innocence but I know it to be an outcome of need rather than a reality. In his poem 'The Way We Live Now',[7] William Grono captures a communal voice of Western Australians in the late 1960s at the height of the Poseidon boom which made everyone a speculator:

> Yes, we like it here.
>
> Sometimes the shrewdest of us find the time,
> after the gardening, before television,
> sipping beer on enclosed verandahs,
> to speculate on the future.

Despite the racism, violence and corruption evident in Australia's West in the 1970s and '80s—the corruption typified in the rise and fall of Alan Bond—writer Robert Drewe found himself 'seduced again', as I have been, by a combination of natural forces, when he returned to the West:

> I walked the length of the beach up to the Royal Perth Yacht Club, with its massed wealth floating serenely in the shallows, and back to Mounts Bay Road. On my right the city skyline stood out sharply against the sky (especially the letters BOND, in dark blue, atop one building) and on my left the tower of the university, with its striking harmonious architecture and red ochre tiles, was visible through the gum trees. A magpie carolled in the distance, right on cue. It was quiet and still and as I strolled past where the old Crawley Bay tea-rooms once stood two butterflies flapped lightly into my face. They were copulating on the wing, fused gently together and just too languid to get out of my way.
>
> Talk about symbolism! I thought. 'I've got to get back here'. Seduced again.[8]

I return to my home state whenever I can, but feel its distance. Sometimes I think warily of John Hepworth's anecdote about his return visit to Perth:

> The fella standing at the bar next to me looked an understanding sort of sandgroper. 'This is the first time I've been home to Perth in twenty-four years', I said shyly. 'Well, what do you want', he snarled, 'a fuckin' medal or your fuckin' head read?'[9]

Recently, I took the new direct flight from Canberra to Perth. Gale force westerly winds tried to force me back east. The plane jolted, dipped and shuddered. It was worse than the heavily corrugated dirt road which I had driven across in the early 1960s before the Nullarbor highway was built. The Boeing 747 finally won its way west, but with mighty resistance from the elements.

These westerlies have blown throughout my life, sometimes with the palliative care of the Fremantle Doctor, sometimes ripping off roofs, cutting swathes through the suburbs. They are 'fresh' westerlies. My mother used to leave front and back doors open to let the fresh winds blow through our house. I need them, or the memory of them, to keep that distant, close place alive. But it can be revived sometimes too through the words of writers such as Randolph Stow or Tim Winton. Here is Winton recalling his boyhood suburban home and the power of wind:

> My house had no view; I was landlocked by picket fences and parked cars and homework, but in the afternoons I could smell the Fremantle Doctor coming in across the treetops, stirring the curtains and the copper-boiled washing. It came as sweet relief, cool and merciful, and at night as it moderated to a gentle breeze it brought the coast upon it in the scents of brine and seagrass. The pounding of the swell against the land's edge was so clear it seemed the sea was only a dune away. I didn't need a map to know where I was. In the atlas I lived in a dot, but with that breeze on my back I had a life and a place.[10]

Idealising the places that have formed us is a dangerous pursuit, no doubt. But to give these places a role in the continuing drama of a life is necessary for some of us. Despite some lean seasons, I remain faithful to the West Coast Eagles football team. When they travelled to Canberra one recent winter to play the quasi-home team, the Kangaroos, it was snowing in the Brindabellas. Predictably, in these conditions my team's muscles seized up in the cold and they lost.

West Australian journalist Matt Price generously observed that 'West Coast are like any vintage red; they operate much better at room temperature'.[11] In the Bradman stand at Manuka Oval, suitably scarfed and rugged up, I realised that I could handle the cold. A decade in the new place has implanted another set of expectations, sense impressions and memories that can live in generally peaceful co-existence with my western existence. When the wind blows in from the west, I just have to remember that it's a kind of easterly. But when I look to the mountains I know they are more than sand dunes.

Some Dynamics of Literary Placemaking

Emotional and familial relationships with places indicate patterns of belonging and ways in which value is accorded. A major challenge for writers is to convey a deep subjectivity in their relations to place which is neither glib nor programmatic but which expresses the whole of personality engagement felt by many people towards the places they have known. A leading exemplar of this kind of writing is the American author Barry Lopez.

When I met Barry Lopez in Perth in the early 1990s, we walked along a line of cork oaks by the Swan River at Matilda Bay in the grounds of the University of Western Australia. Almost at once, we both bemoaned the trends in universities that turned our students from appreciating such places; especially the current Anglo-American tendency in literary studies towards high theory and abstraction. We discussed the Canadian humanistic geographer, J Douglas Porteous, who had expressed a counter-belief in 'a world that cries out for involvement, empathy and deeper meaningfulness' rather than abstraction and distance.[1] For his part, Barry was concerned to construct a 'real geography' in his travel writings allied with an awareness of contemporary literary technique.

The voice adopted by Barry Lopez in his book *About This Life*[2] is neither intensely personal nor coolly dispassionate. Like Chekhov, the author has learnt that relatively cool writing, which evokes situations and their associated sense impressions can build an emotional atmosphere more effectively than writing which gushes.

The introduction to Lopez's 'journeys on the threshold of memory' gives autobiographical detail about the author's birth in New York, his move to Southern California when he was three, images of their first house, his parents' divorce and his father's departure, never to be seen again—but happily soon replaced with a man he was pleased to call his father. A key element in Barry Lopez's testimony is his attempt to fix memory through evocation of remembered places—the first house, boys' adventures in the fruit orchards of the San Fernando Valley, hiking in the Santa Monica Mountains, bike riding, hitching rides on slow freight trains and trips by car with his mother and brother on weekends into the Mojave Valley and summer camps at Big Bear Lake. These names, places and the physical adventures and sensations associated with them (of smell, sound, touch and hearing as well as sight) emerge from an apparently effortless recall of a childhood in which the physical world was experienced as if for the first time. Whether presented in visionary or relatively physical terms—in Blakeian or Wordsworthian terms—such recalls of childhood are often said to express a romantic temperament. But in the case of Lopez, and as I will later suggest, the Australian Roger McDonald, romanticism is tempered with knowledge and close observation.

Here is a characteristic paragraph by Lopez from an essay in *About This Life* called 'The American Geographies':

> The real American landscape is a face of almost incomprehensible depth and complexity. If one were to sit for a few days, for example, among the ponderosa pine forests and black lava fields of the Cascade Mountains in western Oregon, inhaling the pines' sweet balm on an evening breeze from some point on the barren rock, and then were to step off to the Olympic Peninsula in Washington, to those rain forests with sphagnum moss floors soft as fleece underfoot and Douglas firs too big around for five people to hug, and then head south to walk the ephemeral creeks and sun-blistered playas of the Mojave Desert in southern California, one would be reeling under the sensations. The contrast is not only one of plants and soils, a different array, say, of brilliantly colored beetles. The shock to the senses comes from a different shape to the silence, a difference in the very quality of light, in the weight of the air. And this relatively short journey down the West Coast would still leave the traveller with all that lay to the east to explore—the anomalous

sand hills of Nebraska, the heat and frog voices of Okefenokee Swamp, the fetch of Chesapeake Bay, the hardwood copses and black bears of the Ozark Mountains.[3]

This paragraph is characteristic of Lopez because of the way it extends the genre of advertising travelogue to convey an alert and lively sense of contemplative wonder as it brings forward specific instances of human interactions with landscape. Point-of-view, imagery and speech rhythms conduce to an effect of naturalness, though this is also an adroitly turned piece of rhetoric. Engagement of the senses, including what Porteous calls 'smellscape' and 'soundscape' is a key element. The tactile effect of 'sphagnum moss floors soft as fleece underfoot' is cunningly timed and sonically reinforced. The physical engagement of a human body with names and evoked places is figured dramatically throughout the paragraph and especially in the image of 'Douglas firs too big around for five people to hug'—an image that graphically relates human to non-human scales and is a faintly humorous exaggeration of the stereotypical tree-hugging greenie.

Lopez's writing at its best manages a certain balance of substance and authority without sounding mawkish or pompously didactic. This balanced tone is evident in his brief evocation of the Mojave Desert in the paragraph I have quoted. 'The shock of the senses', his persona summarises, 'comes from a different shape to the silence, a difference in the very quality of the light, in the weight of the air'. The rhythms and repetitions of phrasing in that sentence contribute to a drama of shifting moods, suggesting the value and significance of aesthetic and emotional intelligence as a counterweight to the tones of a more objective, scientific certitude. Underlying this paragraph, and much of Lopez's writing going back to *Arctic Dreams*[4] and *River Notes*,[5] is the journey motif. Lopez's geographic excursions are remarkably 'real' because the authorial guide is empathetic, knowledgeable, perceptive and always open to wonder. His persona suggests that nature is always both 'out there' and 'in here'.

Much of the 'edge' in contemporary Australian writing about the physical environment derives from its opposition to the notion and reality of cities. Indeed, the city/bush antinomy is one of the most persistent rhetorical oppositions in Australian writing, with different degrees of authority being given to each at different periods of our

post-occupation history. In our early twenty-first century obsession
with globalisation and the role of cities in responding to its
challenges, the bush is often represented at the margins of debate or
conversation. Think of the glamour of Sydney's Kings Cross versus
almost any country town, agricultural region or unsettled area in
Australia's interior. Yet a fine anthology of literary writings about
Kings Cross, *In the Gutter ... Looking at the Stars*,[6] also demonstrates
the presence of the inescapable otherworld of nature beyond the
sinful, Babylonian metropolis. The 'natural' life beyond an artificially
enclosed urban precinct might be temporarily suppressed but
emerges in dreams and fantasies of a larger 'wild world' against
which the restrictive urban one can be set. Kenneth Mackenzie's
protagonist in *The Refuge*, for instance, enters the Cross as into a
dreamworld where, 'like the beetle or the butterfly from its chysalis,
he was ready to emerge, full of plans for conquest',[7] but the harbour
and the ocean beyond provide the larger rhythms and reminders of
mortality. The snakes with which Roberta Sykes does her rhythmic
dancing in the Cross are both a security against rapists and a
reminder of a wider natural world.[8] Merlinda Bobis's Filipina
fruitstall operator has continual reminders of her other world in the
papayas which are never as good as those 'back home'.[9] Often,
another larger, more natural world is seen to lie behind and beyond
the distorted intensities and temporary excitement of sin city.

Indigenous Australian tale tellers and their interpreters have
frequently invoked a Dreamtime that seems in accord with a natural
life beyond the cities. However, contemporary Aboriginal writers
can seldom escape the influence of cities on that slower, more
expansive view of a natural world. Herb Wharton's stories, deriving
from his experience as a drover in the cattle camps of the Northern
Territory and Queensland, exemplify this tension and source of
dramatic conflict. He faces the issue squarely in a humorous and
satiric story called 'Dreamtime Future: Bungo the Money God' in
his collection *Where Ya' Been, Mate?*[10] Wharton presents a city,
rather like Brisbane, as the source of a new Dreamtime myth, where
Bungo the Money God is worshipped above all other gods. His
worshippers build a drab stone building over 'His resting place'
which they call the Treasury Building. When the Aboriginal visitors
to the city return to their home in the outback they start a
Corroboree of the Money God Bungo—and charge an admission
fee of $2. Wharton humorously depicts a polarity of values,

outlooks and notions of civilisation between Indigenous Australian bushdwellers and materialistic city slickers which persists through our culture and affects ways of perceiving country and city. This rhetoric of opposition shows an apparently inevitable domination of city over country, with humour as a safety valve.

Another kind of sensibility concerned with these issues in contemporary Australian writing is that of the immigrant from an Asian country. Indonesian Australian journalist and fiction writer, Dewi Anggraeni's novella 'Uncertain Step' from her volume *Stories of Indian Pacific*[11] registers the shock often felt by immigrants or visitors from the crowded cities of Asia when confronted with the open spaces of unsettled Australia. In this story, Aryani, a young woman in her early thirties from Bandung flies to Kalgoorlie to meet Steve, a divorced Australian teacher who had proposed marriage to her in Indonesia. They meet in Kalgoorlie and drive east across the Nullarbor Plain. Her journey across the treeless landscape is towards a possible marriage with this man with whom she has not yet slept. Her thoughts are registered:

> There is no adventure in this road. There aren't any turns to make you anticipate what'll come into view, neither are there any hills to obscure what is ahead. Yet, I don't know what'll happen in my life next. Aryani begins to seek security in the monotony of the drive.[12]

Aryani, who has read widely in Australian as well as other literatures, asks Steve if this is Henry Lawson's country but he laughs good humouredly and says no, they are close to the south coast whereas Lawson's country was western New South Wales. Aryani has nevertheless responded intuitively to the desolate spirit of Lawson's literary landscapes. She feels gloomy: 'This is how my life's going to be. At first relative monotony with occasional sparks, then emptiness'.[13] Aryani dreams of returning home to her family and friends in Bandung as a fallen woman, a divorcee. To her highly educated, urban sensibility, she and Steve seem to enter 'a surrealist painting. Dead trees and yellowy dry grass, symbolic of the skeleton of her elusive happiness.' She is jolted by the sight of eagles and crows flying above the skeletons of animals and feels vulnerable and worthless. The long drive is not without its adventures though. Aryani and Steve sleep together for the first time in a motel at

Madura. And later, Aryani's interior landscape brightens up when they approach the hills outside Adelaide, with their reminders of Bandung. Here, she feels, may be a livable environment.

I have cited Anggraeni's novella at some length here because it reinforces a view held by many immigrants, including those from Asian countries, that non-urban Australia is unremittingly harsh and desolate. Moreover, Immigration Department data show that between 1996 and 2001, 61 percent of immigrants given permanent residence chose to live in Sydney and Melbourne, with Perth as the next most popular city with 12 per cent. Images of regional and rural Australia are often negative in these people's minds, but this is a pattern that may change as refugees and other immigrants live and work successfully in country areas. Afghan asylum seekers with meatworkers' jobs in rural New South Wales are a recent example of successful integration. Burmese-Scottish Australian Colin McPhedran's haunting memoir *White Butterflies*,[14] which recounts his trek through the mountainous refugee trails from Burma to India, escaping from the Japanese in 1942 while his mother, sister and brother die, ends with a happy experience. After arriving in Sydney, Colin as a young man catches a train and finds himself alighting in the Southern Highlands at Bowral. The topography and vegetation remind him of the hill station in Burma from which he and his family had left so hurriedly to set out on their tragic trek. This involuntary act of remembering turns to a sense of belonging. Colin stays, and Bowral and the Southern Highlands become his home. Places transposed in memory inform the most significant choice in a young man's life.

Deep subjectivity in the representation of place occurs in a variety of ways. Often, as in Colin McPhedran's intuitive response to Bowral, powerful images from childhood recur and inform adult perceptions and choices. One of the best documented reflections of childhood as the seedbed of later responses to landscape occurs in Dorothy Hewett's memoir *Wild Card*, as suggested in Essay 6 of this book. Like Judith Wright, Hewett was profoundly influenced in her attitudes to the land by her father.

The trajectory of Hewett's narrative is similar to many of those in Peter Read's *Returning to Nothing*,[15] in which formerly loved places which have disappeared through flooding, cyclones or human intervention are grieved over by those who return to these sites, either physically or in memory.

The interweaving of narrative, image and idea to reveal a depth of response to the natural environment is a difficult task for the literary artist. But an Australian book which has achieved this combination remarkably successfully is novelist Roger McDonald's *The Tree in Changing Light*.[16] This work is not a novel, though it employs novelistic techniques: it is a mixed-mode book of stories, essays, descriptive passages, memoir and fragments of philosophy which together reveal the deep subjectivity of its author's interactions with the physical environment. Like some of Barry Lopez's excursions into 'real geography', McDonald's text also shows a practical respect for solid objects in the physical world. While the book in some respects resembles the genre of Pascal's *Pensees*, and it dramatises a similar search for meaning, identity and even faith, it is more solidly grounded in a world of work and practical activity.

The Tree in Changing Light presents its author in a particular stage of the life-cycle. Having ceased temporarily from travel he puts down roots—the metaphor is both a deliberate commonplace and a literal expression of real-world activity. The book's dramatic centrepiece is McDonald's planting of trees on a property at Braidwood, 80 kilometres east of Canberra in the Monaro region of New South Wales. While the farm near Braidwood is the central locale, a kaleidoscope of observations and memories from earlier phases in the writer's life, or encounters with other people, give a layered context to the vividly rendered Braidwood scenes.

As with some other writers, memories of childhood fuel adult searches for meaning, significance and value. In McDonald's childhood, as the son of a Methodist minister, he lived in the 1940s and 1950s in a number of small towns of western New South Wales including Young, Temora and Bourke. The imagining of trees, so scarce in those areas, transmutes into a way of thinking about family history, and vice versa:

> Family history as it expresses itself in an individual can feel like something coming from nowhere, because the roots are buried. It is only now, in midlife, that I feel this matter of trees as part of a line of continuation. My mind sinks back; it feels like drawing water up through fine capillary veins and leaves uncurl, and then those leaves hanging edge-on to the hard Australian sunlight. I like to think of the earth around the roots being kept damp by a sprinkler disgorging cold, silver water.[17]

The tree serves here as a metaphor for autobiography or life-writing, in which one draws sustenance from the ground of one's being; but it avoids being a merely self-centred reflection for it holds continual reminders of its physical activity and need for material sustenance.

As he replays the spools of childhood, McDonald pictures a scene from the playground of his school at Bourke in far western New South Wales:

> I remember trees away in the smashed-glass glare of wheatfields: yellow box, white cypress, kurrajong. Lone sentinels shimmering in heat haze. And playground eucalypts in asphalt, their leaves pungent after rain. A tree at Bourke, it must have been a red gum, growing tall in the dirt-surfaced playground there; Aboriginal kids eating grubs from under the bark and boasting about it; our teacher taking us out to sit around under its thin shade and asking me to read out a story I had written—a 'composition'. I remember how everyone listened.[18]

Trees, nature, the Aboriginal presence and its lessons are foregrounded here in a passage that offers a more hopeful picture of Bourke and beyond than Lawson's famous mythologising of a desolate, treeless environment where everything seemed hopeless, even when it rained:

> Sky like a wet, grey blanket; plains like dead seas, save for the tufts of coarse grass sticking up out of the water; scrub indescribably dismal—everything damp, dark and indescribably dreary.[19]

Manning Clark remarked perceptively of Lawson's writing about place: 'he was a man for atmosphere, a man to notice what a country did to a man. He never attempted a detailed description, never noticed that tiny point which illustrated a whole scene'.[20]

Writing out of a more rooted sense of his childhood in this country, around which associations of a mythical outback lingered, McDonald offered a different dynamic of placemaking. His treatment of place is characterised by a combination of practicality, local knowledge and aesthetic appreciation. The relationship of work to an appreciation of landscape is manifest in McDonald's case. He had been interested in forestry from the age of seventeen, when he had declared a wish to study and work in that field but had been dissuaded because his aptitudes were in the humanities rather than science. Instead, he became a teacher, broadcaster, book editor and writer. But the old dream persisted and became operable when he and his wife, the poet Rhyll McMaster, took up a three hundred and twenty acre property called Spring Farm near Braidwood in the early 1980s, where they spent eleven years and brought up three daughters.

One of the threads through McDonald's book is the search for vocation. Vocation implies more than seeking a job or making a living—it involves a search for significant and meaningful activity, some occupation which, according to a residual but fading Christian belief, might give one a sense of having been 'called' to do it. In McDonald's case, this involves a recognition, and a seeking-out, in the past and present, of mentors who have led him to feel the romance and to know something of the science of trees. McDonald's itinerant clergyman father is recognised as the first of these mentors in the tree-recognition games he encouraged his son to play: 'leopard tree, bloodwood, wilga, quandong' and then 'peeling the sour red quandong flesh, insubstantial as a thumb-scraping, and drying the seeds that were ridged like a model of the human brain'.[21]

McDonald's chief mentor is a professional forester, Wilf Crane, who worked for CSIRO in Canberra and who traced boron deficiency as a common problem. The author explains:

> [Crane] made tree guards and grow-tubes and was open to every conceivable way of giving a tree a good start in life. He was a mover in Greening Australia. The fullest expression of himself was to be out planting in the rain. When people talked about 'making things hard for a tree', depriving them of nutrition to 'toughen them up,' he asked if they would do it to a child.[22]

In a section called 'Life of a Tree Planter', McDonald celebrates and elegises Wilf Crane's life, which ended suddenly when his Volksplane crashed at Bungendore near Canberra in 1992. It is one of the most finely woven and moving parts of McDonald's book—more integral to the whole than his more obviously literary celebration of his female mentor figure, Judith Wright.

Knowledge of the landscapes, soil and vegetation of a region through working with them is crucial to McDonald's writing in *The Tree in Changing Light*. Similarly, Wallace Stegner's knowledge of Rocky Mountains geography and climate informs his lyrical evocations of the American West.[23] McDonald's knowledge of tree

planting is combined with an understanding of the ideologies of
colonial and post-colonial plantings and their effects. 'Introduced
trees', he notes, 'had been planted on Spring Farm for well over a
hundred years', including 'Lombardy poplars, along with willows,
black locusts or robinia, elms, hawthorns, Monterey cypresses,
arbutus or Irish strawberry, Canary Island pine, and tree of heaven
in a pungent, impenetrable stand'.[24] At a time of national awareness
in Australia in the early 1980s, McDonald did not slavishly follow
nativist fashions. The first tree he plants on the farm, at the age of
forty, is a linden or European lime. But he develops an historical
knowledge of early European settlement of the region in the 1820s,
and dreams of how the present, frost-exposed landscape might be
restored to something like its pre-colonial state:

> I had a fantasy, never fulfilled, of getting some of the paddocks
> back to the way the landscape would have once looked. A reedy
> creek, wildfowl, banksias despite the fierce cold, and glittering black
> sallees in the frost hollows—a tree with an almost mystical
> attachment to the coldest places, with olive and green tones in the
> bark, almost like streamed shellacked paint. Here and there in the
> paddocks, at a rate of a few to the acre, there would have been huge
> old ribbon gums—or water gums to use the common name for
> them. I saw them swarming with native beehives.[25]

One of the effective techniques in *The Tree in Changing Light* is an
impressionistic treatment of visionary or dream-like moments—a
treatment that recalls Wordsworth's 'spots of time'. Epiphanic
fragments hint at the elusive mystery of trees and their impact on
humans. Some are quotations from other writers. But McDonald is
expressive in his own voice too as he recalls a moment at night on
the inland plains:

> Coolabah trees went walking on a night of low moon on a
> floodplain of the Darling River. Out beyond the shearers' quarters
> they gathered like a population coming in, getting home through
> the river mist.[26]

Or the moment of visionary transfiguration, with its reminder of
human mortality, with which the books ends:

> Light, upon which the tree depended, and which the tree's function
> was botanically described as being solely to catch, stood blazing
> behind the tree and the tree disappeared.[27]

I find Roger McDonald's *The Tree in Changing Light* an important book at a personal level because it helps to shape my relationship to my adoptive Monaro region, where I have lived for over a decade. In the context of literary history, this book suggests ways for other writers to explore a variety of modes of environmental writing that are not merely external description or decoration. Like some of the works described earlier, it shows the value of expressing a deep subjectivity in human responses to the environments we inhabit.

Reconciling the Accounts: Jack Davis, Judith Wright, A D Hope

As new directions are sought for Australian Studies into the twenty-first century, we must assert that the past matters. The literary past matters especially, since much of the virtual reality that literary texts create can be imagined as a continuous present and taken with us into different contexts and domains. But the understanding of these images, episodes and ideas will be enhanced by a recognition of their embeddedness in the times and places of their creators' lives and circumstances. Hence the value of literary history and biography. With these considerations in mind, I propose to revisit three Australian writers who died in the first year of the twenty-first century but who lived through much of the twentieth, with a view to considering what legacy they offer—some of their images and ideas, the traditions they represent and the challenges with which they present us. The authors are Jack Davis, Judith Wright and A D Hope. The three writers represent distinct intellectual, artistic and socio-political traditions which at certain points seem to clash and conflict. Each has a distinctive literary voice and presence. All three have made major contributions to Australian literary culture from different parts of the country.

At first sight, the writings and statements of Hope, Wright and Davis may seem to place them at loggerheads. No one has probed the sources of western civilisation (and its discontents) more quizzically than the first of these authors, A D Hope. Thoroughly imbued with classical notions of British and European cultural standards, and supported by his role as Professor of English at the Australian National University, Hope clashed with the environmental and Aboriginal-inspired Jindyworobaks and had the temerity to ridicule Patrick White's writing style as sub-literate (while also acknowledging him as a genius). By contrast, Judith Wright's romanticism, her ultra-green environmental values and her pro-Aboriginal stance took her on a collision course with Hope's value system; the divergence of paths taken seemed to increase with Wright's conscious decision to take an activist's role in public campaigns for Indigenous people and environmental issues, in contradistinction to Hope's preference for a more contemplative, less interventionist approach for the writer. By contrast with Wright's rural, aristocratic upbringing in New England and the 'double tree' of her Australian and British inheritance, and Hope's Eurocentricism, the Aboriginal Jack Davis remained firmly planted in Australia, though conferences and tours of his plays occasionally took him overseas in his later years. His poetry and plays are firmly located in the Western Australia of his upbringing, among Indigenous and mixed communities. His writings often take up the cause of Aboriginal Australians against exclusivist notions of European Australian 'civilisation', as they address the tragic impact of the dominant immigrant culture over that of Indigenous Australians.

The literary work of Hope, Wright and Davis has been brought to the notice of Australians chiefly through the loosely organised but influential institution of Australian literature. A readership of mainly school and university students has often been encouraged to read a tailored selection of texts based on a syllabus (often presented in thematic form) and their teachers' knowledge and understanding. It should be said at the outset that each of the three writers has been accepted at the highest levels of the Humanities establishment in Australia: all three were invited Honorary Fellows of the Australian Academy of the Humanities. However, reference to the more established figures of Hope and Wright occurs more frequently in literary histories of Australia. It is also noteworthy that the Writers Walk at Circular Quay in Sydney contains plaques for Hope and Wright but not for Davis.

With some of these factors in mind, I will reverse the usual order of priority and consider first Jack Davis's contribution to Australian literature and society. Before that, I should confess that I knew each of these writers a little—Jack through the Black Swan Theatre Company in Perth, Judith through dancing with her at an Australian literature conference in Armidale and Alec through university lectures in Perth, and driving dangerously with him after a long red-wine lunch in Canberra. I suspect that these occasions were more momentous for me than for the three writers, though Judith Wright, in her Spanish shawl, may have remembered vividly missing out on the Frank Moorhouse medal for ballroom dancing because of her less poetic partner.

In the 1980s and early '90s, Jack Davis was a striking figure with a shock of white hair and blue eyes. Born in Perth in 1917, he was the fourth of eleven children to Aboriginal parents who originally came from the North-West of Australia. On his mother's side, there was a descent from the nineteenth-century Afghan community which ran camel transport in the Western desert. Jack said that his grandfather on his father's side was a Sikh whose family name was Bung Singh, but his father 'Australianised' himself by adopting the name of a white squatter (Davis) and was simply known as Bill.[1] Both of Jack Davis's parents were taken from their tribal families and brought up by white families until they were fourteen or fifteen. His mother remembered being taken from her mother when she was seven and given by the police to a pioneer white family in Broome, where she worked as a servant.

When Jack Davis was less than a year old, he travelled to the South-West of Western Australia with his family, where his father was appointed foreman of a timber mill at Yarloop. Jack went to school at Yarloop. This 'bush childhood', and the period after he left school from age fifteen to seventeen were happy times, as Keith Chesson's biography demonstrates, and as Davis reveals in poems such as 'The Children' and 'Retrospect' in *The First-born and Other Poems* (1970).[2] The view is confirmed in his interview with Richard Beilby.[3]

After primary school and before his son Jack started working for a living, Bill Davis arranged with the Chief Protector of Aborigines, A O Neville, for the boy to go to the Moore River Native Settlement to learn trade and other skills. Davis recreated scenes from that period in his plays *Kullark* (Home)[4] and *No Sugar*.[5] He also set a trend by characterising Neville as an authoritarian representative of white attitudes and values of his time. The characterisation of Neville (and his administrator Neal) has been made possible partly because of the written documents Neville left which—like those of George Augustus Robinson a century earlier in Tasmania—enabled novelists such as Robert Drewe in *The Savage Crows* (1976) and Mudrooroo in *Doctor Wooreddy's Prescription for Enduring the Ending of the World* (1983) to similarly characterise Robinson as a representative figure of his times—an ironic figure both threatening and ridiculous in hindsight. Social historians and the novelist, Kim Scott, in his Miles Franklin Award-winning novel *Benang* (1999) have given their own interpretations of Neville and his times. In an ABC interview, Scott described Neville as an emblematic figure of the 1920s and '30s.[6] Neville believed in the social Darwinist notion of survival of the fittest, that 'full blood' Aborigines would die out and that he could best 'protect' the 'half-castes' and other part-Aborigines by assisting that process. Thus Aboriginal women were sent out from the missions into 'service' and would often become pregnant to white men, contributing to the 'breeding out' of the Aboriginal race. This is the kind of assimilationism against which Judith Wright and others protested. Kim Scott, with his traces of Nyungah ancestry, wrote, in Jack Davis's wake, *Benang*, his novel of dispossession and hopelessness, as a partial response to these historical events and as a way of articulating his sense of self. Sally Morgan's autobiographical *My Place* (1987) also emerges from these historical conditions. In the hands of such writers, literature becomes a means of self-discovery, truth-telling and protest against prevailing attitudes and values of the dominant culture. Davis and his successors knew they were writing principally for the dominant white culture and it was their values which were being challenged and changed by such writing.

In a typically fair-minded attempt to balance the accounts, Jack Davis recorded the positive as well as the negative aspects of the Moore River Native Settlement and the mission stations in various parts of Australia. He readily conceded that the missions were where many Aboriginal children learnt literacy skills: 'At least on these missions and settlements', Davis wrote, 'some of our people learned to read and write in English. Outside these institutions it was considered improper for Aboriginal children to attend school. They thrust pencils and paper before us to write, and write we did'.[7] Reading and writing became a solace and a strength for Davis, as it did for Indigenous short story writer Herb Wharton on the other side of the continent in Queensland. Another blessing of the Moore

River interlude for Davis was the opportunity to meet others of Aboriginal descent from whom his upbringing had largely excluded him. A 'full-blood' Aborigine from the North-West, Warru, fascinated him. Davis learnt a new vocabulary of Bibbulmun words and phrases from Warru, went hunting in the bush with him, listened to his songs and wrote them down.[8] The imaginative adolescent became emotionally engaged with Indigenous people to whom he began to feel connected. Many years later, Davis met Warru in the city, Perth. The older man was alcoholic, blind, picking up cigarette butts in the street. A little later, Warru was found dead in Wellington Square. The figure of this man, who came from the same area in the North-West as Davis's father, has an emblematic presence in Davis's plays and verse.

Jack Davis became a father-figure of the revival of Black Australian writing from the 1970s, as Kath Walker, or Oodgeroo, became a mother-figure. (Davis perhaps shares this role with Kevin Gilbert, a more confrontational, polemical writer than Davis. The gentle figure of David Unaipon, whose face appears on the Australian $50 note, is perhaps the grandfather figure). One of the noticeable characteristics of Davis's plays, prose and verse, which he shares with other writers of Indigenous extraction is its powerful sense of place. I have mentioned Davis's bush childhood in the hardwood forests of the South-West, but the vast spaces of the North also captured his imagination when he worked in the Gascoyne in the 1940s. He had no trouble dealing with the isolation. Working on an out-camp on a cattle station for two years, Davis says he saw the Boss 'about eight or nine times'. His sense of humour is evident in his remark that, having no calendar he missed Christmas Day, arriving back at the station on 26 December, when 'most of the fun was over'. 'But that was nothing', he adds, 'It was the country I liked':

> This place where I was, was break-away country, the valley floor was down about three to four hundred feet; and the hills, which were sheer, were all around me. It was really beautiful country, stark, the green of Spinifex; and when it did rain, which was seldom, the grass would green up very quickly, flowers would come out, live perhaps three or four days and then die. I used to feel that that particular piece of country was my own and there was many and many a piece of verse which I wrote and which I unfortunately lost or destroyed myself.[9]

But he was not in total isolation in this landscape, for, as he puts it, 'sometimes the tribes came through'. On one occasion, some 450 Aboriginal men, women and children camped nearby on their annual 'pingai', or walkabout, and Jack shot a scrub bull for them. He remembers the scene idyllically:

> ... the pool down the bottom of the hill with the gum-trees around it, their moving around in the moonlight, the windmill behind them where they could get water if they wanted it, although they had the creek, small fires dotted over the hill itself—a small hillside where they camped—you could hear them talking their own language and now and then there'd be a burst of laughter.[10]

Davis could think of such country as 'Eden' and felt the Aborigines' continuous presence there: 'We had been here at the creation and through countless cycles of the seasons, and had experienced the land's harshness as well as its bounty since time immemorial'.[11]

Davis felt a sense of camaraderie with the other black stockmen with whom he worked in the North. His poem 'Aboriginal Stockmen' in *The First-Born*[12] expresses a sense of mateship with these tough but light-hearted men who kept control of the cattle and kept their dreams to themselves. But many poems deal with the difficult lives of Indigenous people and the injustice and suffering wrought upon them by white Australians. The poem 'Family', for instance, was evoked by 'the sentencing of two Aborigines to three months gaol for leaving a country reserve without permission'[13] at a time when curfews were imposed. This poem leads forward to the *John Pat and Other Poems* volume (1988),[14] with its poems of protest against wrongly imprisoned Aborigines and their brutal treatment. The title poem, with its haunting refrain about the death of a young Aboriginal man in the Roebourne police cells in 1983, was set to music by Archie Roach. The first stanza gives a good introduction to the poem's laconic power:

> Write of life
> the pious said
> forget the past
> the past is dead.
> But all I see
> in front of me

is a concrete floor
a cell door
and John Pat.[15]

One of the least remarked aspects of Jack Davis's outlook is his Christianity. During the second world war, Davis returned to the South-West and joined the Brookton Aboriginal Church, taught in the Sunday School there and considered entering the ministry.[16] He continued this interest with the Aboriginal Church in Perth which was then affiliated with the Aboriginal Advancement Council. He became manager of its community centre and President of the AAC. The expression of a Christian outlook in Davis's writing is typically practical and ethical and without any sentimental religiosity. This applies, too, to his concern for environmental issues, which derived from his experience of subsistence living in the bush during the depression years, when white and black people alike struggled for a living. Jack Davis claimed that he found a proper equilibrium in race relations not during a period of economic prosperity in Australia but during the depression of the 1930s—the happiest time in his life. According to Davis's account, Aboriginal people then had a temporary advantage in that they could hunt and eat well in the bush while men in the cities were out of work:

> They were really wonderful times when I look back because we had so much freedom, didn't have to worry about social service or anything like that because we did actually keep ourselves. All we had to have was flour, tea and sugar, a few spuds and onions.[17]

Jack Davis's temperament and outlook led him towards building bridges of understanding between black and white Australians. Betty Meehan and Rhys Jones have summed up the importance for Davis of moves towards reconciliation and his active involvement in them:

> Despite the trials of his life, Davis held no bitterness and was strongly supportive of non-Aboriginal peoples' involvement in the political and artistic issues of reconciliation. With failing health due to diabetes and heart problems, he still remained an activist, protesting against the clear felling of old forests in the south-west and against Western Australia's laws of mandatory sentencing.[18]

Davis's legacy to Australian Studies in the twenty-first century, then, is a close-to-the-earth outlook, a concern for the underdog and reminders in his writing of a humorous, poetic and at times theatrical personality. His work in education and protest movements from the 1970s, especially, showed faith in the advancement of both Aboriginal and white Australians towards an ideal of active communication across barriers of class and race.

Judith Wright's early life as the daughter of a New England squatter was a radically different rural beginning from Jack Davis's struggling, working-class upbringing in Western Australia. The dynamics of Wright's later sense of guilt and deprivation in being prevented as a child from playing or conversing with Aboriginal children is one of the interesting aspects of her life. (Here, as elsewhere, Veronica Brady's sympathetic and comprehensive biography of Judith Wright is a reliable guide.[19]) Wright's feeling for landscape, which was enhanced during her later friendship with Kath Walker (or, as she became known from 1988, Oodgeroo Noonuccal) was evident in Wright's first book of poems *The Moving Image* (1946) in her now famous lines from 'South of My Days':

> South of my days' circle, part of my blood's country,
> rises that tableland, high delicate outline
> of bony slopes wincing under the winter,
> low trees blue-leaved and olive, outcropping granite—[20]

Wright's poetry, by which her reputation was made, sets the relative stability of landscape against human crises and dramas, wars and threats of nuclear destruction. But damage to the environment and discrimination against Aborigines, the original owners, increased Wright's sense of the fragility of all human existence. There are both personal and public dimensions to Wright's work. On the one hand, childbirth, lovemaking, the relationship between a daughter and her mother, or philosophical reflections, offer lyrical and epiphanic moments behind which lie the darkness and finality of death, which her own mother's death when Judith was twelve, and the war years, must have intensified. Her sense of liberation in land and seascapes may be directly related to the dark, enclosed rooms of her mother's slow dying in Judith's childhood years.

At significant moments in her writing career, Wright put poetry aside to concentrate on polemical treatises on major public issues. While she valued poetry, she did not fetishise it and she had little hesitation in telling people if she thought they were reading her work wrongly. Her well-known criticism of what she considered to be misreadings by teachers and others of her poem 'Bullocky'—that they were mistakenly interpreting it as a celebration of the myth of the heroic pioneer rather than as a poem about a madman—and her withdrawal of the poem from anthologies indicate her serious intention that influential poems should carry the 'right' message, and that she should not be perceived as indulging in white ancestor worship.

I have argued elsewhere that Judith Wright is a moralist with an overarching ecological vision that informs her work.[21] While she fought for local issues she saw that the underlying threat was economic rationalism: in her view, merely economic rather than humanistic values would destroy the future of the universe. As an active foundation member and leading figure in the Australian Conservation Foundation she took part in many campaigns, but pre-eminently to save Fraser Island and the Barrier Reef.

The Coral Battleground is a knowledgeable and eloquent reminder of Wright's commitment to the Australian environment:

> Not a town but was putting undiluted and untreated sewage into creeks and rivers. Oil slicks from ships' tanks were often reported. The reef was suffering, the illnesses of civilization were already changing it. What chance had we of keeping it as it had been, or even as it is now.[22]

Wright did not belong to political parties but she had no hesitation in telling governments of all persuasions that they must improve their act in regard to the environment. She combined passion with solid argument, images with ideas. Wright was 'green' before the term had any currency, and she helped to form the Wildlife Preservation Society of Queensland in the early 1960s. By the early 1970s, when Jack Mundey's New South Wales Builders' Labourers' Federation's 'green bans' were used to halt destruction of certain buildings and landscapes and popularised the term 'green' in its modern political sense around the world, Wright had long been a battler in the field.[23] Her legacy is a wide-ranging vision that conveys thought and feeling with rhetorical flair and precision. Her outlook is summarised in *The Coral Battleground*: 'It was easy to see that the shibboleths of growth and progress needed a balancing force, if the future was going to be lived in a world fit for humans'.[24]

Judith Wright's commitment to the causes of Indigenous Australians recurs throughout her writings but nowhere more forcefully than in expressions of her deep friendship with her 'spirit sister', Kath Walker, or Oodgeroo. In 'Two Dreamtimes', Wright addresses her directly:

> Kathy my sister with the torn heart,
> I don't know how to thank you
> for your dreamtime stories of joy and grief
> written on paperbark.[25]

In a sense, Kath Walker represents a return of the repressed for Judith, the little girl who was not allowed to play with 'the dark children' who camped on her parents' sheep and cattle property. Veronica Brady refers to Walker (later Oodgeroo) as 'a kind of 'touchstone' to whom [Wright] mentally referred ideas and projects and from whom she drew many of these ideas'.[26] Oodgeroo's death in 1993 (not long after Kevin Gilbert died) was an enormous loss: Wright could never return to the 'easy Eden dreamtime' of their conversations.

But she had another soulmate in her public struggles for proper justice for Aboriginal people. This was H C (Nugget) Coombs—a man who has been called, with some accuracy, the last of Australia's great public servants. The corporatisation of Australia's public service, with its tendency to narrow the scope of accountability to what a financial accountant could account for, has unfortunately given the term 'public service' a somewhat hollow ring beside the public achievements of Nugget Coombs, whose view of economics was that it concerned not just 'getting and spending' but managing and caring for the earth's resources, physical and human, for the good of all.[27] Wright and Coombs became close friends and fought alongside each other, with their combined literary and bureaucratic skills, for issues ranging from opposition to the Ranger Uranium mine, to protection of the Barrier Reef and support of indigenous rights. Through all the arguments and debates about treaties, Aboriginal sovereignty and land rights in the 1980s and '90s, Wright supported and was supported by Coombs, but she also read and corresponded with Aboriginal authors such as Jack Davis and Kevin Gilbert. Publicly and privately, she was on their side. When her conservationist and Aboriginal interests seemed to conflict she made it clear that she stood for the best that could be achieved for Aboriginal Australians. As Tim Bonyhady has pointed out, Wright resigned from the Wildlife Preservation Society in 1991 when it failed to support Aboriginal rights.[28]

Wright's legacy to twenty-first century Australian Studies is likely to be felt in several main areas. The first is as a writer. Whatever directions the institution of Australian literature takes, Wright's poetry from *The Moving Image* (1946) to *Phantom Dwelling* (1985) will contribute to a sense of the power of words to shape personal, relational and public lives. Second, her personal witnessing and public support for the conservation of the Australian environment will continue to resound. Third, her example highlights the crucial importance of listening and responding to Aboriginal voices and concerns. There is a fourth area, too, in gender studies. As Veronica Brady has noted, Wright was 'never a doctrinaire feminist',[29] but she joined the Sisters publishing group, was supportive of women writers, and poems such as 'Eve Scolds' and 'Eve Sings' reveal her concern for women who are exploited or oppressed.

The role of A D Hope in this tryptic for new-century Australianists is in some ways the most problematic and interesting. Half a century ago, Hope's role would have been the easiest part to describe and justify, for Hope may seem to represent what was once an almost automatic Anglo-Australian recourse to the touchstone of British and European civilisation. In her review of Hope's *Collected Poems* in 1972, Leonie Kramer observed that Hope was one of the least Australian of Australian poets and in her obituary for Hope twenty-eight years later[30] she reminds us that in 'A Letter from Rome'[31]—a poem addressed to her—Hope differentiated himself from other Australian poets' alleged preference for 'the packhorse and the sliprail and the spur'. Moreover, in his best-known poem, 'Australia' (1939), Hope reveals 'a persistent scepticism about the value of his country's literary achievements' when he refers to Australia as 'A nation without songs, architecture, history'. Yet as David Brooks observed in his edited collection of essays on Hope, *The Double Looking Glass*, Hope did indeed produce in his sixties and seventies 'a distinctively Australian body of work that can be seen, under subsequent critical lights, to draw out retrospectively the implicit Australianness of the work that preceded it'.[32] A late developer, Hope is a more surprising and more various person and writer than portraits of him sometimes suggest.

Hope did not return reflectively in his poetry to Cooma, the small highland town of his birth until the late 1970s with his poem 'Beyond Khancoban', in which he wrote:

> ... I think of the spot
> To which I return, from which long ago I was made,
> Cooma, and wonder whether it made me or not.

The poem concludes with the resonant stanza:

> Man is made by all that has made the history of man,
> But here the Monaro claims me; I recognise
> Beyond Khancoban the place where a mind began
> Able to offer itself to the galaxies.[33]

The regional claim for Cooma and the Monaro here is interesting, followed by its expansion into a universal perspective. But Hope's boyhood was spent also in Tasmania, from the age of four to fourteen, before his family moved to Sydney. Perhaps the deepest imprint on him was made by island Tasmania. Kevin Hart has shown convincingly that Hope 'returns again and again to images of islands, places offering poets an ideal community as well as a refuge from increasing incursion of popular and mass cultures'.[34] There are interesting similarities and differences between Hope and Edwin Thumboo, the Singapore poet-professor, in their uses of island imagery.[35] If a Eurocentric outlook sometimes blinded Hope to local pleasures, this is greatly compensated by later poems of pleasurable humour and feeling, such as 'Hay Fever' and 'Country Places'. The coda to the latter poem laments in a somewhat Judith Wright manner (but less earnestly) the destruction of trees and water courses in the name of economic development:

> Alas! my beautiful, my prosperous, my careless country,
> She destroys herself: the Lord will come too late!
> ...
> Even Sweet Water Creek at Mullengandra,
> If I went there now, would it live up to its name?[36]

None of Hope's later work however denies his resonant earlier discovery, in his early fifties, of an alliance with Italy, and especially Rome—and through Rome with Western civilisation. If Hope was alert to 'the chatter of cultured apes/Which is called civilisation over there' (in Europe), as he put it in his pre–second world war poem,

'Australia',[37] he also realised the significance and power of Western civilisation for Australians—a recognition that has re-emerged in a number of Australian university courses and programs in the new century. Like another protestant sceptic, the Australian born Londoner, Peter Porter, Alec Hope discovered Italy on furlough from Britain, somewhat belatedly (see Essay 11). In both cases, these Australian poets were converted by art and history—as another provincial Protestant, George Eliot's Dorothea in *Middlemarch*, had been converted almost a century earlier. Hope expresses the link he feels with this northern hemisphere world, and Italy in particular, in organic, Wordsworthian imagery:

> ... I sensed some final frontier passed,
> Some seed, long dormant, which has stirred and sprouted,
> Some link of understanding joined at last ...
> Laugh at these intimations if you will;
> The days go by and they are with me still.[38]

At this point, in the late 1950s, Hope remains a reluctant Australian, ambivalent about his deepest loves and loyalties, as he had shown himself to be in his endorsement of Australian literature as a full subject of study at Canberra University College (later the Australian National University) in the mid-1950s. Duty speaks, rather than love. This tone extends to his mention of Australia in 'A Letter from Rome':

> And as I walk I think of my own land
> To which I must return when this trip's over.
> She speaks a language that I understand
> And wakes no love that 'moves with the remover'.[39]

At the same time, the age of heroic Rome has passed, and the poet is aware that he lives in

> ... the age of plastics and alloys
> Which bring combustion engines in their train
> To fill with hideous and inhuman noise
> All your once pleasant cities of the plain.[40]

Who speaks for Europe now, he asks, in 'this yawp of Babel'? Hope's Rome, which he has entered on Byron's coat-tails (even to using the *ottava rima* verse form) is the Rome of history and the eternal presence of art, as in Vivaldi's music ('Vivaldi, Bird and Angel') or in Casserius's engravings ('On an Engraving by Casserius').[41]

As a critic as well as a poet with a long view, Hope retained a sceptical and ironic view of Australian artists and their achievements, including his own. Nevertheless, he was a great encourager of younger writers. But he was not a barracker. He knew the depth of British and European culture and this outlook contributed to his satiric portrait of a nationalist 'barracker', A A Phillips, as the principal dunce of his *Dunciad Minor*.[42] This outlook contributed also to his description of Rex Ingamells and the Jindyworobaks as 'the Boy Scout School of Poetry' (in 1942) and his description in 1956 of elements of Patrick White's prose style as 'pretentious and illiterate verbal sludge'.[43]

Hope's response to, and reception by feminists is interestingly ambivalent. A late poem 'Botany Bay, or the Rights of Woman' (from *The Age of Reason*, 1985) quotes Mary Wollstonecroft and presents the Australia of our convict origins as a place of hope rather than of despair for women:

> They say one false step's ne'er retrieved. I think
> It is, if folk are not pushed to the brink.
> That's why I like this land where they can grow
> In ways that let them have a second go
> ...
> A chance at a new life on a new shore
> Was something, certainly, but even more
> Those virtues which the Age of Reason presents:
> Intelligence, enterprise, and common sense![44]

These then are the classical European and Australian values which underlie much of Hope's work—intelligence, enterprise and common sense. But such aspirations were pulled hither and yon in the earlier days of his *Sturm und Drang*, both in his verse and prose.

Hope's editor and biographer, Ann McCulloch, has remarked that Hope's views are 'essentially and perhaps inevitably male'. She sees this in the way he subscribes to the Faustian and Don Juan myths, but she also claims that this does not prevent him having insight into the way women think and feel.[45] Echoing the finding of some previous commentators and critics, McCulloch observes that Hope's poetry is both romantic and classical, expressing men and women in a state of becoming, often desiring transcendance. Hope and Judith Wright were products of their times in seeing a polarity in men and women and neither seems particularly interested in the 'unisex' or androgynous options which intrigue the present generation. Yet they *were* different in their ways of perceiving and understanding the world and its people. Fay Zwicky has described Wright as 'metaphysical' and Hope as 'metabiological', by which she meant that Hope 'seems to start with our heads ... to involve biological considerations [and] to consider motives' whereas Wright 'seems more likely to salute the vague concept of 'human nature' in pointing to the continuing and repetition of fundamental human responses'.[46]

Hope lived for writing. With a touch of his usual exaggeration for rhetorical and epigrammatic effect, he said that 'Living is merely writing at second-hand'.[47] It is doubtful whether Jack Davis or Judith Wright would have given such precedence to the written word as an art form that precedes and shapes living. Both of them were more aware of, and concerned with, the *effectiveness* of their writing, how they could bring about changes in society, though they were also painfully aware of the limitations of the changes they could bring about. This outlook is evident in Wright's focus on the ethics rather than the style of Jack Davis's poetry in her introduction to his second volume of poems, *Jagardoo*:

> The dispossessed [Aboriginal] people are increasingly huddled on the fringes of the towns and cities, where they must live despised lives in what Davis calls 'the stench and pitch of poverty' ... Yet the surprising thing about [Davis's] book is not in its expression of dispossession and injustice, but in its refusal of any final bitterness and violence ... So the book becomes a plea, rather than a threat; an assertion of humanity rather than a curse or a baring of teeth.[48]

There is no better or more powerful statement than this of Wright's sense (derived in part from her reading of Davis and other Indigenous writers) of a shared humanity with Aboriginal people, men and women.

Hope stood for the written word as art. It is in this light that his attack on the Jindyworobaks should be viewed. Hope was offended, above all, by the poor quality of the writing by many of the Jindys. Despite his conviction that 'there is a sound core of common sense in the Jindyworobak case' he was offended by, for example, Rex

Ingamells's 'versified journalese' and 'flat-foot verbiage'. On the other hand, he praised Ian Mudie's verse while finding in its expression of patriotism, in 1942, 'traces of the fanaticism of the Hitler Youth Movement'.[49] Hope's wartime attempts, including here, to reject the kind of nationalistic fervour that kills artistic expression mellowed, as we have seen, under the auspices of a different kind of 'new nationalism' in the 1970s and '80s. But he remained a resistant spirit, and something of an intellectual nomad, most at home in an era of internationalism.

In the international sphere, Hope and Wright have probably had the greatest influence of the three, though Davis's work received significant notice in the 1990s. What kind of influence can a writer like Hope leave on Australia and Australianists? I am reminded of academic and writer Yasmine Gooneratne's comment that when she was trying to decide where to emigrate to from her troubled Sri Lanka, she heard that A D Hope lived in Australia and thought that Australia must therefore be a civilised country. Writers of Hope's ability and stature can give depth and stability to a civilisation.

In a new spirit of reconciliation, then, we should give due thanks and praise for a remarkable trio of Australian writers—Davis, Wright and Hope—who all died in the first year of the new century. Their experience spans the West, East, North and South of the Australian continent. Their literary work, which spans much of the twentieth century, enables us to speak with justifiable pride, in international forums and publications, of outstanding cultural achievements which enable a wider world to understand better the civilisation, problems and way of life of Australians.

Endnotes

Chapter 1
Living Spaces: Some Australian Houses of Childhood

This essay was first published in *Kunapipi*, vol xvi, no 2, 1994.

1   See Gaston Bachelard, *The Poetics of Space, Beacon Press*, Boston 1958. For an Australian application see Elizabeth Ferrier, 'From Pleasure Domes to Bark Huts: Architectural Metaphors in Recent Australian Fiction', *Australian Literary Studies*, vol 13, 1, May 1987, pp 40–53.
2   Eric Rolls, *Celebration of the Senses*, Penguin, Ringwood, 1985, p 142.
3   Frank Moorhouse, *The Electrical Experience: A Discontinuous Narrative*, Angus & Robertson, Sydney, 1974, pp 65–74.
4   Frank Moorhouse, 'The Commune Does Not Want You', *Tales of Mystery and Romance*, Angus & Robertson, Sydney, 1977, pp 134–41. See also Essay 19.
5   Fiona Giles (ed.), *From the Verandah: Stories of Love and Landscape by Nineteenth Century Australian Women*, McPhee Gribble/Penguin, 1987.
6   David Malouf, *12 Edmonstone Street*, Penguin Books, Harmondsworth, 1985. For further discussion see Martin Leer, 'At the Edge: Geography and the Imagination in the Work of David Malouf', *Australian Literary Studies*, vol 12, May 1985, pp 3–21.
7   Malouf, op cit., p 19.
8   ibid., p 20.
9   ibid.
10 ibid., p 21.
11 David Malouf, *Johnno*, Penguin, Harmondsworth, 1976, p 4.
12 See Bruce Bennett, *Spirit in Exile: Peter Porter and his Poetry*, Oxford University Press, Melbourne, 1991, p 31.
13 ibid., p 8.
14 Dorothy Hewett, *Wild Card: An Autobiography 1923–1958*, McPhee Gribble/Penguin, 1990, p 271. See also Essay 6.
15 ibid., p 273.
16 Les A Murray, *The Daylight Moon*, Carcanet, Manchester, 1988, p 18.
17 Tim Winton, *Land's Edge*, Pan Macmillan Australia, Sydney, 1993, p 8.
18 ibid., p 12.
19 Jack Davis, *A Boy's Life*, Magabala Books, Broome, 1991, p 8.
20 Keith Chesson, *Jack Davis: A Life-Story*, Dent, Melbourne, 1988, Chap 2.
21 Sally Morgan, *My Place*, Fremantle Arts Centre Press, Fremantle, 1987.
22 ibid., p 42.

23 See Christina Stead, *Ocean of Story*, Penguin, Ringwood, 1986; and Helen Garner, *Postcards from Surfers*, McPhee Gribble/Penguin, 1985.
24 See Frank Moorhouse, *The Coca-Cola Kid*, Angus & Robertson, Sydney, 1985.
25 See Clifford Geertz, 'Thick Description: Toward an Interpretive Theory of Culture', *The Interpretation of Cultures: Selected Essays*, Basic Books, New York, 1973. The idea of localism as a site of knowledge is further developed in *Local Knowledge: Further Essays in Interpretive Anthropology*, Basic Books, New York, 1983.
26 Julienne Hanson and Bill Hillier, 'Domestic Space Organization: Two Contemporary Space-Codes Compared', *Architecture and Behaviour* 2, (1982), pp 5–25.
27 The Urban Research Program at the Research School of Social Sciences, under the direction of Professor Patrick Troy, held regular seminars on such topics at the Australian National University, Canberra in the 1990s.

Chapter 2
Australian Myths

An earlier version of this essay appeared in *Australian Civilization*, Richard Nile (ed.), Oxford University Press, Melbourne, 1994.

1   *New Encyclopaedia Britannica*, University of Chicago, Chicago, 1982, Micropaedia, vol 4, p 394.
2   The Australian Studies course in the TV Open Learning program was produced by Griffith University and A&C Television in 1992.
3   See Robin Gerster, *Big-noting: The Heroic Theme in Australian War Writing*, Melbourne University Press, Melbourne, 1987; Alan Seymour and Richard Nile (eds), *Anzac: Meaning, Memory and Myth*, Sir Robert Menzies Centre for Australian Studies, University of London, 1991.
4   Bob Hodge and Vijay Mishra, *The Dark Side of the Dream: Australian Literature and the Postcolonial Mind*, Allen & Unwin, Sydney, 1991.
5   For example, Gareth Griffiths, 'The Dark Side of the Dreaming: Aboriginality & Australian Culture', *Australian Literary Studies*, vol 15, no 4, 1992, pp 328–33.
6   J J Healy, *Literature and the Aborigine in Australia*, University of Queensland Press, St Lucia, 1978; Adam Shoemaker, *Black Words, White Page: Aboriginal Literature 1929–1988*, University of Queensland Press, St Lucia, 1989.
7   Shoemaker, *Black Words, White Page*, p 279.
8   See Adam Shoemaker, 'Tracking Black Australian Stories', in Bruce Bennett and Jennifer Strauss (eds), *The Oxford Literary History of Australia*, Oxford University Press, Melbourne, 1998, pp 340–1.
9   Peter Pierce (ed.), *The Oxford Literary Guide to Australia*, Oxford University Press, Melbourne, 1987, p 99.
10 Les Murray (ed.), *The New Oxford Book of Australian Verse*, Oxford University Press, Melbourne, 1987, p 245.
11 Colin Johnson, *The Song Circle of Jacky and Selected Poems*, Hyland House, Melbourne, 1986. Colin Johnson (Mudrooroo Narogin), *Dalwurra: The Black Bittern*, Centre for Studies in Australian Literature, University of Western Australia, Nedlands, 1988. Arguments about Mudrooroo's Aboriginal identity in the late twentieth century and early twenty-first century have reduced his status as a spokesman for the Aboriginal

community but his work remains an important statement of views and perceptions in the 1980s and '90s.

12 See Kath Walker, *My People: A Kath Walker Collection*, Jacaranda Press, Brisbane, 1970; Sally Morgan, *My Place*, Fremantle Arts Centre Press, Fremantle, 1987; Jack Davis, *The First-born and Other Poems*, J M Dent, Melbourne, 1983, and *Kullark (Home) and the Dreamers*, Currency Press, Sydney, 1982.

13 Ernie Bridge, *The Great Australian Dream*, cassette tape-recording arranged and directed by Ernie Bridge, DR 9001, Perth (1990).

14 Mudrooroo Narogin, *Writing from the Fringe: A Study of Modern Aboriginal Literature*, Hyland House, Melbourne, 1990, pp 179–94.

15 Sneja Gunew and Kateryna O Longley (eds), *Striking Chords: Multicultural Literary Interpretations*, Allen & Unwin, Sydney, 1992.

16 See Gunew, *Striking Chords*, pp 44–6.

17 ibid., p 45.

18 Julius Kovesi, 'Nature and Convention', Proceedings from the First New Norcia Humanities Symposium, Perth, 1985.

19 ibid.

20 Bruce Bennett, 'An interview with András Domahidy', *Westerly*, vol 37, no 2, 1992, pp 40–1.

21 ibid., pp 36–7.

22 András Domahidy, *Shadows and Women*, Aeolian Press, Claremont, WA, 1989 (trans. Elizabeth Windsor), pp 79–80.

23 Bennett, 'An interview with András Domahidy', pp 38–9.

24 ibid., p 39.

25 In 1988, for example, the proportion of Asians in the Australian population (2–3 per cent) was predicted to grow to around 10–15 per cent by 2030. Department of Immigration, Local Government and Ethnic Affairs, *Australian Population Trends and Prospects*, Australian Government Publishing Service, Canberra, 1988, p 102.

26 Alison Broinowski, *The Yellow Lady: Australian Impressions of Asia*, Oxford University Press, Melbourne, 1992.

27 Annette Hamilton, 'Fear and desire: Aborigines, Asians and the national imaginary', in David Walker et al. (eds), *Australian Cultural History*, vol 9, 1990 (special issue: *Australian Perceptions of Asia*), p 16.

28 Bruce Bennett and Dennis Haskell (eds), *Myths, Heroes and Anti-heroes: Essays on the Literature of the Asia–Pacific Region*, Centre for Studies in Australian Literature, University of Western Australia, Nedlands, 1992.

29 Satendra Nandan, 'The Mahabharata in modern fiction', in Bennett and Haskell, *Myths, Heroes and Anti-heroes*, pp 201–9.

29 Sharifah Maznah Syed Omar, 'The myth of divine kingship in Malay history', in Bennett and Haskell, *Myths, Heroes and Anti-heroes*, pp 28–35; Orie Muta, 'Myths, heroes and anti-heroes in Japanese culture', ibid., pp 36–46.

30 F Sionil Jose, 'Notes on the writing of *Po-On*', ibid., p 169.

31 See, for example, Richard Rossiter, '"Heroines" in Australian fiction'; Suzette Henke, 'Constructing the female hero'; Sue Hosking, 'Two corroborees'; and Veronica Brady, 'Heroes against empire' in Bennett and Haskell, *Myths, Heroes and Anti-heroes*. See also Hodge and Mishra, *The Dark Side of the Dream*, and Shoemaker, *Black Words, White Page*.

32 Bruce Bennett (ed), *A Sense of Exile: Essays in the Literature of the Asia–Pacific Region*, Centre for Studies in Australian Literature, University of Western Australia, Nedlands, 1988.

33 Meenakshi Mukherjee, 'The exile of the mind', in *A Sense of Exile*, pp 7–14.

34 Kirpal Singh, 'The only way out: Sense of exile in the poetry of Ee Tiang Hong' in *A Sense of Exile*, pp 33–42.

35 Ee Tiang Hong, *Tranquerah*, Department of English Language and Literature, National University of Singapore, Singapore, 1985.

36 Singh, 'The only way out', p 37.

37 ibid., p 47.

38 Ee Tiang Hong, 'Coming to', *Westerly*, 3, 1986, pp 56–7.

39 See 'Place region and community: An introduction' in Bruce Bennett, *An Australian Compass: Essays on Place and Direction in Australian Literature*, Fremantle Arts Centre Press, Fremantle, 1991, pp 11–23.

Chapter 3
Nostalgia for Community: Tim Winton's Essay and Stories

This essay first appeared in *Tilting at Matilda: Literature, Aborigines, Women and the Church in Contemporary Australia*, Dennis Haskell (ed.), Fremantle Arts Centre Press, 1994.

1 Tim Winton, *Land's Edge*, Pan Macmillan, Sydney, 1993. Photographs by Trish Ainslie and Roger Garwood. The talk referred to here took place at University House, Australian National University, Canberra, on 30 November 1993.

2 ibid., p 34.

3 ibid., p 9.

4 ibid., p 14.

5 Robert Hefner, 'Winton on cloud nine after reviews', *Canberra Times*, 21 April 1991, p 23.

6 ibid.

7 Tim Winton, *Cloudstreet*, McPhee Gribble/Penguin, Ringwood, 1991.

8 David Butstone, 'Spinning Stories and Visions', *Sojourners*, 21, 8, 1992, pp 18–21. Cited in *Reading Tim Winton*, Richard Rossiter & Lyn Jacobs (eds), Angus & Robertson, Sydney, 1993, p 13.

9 *Reading Tim Winton*, p 6.

10 Tim Winton, *Scission*, McPhee Gribble/Penguin, Ringwood, 1985; page references are to this edition.

11 ibid., pp 23–4.

12 ibid., p 26.

13 ibid., p 29.

14 Beth Watzke, 'Where Pigs Speak in Tongues and Angels Come and Go: A Conversation with Tim Winton', *Antipodes*, December 1991, pp 98–9.

15 ibid.

16 For example, Susan McKernan, 'Death and Disarray', *Australian Book Review*, no 71, June 1985, p 21.

17 *Scission*, p 38.

18 ibid., p 103.

19 ibid., p 49.

20 See Peter Kemp, 'Abattoir Extremities', *Times Literary Supplement*, 4718, 3 September 1993, p 23.
21 Tim Winton, *Minimum of Two*, McPhee Gribble/Penguin, Ringwood, 1987; page references are to this edition.
22 See 'Flannery O'Connor', *Reference Guide to Short Fiction*, Noelle Watson (ed.), St James Press, Detroit & London, 1994, pp 394–6.
23 *Reading Tim Winton*, p 2.
24 Beth Watzke, 'An Interview with Tim Winton', *AWP Chronicle*, 24, 6, 1992; cited in *Reading Tim Winton*, p 3.
25 *Minimum of Two*, p 46.
26 ibid., p 76.
27 ibid.
28 ibid., p 92.
29 For example, see Robert Drewe, 'Seduced Again', *Bulletin*, March 1977; reprinted in *Wide Domain: Western Australian Themes and Images*, Bruce Bennett & William Grono (eds), Angus & Robertson, Sydney, 1979, pp 181–4.
30 Tim Winton, *Cloudstreet*, McPhee Gribble/Penguin, Ringwood, 1991, pp 422–4.
31 *Minimum of Two*, p 93.
32 Cf 'I ... couldn't commit myself to [religious affiliation] for various reasons. I'm a non-conformist by nature ... my affiliation is to the Creator, not to any institution'. Tim Winton to Frank Sheehan (narrator), *Encounter*, 3 May 1992, ABC Radio discussion of *Cloudstreet*, quoted in *Reading Tim Winton*, p 31.

Chapter 4
Expatriate Voices

This essay was first published in *Voices* (National Library of Australia, Canberra), vol IV, no 3, Spring 1994.

1 Colin Roderick, *Miles Franklin: Her Brilliant Career*, Rigby, Adelaide, 1982.
2 Jill Roe (ed.), *My Congenials: Miles Franklin and Friends in Letters*, State Library of New South Wales, Pymble, NSW, and Angus & Robertson, 1993, vols 1 and 2.
3 Marjorie Barnard, *Miles Franklin*, Hill of Content, Melbourne, 1967, p 146.
4 ibid., p 134.
5 *My Congenials*, op cit., p 255.
6 Geoffrey Serle, *The Creative Spirit in Australia: A Cultural History*, William Heinemann, Melbourne, 1987, p 124.
7 ibid.
8 ibid.
9 *A One Night Stand with Clive James*, Australia and New Zealand Tour 1994, program brochure. The poem 'Go Back to the Opal Sunset' was previously published in *Other Passports: Poems 1958–1985*, Jonathan Cape, London, 1986.
10 See, for example, Part One of *The Dreaming Swimmer: Non-Fiction 1987–1992*, Jonathan Cape, London, 1992. See also Essay 8 in this book.
11 Barry Humphries, *More Please: An Autobiography*, Penguin, Ringwood, 1993.
12 ibid., p 308.

13 ibid., p 311.
14 See also Barry Humphries, *The Life and Death of Sandy Stone*, Pan Macmillan, Chippendale NSW, 1990.
15 Germaine Greer, *Daddy We Hardly Knew You*, Hamish Hamilton, London, 1989.
16 ibid., p 33.
17 Germaine Greer, 'Home is an Illusion', *Guardian Weekly*, 24 October 1993, p 12.
18 ibid.
19 See Bruce Bennett, *Spirit in Exile: Peter Porter and his Poetry*, Oxford University Press, Melbourne, 1991.
20 Peter Porter interview with Bruce Bennett, Canberra, 17 March 1994.
21 Rosemary Sorenson, 'Short List Excludes Sensible Interpretation', *Sydney Morning Herald*, 30 April 1994.
22 ibid.
23 Peter Craven, 'Homage to Freedom on Another Front', *The Australian*, 8 June 1994, p 28.
24 Liam Davison, 'Landscape with Words—Writing about Landscape', *Overland* 134, Autumn 1994, pp 7–8.
25 ibid., p 10.

Chapter 5
Ee Tiang Hong's *Nearing a Horizon*

This piece was first published as a Foreword to Ee Tiang Hong's *Nearing a Horizon*, UniPress, Singapore, 1994.

1 Ee Tiang Hong, *Nearing a Horizon*, Uni Press, Singapore, 1994.
2 Bruce Bennett, 'The Subdued Ego: Poetry from Malaysia and Singapore', *Meanjin* 37, 2, July 1978, pp 240–6.
3 Ee Tiang Hong, *Myths for a Wilderness*, Heinemann Educational Books, Singapore, 1976, p 59.
4 Jack Davis, *Kullark (Home)* and *The Dreamers*, Currency, Sydney, 1982.
5 Tim Winton, *Cloudstreet*, McPhee Gribble/Penguin, 1991.
6 Randolph Stow, *A Counterfeit Silence*, Angus and Robertson, Sydney, 1969.

Chapter 6
Dorothy Hewett's Garden and City

This essay was first published in *Dorothy Hewett: Selected Critical Essays*, Bruce Bennett (ed.), Fremantle Arts Centre Press, 1995, pp 19–31.

1 J Nicholas Entrikin, *The Betweenness of Place: Towards a Geography of Modernity*, Macmillan, London, Intro.
2 E Relph, *Place and Placelessness*, Pion, London, 1976, p 5. See also R J Johnston, *Philosophy and Human Geography*, Edward Arnold, Melbourne, 1983.
3 Eudora Welty, 'Place in Fiction', *The South Atlantic Quarterly*, 55: 1, January 1956, pp 55–72.
4 Margaret Williams, 'A Debt Repaid: Dorothy Hewett's Pastoral Plays', in Peter Holloway (ed.), *Contemporary Australian Drama*, rev edn., Currency Press, Sydney, 1987, pp 486–97.
5 ibid., p 487.

6 Dorothy Hewett, 'The Garden and the City', *Westerly*, 27, 4, December 1982, pp 99–104.
7 ibid., p 99.
8 When this essay was written Hewett was 70. She died at age 79 in the Blue Mountains in 2002. See *Westerly*, vol 47, November 2002, pp 17–19.
9 Interview with Bruce Bennett, Faulconbridge, NSW, 18 May 1993.
10 See Peter Porter, *Possible Worlds*, Oxford University Press, Oxford, 1989, pp 10–11.
11 Dorothy Hewett, *Wild Card: An Autobiography 1923–1958*, McPhee Gribble/Penguin, Ringwood, Victoria, 1994, p 4.
12 Martin Leer, 'Imagined Counterpart: Outlining a Conceptual Literary Geography of Australia', in Giovanna Capone (gen. ed.), *European Perspectives: Contemporary Essays on Australian Literature*, University of Queensland Press, St Lucia, Qld, 1991, p 8.
13 Interview with Bruce Bennett, Faulconbridge, 30 May 1993.
14 'The Garden and the City', p 100.
15 Don Anderson, *Southerly*, 29, 1, 1969, p 75.
16 ibid.
17 These poems appear in Hewett's collection, *Peninsula*, Fremantle Arts Centre Press, Fremantle, 1994.
18 C T Stannage, *The People of Perth: A Social History of Western Australia's Capital City*, Perth City Council, Perth, 1979.
19 ibid., pp 7–9.
20 Dorothy Hewett, *Rapunzel in Suburbia*, Prism, Sydney, 1975; 1976.
21 See Nicholas Hasluck and Fay Zwicky, 'Poetry', in Bruce Bennett (ed.), *The Literature of Western Australia*, University of Western Australia Press, Nedlands, 1979, p 170.
22 See Elizabeth Kenworthy Teather, 'Early Postwar Sydney: a comparison of its portrayal in fiction and in official documents', *Australian Geographical Studies*, 28: 2, October 1990, pp 204–23.
23 See *Alice in Wormland*, Paper Bark Press, Paddington, NSW, 1987, p 49.
24 Dorothy Hewett, *The Toucher*, McPhee Gribble/ Penguin, Ringwood, Victoria, 1993, p 200.
25 David English, 'Deep Water Explorer', *Weekend Australian*, The Weekend Review, 19–20 June 1995, p 6.

Chapter 7
Poet and Statesman: Paul Hasluck

This essay first appeared in *Paul Hasluck in Australian History*, Tom Stannage, Kay Saunders and Richard Nile (eds), University of Queensland Press, St Lucia, 1997.

1 Paul Hasluck, *Mucking About: An Autobiography*, University of Melbourne Press, Carlton, Melbourne, 1977, p 284.
2 ibid., p 284.
3 Nicholas Hasluck, *Quarantine*, Macmillan, South Melbourne, 1978.
4 Paul Hasluck, in 'Then and Now—Talking', *Quadrant* 36, 9, September 1992, p 61; reprinted in Paul Hasluck, *The Light that Time has Made*, National Library of Australia, Canberra, 1995.
5 Paul Hasluck, *The Poet in Australia: A Discursive Essay*, Melbourne, 1969.
6 Hasluck, *Mucking About*, p 11.

7   ibid., p 74.
8   ibid., pp 74–75.
9   ibid., p 76.
10 ibid., p 82.
11 ibid., p 83.
12 ibid., p 82.
13 Paul Hasluck, 'An Eagle's Feather', *Westerly*, vol 27, no 2, 1982, pp 96–8.
14 ibid.
15 Hasluck, *The Poet in Australia*, p 2.
16 Paul Hasluck, Review of John La Nauze, *Walter Murdoch: A Biographical Memoir*, in *Studies in Western Australian History*, no 2, 1978, pp 75–8.
17 Hasluck, *The Poet in Australia*, pp 2–3.
18 Paul Hasluck, *Into the Desert*, Freshwater Bay Press, Claremont, 1939.
19 A D Hope, *Collected Poems 1930–1970*, Angus and Robertson, Sydney, 1966, Introduction, p viii.
20 Paul Hasluck, *Collected Poems*, Hawthorn Press, Melbourne, 1969.
21 ibid., foreword, p vii.
22 ibid., p 117.
23 Hasluck, *Mucking About*, p 266.
24 See 'The Australian Soil', *Collected Poems*, p 55.
25 Hasluck, *Mucking About*, pp 282–84.
26 Paul Hasluck, *Dark Cottage*, Freshwater Bay Press, Claremont, 1984.
27 Judith Wright, *Phantom Dwelling*, Angus & Robertson, Sydney, 1985.
28 See Dorothy Hewett, *The Chapel Perilous*, Currency Press, Paddington, 1972, Act Two, p 86. Hewett's alter ego, Sally Banner, defends her defiant honesty with the statement: 'I walked naked through the world', but her accusers find her guilty of not considering 'the outraged reticence of others'.
29 Hasluck's engagement with Hewett's verse is evident in *The Poet in Australia*, pp 36–7. Although repelled at first by her poem 'Rapunzel in Suburbia', he admitted to being drawn to the 'emotional intensity' in 'the experience behind the verse'.
30 Paul Hasluck, *Crude Impieties*, Victoria, 1991.

Chapter 8
Clive James, Humour and Empire

This essay was first given as a paper at the 13th Triennial Conference of the Association for Commonwealth Literature and Language Studies, Hyderabad, in August 2004. It is reproduced by permission of Sage Publications Ltd, from the *Journal of Commonwealth Literature*, vol 40, no 3, 2005. © Sage Publications 2005.

1   Peter Porter, *Dragons in their Pleasant Palaces*, Oxford University Press, Oxford, 1997, pp 19–20.
2   Clive James, *The Book of My Enemy: Collected Verse 1958–2003*, Pan Macmillan/Picador, London, 2003, p 322.
3   Clive James, *At the Pillars of Hercules: Critical Essays*, Faber and Faber, London, 1979, p 190.
4   ibid., p 191.
5   ibid., p 51.
6   ibid., p 54.

7 ibid.
8 Peter Porter, *Collected Poems*, vol 1: 1961–1981, Oxford University Press, Oxford, 1999, pp 198–200.
9 *At the Pillars of Hercules*, p 59.
10 See Bruce Bennett, *Spirit in Exile: Peter Porter and his Poetry*, Oxford University Press, Melbourne, pp 96–7.
11 Clive James, *Snakecharmers in Texas: Essays 1980–87*, Jonathan Cape, London, 1988, pp 225–36.
12 ibid., p 228.
13 ibid., p 229.
14 See Ian Britain, *Once an Australian: Journeys with Barry Humphries, Clive James, Germaine Greer and Robert Hughes*, Oxford University Press, Melbourne, 1977, p 117.
15 ibid., The recording was by Arista Records.
16 ibid., p 117.
17 ibid.
18 Clive James, *Even As We Speak: New Essays 1993–2001*, Pan Macmillan/Picador, London, p xiii.
19 ibid.
20 Clive James, *From the Land of Shadows*, Pan/Picador, London, p 166.
21 *Even As We Speak*, p xv.
22 ibid., p xvi.
23 ibid., p xvii.
24 The review was republished in *Snakecharmers in Texas: Essays 1980–87*, Jonathan Cape, London, pp 49–57.
25 ibid., p 56.
26 ibid., p 54.
27 The review was republished in *Even As We Speak*, pp 225–37.
28 ibid., p 225.
29 *Once an Australian*, p 117.
30 For example, in *Even As We Speak*, p 254, James writes that Murdoch has cut himself off from Britain and Australia 'in pursuit of some dreary post-capitalist Utopia in which the hunger to acquire is a spiritual value ...'

Chapter 9
'Nation' and Literary History

An earlier version of this paper was published in *Interrogating Post-colonialism: Theory Text and Context*, Harish L Trivedi and Meenakshi Mukherjee (eds), Indian Institute of Advanced Study, Shimla, 1996.

1 Cherry Ripe, *Goodbye Culinary Cringe*, Allen and Unwin, Sydney, 1993.
2 Cherry Ripe, 'Advance Australia fare, folks', *The Australian*, Saturday, 27 August 1994.
3 ibid.
4 Benedict Anderson, *Imagined Communities: Reflections on the Origin and Spread of Nationalism*, Verso, London, 1983; revised 1991.
5 See Simon During, in Homi Bhabha (ed.), *Nation and Narration*, Routledge, London, 1990.
6 Wang Gungwu, 'Australia's Identity in Asia', in Don Grant and Graham Seal (eds), *Australia in the World: Perceptions and Possibilities*, Black Swan Press, Perth, 1994, p 240.

7 David Perkins, *Is Literary History Possible?*, Johns Hopkins University Press, Baltimore and London, 1992, p 180.
8 Sacvan Bercovitch (gen. ed.), *Cambridge History of American Literature*, vols 1–2, Cambridge University Press, Cambridge and New York, 1994.
9 Sacvan Bercovitch (ed.), *Deconstruction & American History*, Harvard University Press, Cambridge, 1986.
10 Edward Said, *Orientalism*, New York, Pantheon, 1978.
11 Dai Yin, 'The Representation of Chinese People in Australian Literature', PhD Thesis, Murdoch University, 1994.
12 Xiamei Chen, 'Occidentalism as Counter-discourse: "He Shang" in post-Mao China', *Critical Inquiry* 18 (Summer 1992), pp 686–712.
13 ibid., p 688.
14 ibid.
15 Bill Ashcroft, Gareth Griffiths and Helen Tiffin, *The Empire Writes Back: Theory and Practice in Post-Colonial Literature*, Routledge, London, 1989.
16 ibid., p 167.
17 ibid.
18 See Albert Gerard, *Contexts of African Literature*, Rodopi, Amsterdam, 1990.
19 See Mary I Bresnahan, *Finding Our Feet: Understanding Crosscultural Discourse*, University Press of America, Maryland, 1991.
20 Bob Hodge and Vijay Mishra, *Dark Side of the Dream: Australian Literature and the Post-colonial Mind*, Allen and Unwin, Sydney, 1990, p 219.
21 Vicente L Rafael, 'Nationalism Imagery and the Filipino Intelligentsia in the Nineteenth Century', *Critical Inquiry* 16 (Spring 1990), pp 591–600.
22 E San Juan, Jr, 'Philippine Writing in English: Postcolonial Syncretism Versus a Textual Practice of National Liberation', *Ariel: A Review of International English Literature*, 22, 4, October 1991, pp 69–90.
23 ibid., p 72.
24 ibid., p 73.
25 ibid.
26 ibid., p 75.
27 ibid., p 85.
28 ibid., p 86.
29 ibid.
30 ibid.
31 ibid.
32 See William H Epstein, 'Counter-Intelligence: Cold War Criticism and Eighteenth-Century Studies', *ELH*, 2, 1990, pp 63–99. 'Although only some of the Cold War critics were actually trained in counter-intelligence, counter-espionage, and counter-subversion surveillance techniques, all of them participated in critical discourse as if they had been ...' (87).
33 Robert Lecker, '"A Quest for the Peaceable Kingdom": the Narrative in Northrop Frye's Conclusion to the Literary History of Canada', *PMLA*, 108, 2, March 1993, pp 283–91.
34 ibid., p 291.
35 ibid.
36 Lloyd Fernando, *Journal of Commonwealth Literature*, X, 3, 1976, p 57.
37 Anne Paolucci, 'Multi-Comparative Literary Perspectives', *Review of National Literatures*, vol 15, Griffen House, New York, 1989, pp 1–29.
38 ibid., p 1.
39 ibid., p 29.

40 ibid.
41 Diana Brydon and Helen Tiffin, *Decolonising Fictions*, Dangaroo Press, Sydney, 1993.
42 See V K Daniels, B H Bennett and H McQueen, *Windows onto Worlds: Studying Australia at Tertiary Level*, Report of the Committee to Review Australian Studies at Tertiary Level, Australian Government Publishing Service, Canberra, 1987.

Chapter 10
Glimpses of India

Parts of this essay were published in *Unfinished Journeys: India File from Canberra*, Debjani Ganguly and Kavita Nandan (eds), Centre for Research in the New Literatures in English, Adelaide, 1998.

1   Alec Choate, 'Mahatma Gandhi', in *Gifts Upon the Water*, Fremantle Arts Centre Press, 1978, p 40.
2   Nissim Ezekiel, *Collected Poems: 1952–1988*, Oxford University Press, Oxford and Delhi, 1989, p 190.
3   Kenneth Slessor, *Poems*, Angus and Robertson, Sydney, 1957, p 76.
4   Beverly Kingston, 'The Taste of India', in *Australian Perceptions of Asia*, Australian Cultural History, 9, 1990, p 38.
5   ibid., p 142.
6   Edwin Thumboo, *A Third Map: New and Selected Poems*, Uni Press, Singapore, 1993, p 11.
7   ibid., p 116.
8   Satendra Nandan, 'The *Mahabharata* and Modern Fiction', in Bruce Bennett and Dennis Haskell (eds), *Myths, Heroes and Anti-heroes: Essays on the Literature and Culture of the Asia–Pacific Region*, Centre for Studies in Australian Literature, University of Western Australia, Nedlands, 1992, p 205.
9   ibid., pp 207–8.
10 Alur Janaki Ram and Bruce Bennett (eds), *Encounters: Selected Indian and Australian Short Stories*, Pointer Publishers, Jaipur, 1988.
11 *Myths, Heroes and Anti-heroes*, p 210.
12 *A Sense of Exile: Essays in the Literature of the Asia–Pacific Region*, Bruce Bennett (ed.), Centre for Studies in Australian Literature, University of Western Australia, Nedlands, 1988.
13 ibid., p 14.
14 ibid., p 57.
15 ibid., p 58.

Chapter 11
Inner Landscapes: Peter Porter's Later Poetry

This essay was published in a different form in *Antipodes* (USA), vol 14, no 2, December 2000, pp 93–7.

1   After the demise of Oxford University Press's poetry list, Porter's new work has been published by Pan Macmillan under their Picador imprint. Notable volumes include *Max is Missing*, Pan Macmillan, London, 2001, and *Afterburner*, Pan Macmillan, London, 2004. Other work continues to

appear in magazines and newspapers. He has also received honorary Doctorates from Melbourne University and the University of Queensland.

2 Peter Porter, *Collected Poems*, 2 vols, 1961–1981 and 1984–1999, Oxford University Press, Oxford, 1999. This quotation is taken from the *Collected Poems*, vol 2, p 20. Porter's 'later' work is defined here as work that appears in the *Collected Poems*, vol 2. Quotations which follow are from this volume.
3 ibid., p 39.
4 ibid., p 64.
5 *Collected Poems*, op cit., vol 1, p 286.
6 *Collected Poems*, vol 2, p 313.
7 ibid., p 54.
8 ibid., p 110.
9 ibid., p 117.
10 ibid., p 112.
11 ibid., p 150.
12 ibid., p 181.
13 ibid., p 58.
14 ibid., p 27.
15 ibid., p 318.
16 ibid., p 317.
17 ibid., p 188.
18 ibid., pp 176–7.
19 ibid., p 177.
20 ibid.
21 See Bruce Bennett, *Spirit in Exile: Peter Porter and his Poetry*, Oxford University Press, Melbourne and Oxford, 1991, p xiv.
22 *Collected Poems*, vol 2, p 299.
23 ibid.

Chapter 12
The Poet as Traveller: Edwin Thumboo

This essay was first published in *Interlogue: Studies in Singapore Literature*, vol 2, Poetry, Kirpal Singh (ed.), Ethos Books, Singapore, 1999, pp 77–83.

All poems quoted in this essay are taken from Edwin Thumboo, *A Third Map: New and Selected Poems*, UniPress, Centre for the Arts, National University of Singapore, 1993. The volume contains selections from *Gods Can Die* (1977), *Ulysses by the Merlion* (1979) and a new third section *People and Places*.

Chapter 13
Home and Away: Reconciling the Local and the Global

In an earlier form, this essay began as an address at the Indian Association of Commonwealth Literature and Language Studies in New Delhi in November 1997. It was published in *Salt II, In the Mix: International Regionalism and Hypermodernism*, John Kinsella (ed.), Fremantle Arts Centre Press, 1999, pp 231–44.

1 Virginia Woolf, *Mrs Dalloway*, 1925; Penguin, Harmondsworth, 1992, p 49.
2 Pia Tafdrup, *Spring Tide*, Forest Books, London and Boston, 1989, p 35.

3   Phil Butterss (ed.), *Southwords: Essays on South Australian Writing*, Wakefield Press, Kent Town, SA, 1995, p ix.
4   Meenakshi Mukherjee, 'Interrogating Post-colonialism', in Harish Trivedi and Meenakshi Mukherjee (eds), *Interrogating Post-colonialism: Theory, Text and Context*, Indian Institute of Advanced Study, Shimla, 1996, p 7.
5   Bruce Bennett, *Spirit in Exile: Peter Porter and his Poetry*, Oxford University Press, Melbourne, 1991, p xiv.
6   Peggy Nightingale, *Journey Through Darkness: The Writings of V.S. Naipaul*, University of Queensland Press, St Lucia, 1997, p 44.
7   Fiona Carruthers, 'Roaming Writers Deny Cultural Treason', in *The Australian*, October 18–19, 1997, p 19.
8   Peter Porter, 'Foreign Correspondence', *The Australian's Review of Books*, October 1997, pp 7–8.
9   Meaghan Morris, 'Metamorphoses at Sydney Tower', in Eric Carter et al. (eds), *Space and Place: Theories of Identity and Location*, Lawrence and Wishart, London, 1993, pp 383–6.
10 ibid., p 387.
11 ibid., p 392.
12 Peter Read, *Returning to Nothing: The Meaning of Lost Places*, Cambridge University Press, Melbourne, 1996, p 137.
13 ibid., p 33.
14 Benjamin R Barber, *Jihad vs McWorld: How Globalism and Localism Are Reshaping the World*, Ballantine, New York, 1996.
15 Gore Vidal, *Palimpsest: A Memoir*, Random House, New York, 1995, p 169.

Chapter 14
The Trader's Eye: Louis Becke's South Pacific

An earlier version of this essay was first published in *SPAN* 48/49 (Waikato, New Zealand), April and October 1999, pp 150–8.

1   Rod Edmond, *Representing the South Pacific: Colonial Discourse from Cook to Gaugin*, Cambridge University Press, Cambridge and New York, 1997, p 185.
2   Philip Darby, *The Fiction of Imperialism: Reading Between International Relations and Postcolonialism*, Cassell, London, 1998, p 16.
3   A Grove Day, *Louis Becke*, Hill of Content, Melbourne, 1967, p 34. This letter, cited by Grove Day, is held in the Mitchell Library, Sydney.
4   ibid., p 150.
5   H E Maude, 'Louis Becke 1855–1913: The Writer Who Lived His Own Pacific Romances', *Pacific Islands Monthly*, October 1956, p 111.
6   Derek Freeman, *The Fateful Hoaxing of Margaret Mead*, Westview Press, Boulder Co., 1999.
7   Louis Becke, *By Reef and Palm*, 1894; Angus and Robertson, Sydney 1955, p 122.
8   ibid., pp 29–35.
9   Louis Becke, *South Sea Supercargo*, A Grove Day (ed.), Jacaranda, Brisbane, c 1967.
10 *By Reef and Palm*, op cit., p 114.
11 Nicholas Thomas, 'The Beautiful and the Damned', in Ann Stephen (ed.), *Pirating the Pacific: Images of Trade, Travel and Tourism*, Powerhouse Museum, Sydney, 1993, p 56.

12 See Grove Day, op cit., p 45.

13 Robert Dixon, *Writing the Colonial Adventure: Race, Gender and Nation in Anglo-Australian Popular Fiction, 1873–1914*, Cambridge University Press, New York, 1995, p 185.

14 Fay G Calkins, *My Samoan Chief*, University of Hawaii Press, Honolulu, 1962.

Chapter 15
Early Prisoners in Australia: Henry Savery and John Boyle O'Reilly

An earlier version of this essay was published in the *Journal of Australian Colonial History* (University of New England), 2, 2, October 2000.

1 Peter Porter, *Collected Poems*, vol 1, Oxford University Press, Oxford, 1999, p 61.

2 Bruce Bennett, *Spirit in Exile: Peter Porter and his Poetry*, Oxford University Press, Melbourne, 1991, p 94.

3 For example, the *angst* of Thomas Keneally's Halloran in *Bring Larks and Heroes*, 1967, recalls aspects of Quintus Servinton's sufferings, and Jack Chance's exotic adventures in Patrick White's *A Fringe of Leaves*, 1976, parallel some of Moondyne's. These two novels, and others since the 1970s, resist the social pressure to bury Australia's convict past.

4 See Stephen Greenblatt, *Marvellous Possessions: The Wonder of the New World*, Oxford University Press, New York, 1991.

5 Henry Savery, *Quintus Servinton: A Tale Founded upon Incidents of Real Occurrence*, Cecil Hadgraft (ed.), Jacaranda Press, Brisbane, 1962. First published, anonymously, in three volumes, 1830–31, in Hobart Town, Van Diemen's Land, and re-issued in London in 1832.

6 ibid., p 222.

7 Cecil Hadgraft, 'Henry Savery', in A G L Shaw and C M H Clark (eds), *Australian Dictionary of Biography*, vol 2: 1788–1850, Melbourne University Press, Carlton, 1967, p 419.

8 Henry Savery, *The Bitter Bread of Banishment*, formerly *Quintus Servinton*, New South Wales University Press, Kensington, 1983.

9 *Quintus Servinton*, 1962 (introduction), pp xii–xiii.

10 ibid., pp xx–xxi.

11 ibid., pp xxii–xxiii.

12 *The Oxford Literary History of Australia*, B Bennett and J Strauss (eds), Oxford University Press, Melbourne, 1998, p 31.

13 David Burn, *An Excursion to Port Arthur in 1842*, Melbourne, 1972, p 9; reprint from the *Tasmanian Journal of Natural Science*, vol 1, 1842.

14 *Moondyne* was first serialised in weekly instalments in the Boston *Pilot* from 30 November 1878. It was published as a book, *Moondyne Joe* by P J Kenedy and Sons, New York, in 1879. A subsequent edition, *Moondyne*, was published by George Roberts, Melbourne, in 1880. A facsimile of the 1880 edition of *Moondyne*, published by Rigby, Adelaide, in 1975, is referred to in this essay.

15 Robert Hughes, *The Fatal Shore*, Collins Harvill, London, 1987, p 143.

16 A G Evans, *Fanatic Heart : A Life of John Boyle O'Reilly, 1844–1890*, University of Western Australia Press, Nedlands, 1997.

17 *Old Bush Songs*, Douglas Stewart and Nancy Keesing (eds), Angus & Robertson, Sydney, 1981, pp 26–7.
18 Evans, p 101.
19 J B O'Reilly, *Moondyne*, Rigby, Adelaide, 1975, reproduced from the George Robertson publication, 1880. Subsequent quotations from the novel are from this edition and are noted in the text.
20 James Jeffrey Roche, *Life of John Boyle O'Reilly, Together with his Complete Poems and Speeches*, Mrs John Boyle O'Reilly (ed.), Cassell, New York, 1891.
21 Evans, p 210.
22 *Moondyne*, p 197.
23 ibid., p 14.
24 Roche, p 200.
25 *Moondyne*, p 98.
26 Mark Twain, *Following the Equator: A Journey Around the World*, Hartford, Connecticut, 1897, p 169, reprinted in *The Oxford Mark Twain*, S F Fishkin (ed.), New York, 1996.
27 *Moondyne*, p 58.
28 Roche, pp 185–7.
29 *Moondyne*, p 238.
30 ibid., p 127.
31 ibid., p 151.
32 *Quintus Servinton*, p 158.
33 Savery appears to have made several suicide attempts, by drowning and by cutting his throat. See *The Hermit in Van Diemen's Land*, Cecil Hadgraft (ed.), University of Queensland Press, St Lucia, 1964, p 37. Hadgraft also observes that Savery 'must have possessed a strong element of the gambler in his temperament' (p 35).
34 Evans, p 33.
35 The most comprehensive coverage of O'Reilly's writings is contained in Roche, *Life of John Boyle O'Reilly*, op cit.
36 Roche, p v.

Chapter 16
Sharing National Memories: Literary Histories in the Commonwealth

This essay first appeared in *Sharing a Commonwealth*, C S Lim et al. (eds), ACLALS, Department of English, University of Malaya, Kuala Lumpur, 2001.

1 Bruce Bennett and Jennifer Strauss (eds), *The Oxford Literary History of Australia*, Oxford University Press, Melbourne, 1998.
2 See Elaine Showalter, *Hysterical Epidemics and Modern Culture*, Columbia University Press, New York, 1997, chap 5. Subsequent quotes are from this source.
3 See John Bayley, *Iris: A Memoir of Iris Murdoch*, Duckworth, London, 1998.
4 See Daniel Goleman, *Emotional Intelligence*, Bantam, New York, 1995.
5 'New research reveals how moods influence thinking', *Uniken*, 452, no 11, 31 July 1998, p 1. Quotes hereafter are from this source. The author of the comments, Joseph Forgas, is a leading Australian psychologist.
6 Eric Hobsbawm and Terence Ranger (eds), *The Invention of Tradition*, Cambridge University Press, Cambridge and New York, 1983; 1997, p 1.

7 ibid., p 2.
8 Sarah Nuttall and Carli Coetzee (eds), *Negotiating the Past: The Making of Memory in South Africa*, Oxford University Press, Capetown, 1998.
9 ibid., p 2.
10 ibid., p 1.
11 ibid., pp 4–5.
12 ibid., p 5.
13 ibid., p 6.
14 ibid., p 75.
15 ibid., p 83.
16 ibid., p 88.
17 Edward Said, *Beginnings: Intention and Method*, Basic Books, New York, 1975, p 3.
18 W H New, *A History of Canadian Literature*, Macmillan Education, London, 1989.
19 ibid., p 1.
20 ibid., p 20.
21 Terry Sturm (ed.), *The Oxford History of New Zealand Literature in English*, Oxford University Press, Auckland, 1991; 1998.
22 Bennett and Strauss, op cit., p 9.
23 Sturm, op cit., p x.
24 Leonie Kramer (ed.), *The Oxford History of Australian Literature*, Oxford University Press, Melbourne, 1981.
25 W E H Stanner, Boyer Lectures, Australian Broadcasting Commission, 1963.
26 This role was taken by Mudrooroo in *Indigenous Literature of Australia*, Hyland House, Melbourne, 1997, but the author's claims to an Aboriginal parent were undermined by a sister and other Aborigines and Mudrooroo thereafter appeared to relinquish his role as literary historian.
27 Wole Soyinka, *Myth, Literature and the African World*, Cambridge University Press, Cambridge, 1976; Canto edition reprint, 1995, pp xi–xii.
28 See *Postcolonial Identities in Africa*, Richard Werbner and Terence Ranger (eds), Zen Books, London, 1996, pp 1–25, 110–16.
29 Rowland Smith, 'War Literature' in Eugene Benson and L W Conolly (eds), *Encyclopedia of Post-Colonial Literatures in English*, Routledge, London, 1994, vol 2, p 1631.
30 Paul Fussell, *The Great War and Modern Memory*, Oxford University Press, New York and London, 1975.
31 ibid., p 8.
32 ibid., p 29.
33 ibid., p 30.
34 ibid., p 164.
35 Jay Winter, *Sites of Memory, Sites of Mourning: The Great War in European Cultural History*, Cambridge University Press, Cambridge, 1995; Canto edition 1998.
36 Bennett and Strauss, op cit., p 108.
37 ibid., p 240.
38 Leong Liew Goek, 'War Literature (Malaysia and Singapore)', *Encyclopedia of Post-Colonial Literatures in English*, vol 2, pp 1635–6.
39 See Leong Liew Goek, 'Alienation and the Pacific War', in *A Sense of Exile: Essays in the Literature of the Asia–Pacific Region*, Bruce Bennett (ed.), The Centre for Studies in Australian Literature, University of Western

Australia, Nedlands, 1988; 'Fugitives and Prisoners: Narratives of Escape', in Bruce Bennett and Dennis Haskell (eds), *Myths, Heroes and Anti-Heroes: Essays on the Literature and Culture of the Asia–Pacific Region*, The Centre for Studies in Australian Literature, University of Western Australia, Nedlands, 1992.

40 *Myths, Heroes and Anti-Heroes*, p 155.

Chapter 17
A Family Closeness? Australia, India, Indonesia

This essay was first published in *The Regenerative Spirit*, vol 1, Nena Bierbaum, Syd Harrex and Sue Hosking (eds), Lythrum Press, Adelaide, 2003.

1 C J Koch, *Crossing the Gap: A Novelist's Essays*, The Hogarth Press, London, 1987, pp 15–16.
2 Shirley Lim, 'Immigration and Diaspora', in King-Kok Cheung (ed.), *An Interethnic Companion to Asian American Literature*, Cambridge University Press, Cambridge, 1997, p 291.
3 Myra Jean Bourke, Susanne Holzknecht and Annie Bartlett (eds), *Weaving a Double Cloth: Stories of Asia–Pacific Women in Australia*, Pandanus Books, Canberra, 2002.
4 ibid., pp x–xi.
5 Yasmine Gooneratne, *A Change of Skies*, Pan Macmillan, Sydney, 1991, passim.
6 Yasmine Gooneratne, *Masterpiece and Other Stories*, Indialog, New Delhi, 2002, pp 11–12.
7 ibid.
8 ibid., p 13.
9 ibid., pp 95–123.
10 ibid., pp 198–206.
11 ibid., p 200.
12 ibid., p 205.
13 ibid., p 206.
14 ibid., pp 70–83.
15 ibid., p 82.
16 ibid., p 83.
17 *My Mother India*, directed by Safina Uberoi, Chili Films, released by Ronin Films, 2002.
18 Margaret Throsby interview with Safina Uberoi, ABC Classic FM radio, 29 October 2002.
19 ibid.
20 ibid.
21 Bourke et al., pp 195–7.
22 Personal interview, Canberra, 11–12 September, 2002.
23 Bourke et al., pp 186–87.
24 Ien Ang, *On Not Speaking Chinese: Living Between Asia and the West*, Routledge, London, 2001, p 44.
25 Bourke et al., p 188.
26 ibid., p 191.
27 ibid., p 193.
28 ibid., p 195.

29 ibid., p 197.

30 Rosemary Marangoly George, *The Politics of Home*, Cambridge University Press, Cambridge, 1996, p 200.

31 Dewi Anggraeni, *Stories of Indian Pacific*, Indra, Eltham North (Vic), 1992, pp 99–181. See also Essay 21.

32 ibid., p 105.

33 ibid., p 134.

34 ibid., p 135.

35 Blanche d'Alpuget, *Monkeys in the Dark*, Penguin, Ringwood, 1982.

36 ibid., p 16.

37 Personal interview with Blanche d'Alpuget, Fremantle, 29 August 1982.

38 *Stories of Indian Pacific*, pp 183–265.

39 ibid., p 247.

40 *Neighbourhood Tales: A Bilingual Collection of Short Stories*, Indra, Briar Hill (Vic), 2001.

41 ibid., pp 73–80.

Chapter 18
Crossing Cultures: Australia and the Asia–Pacific

An earlier version of this paper was published in *Cultural Interfaces*, Santosh K Sareen, Sheel C Nuna and Malati Mathur (eds), Indialog, New Delhi, 2004.

1 Simon Ryan, *The Cartographic Eye: How Explorers Saw Australia*, Cambridge University Press, Cambridge, 1996.

2 Peter Carey, 'Do You Love Me?' *Collected Stories*, University of Queensland Press, St Lucia, 1994, pp 1–10.

3 Bernard Smith, *European Vision and the South Pacific, 1768–1850*, Oxford University Press, Oxford, 1960.

4 See Ian Donaldson and Tamsin Donaldson (eds), *Seeing the First Australians*, Allen & Unwin, Sydney, 1985, p 26.

5 Mark Twain, *Following the Equator*, 1897.

6 James McAuley, 'Captain Quiros' (1964), in Collected Poems, Angus & Robertson, Sydney, 1971, pp 111–65.

7 A D Hope, 'Australia' (1939) in *Collected Poems*, Angus & Robertson, Sydney, 1966, p 13.

8 See Veronica Brady, *South of My Days: A Biography of Judith Wright*, Angus & Robertson, Sydney, 1998, p 131.

9 Red Edmond, *Representing the South Pacific: Colonial Discourse from Cook to Gauguin*, Cambridge University Press, Cambridge, 1997, p 21.

10 Nigel Krauth (ed.), *New Guinea Images in Australian Literature*, University of Queensland Press, St Lucia, 1982.

11 British New Guinea was administered for the British Government by Australia as Papua from 1906. German New Guinea was taken over by Australia as a mandated territory by the League of Nations in 1921. In 1945, Australia combined its administration of Papua and of the mandate into the Territory of Papua and New Guinea, with Port Moresby as the common capital. From 1946, Australia administered the mandate of New Guinea as a UN trust territory. Self-government in PNG was attained in 1973 and full independence in 1975.

12 Randolph Stow, *Visitants*, Martin Secker and Warburg, London, 1979.

13 Anthony J Hassall, *Strange Country: A Study of Randolph Stow*, University of Queensland Press, 1986, p 127.

14 Robert Dixon, *Writing the Colonial Adventure: Race, Gender and Nation in Anglo-Australian Popular Fiction, 1875–1914*, Cambridge University Press, Cambridge, 1995.

15 See, for example, *The Best of Albert Wendt's Short Stories*, Vintage/Random House, Auckland, 1999.

16 Satendra Nandan, *The Wounded Sea*, Simon & Schuster, Sydney, 1991.

17 Sudesh Mishra, 'Satendra Pratap Nandan', in Eugene Benson and L W Conolly (eds), *Encyclopedia of Post-Colonial Literatures in English*, vol 2, Routledge, London, 1994, pp 1077–8.

18 Satendra Nandan, *Fiji: Paradise in Pieces*, CRNLE, Adelaide, 2000.

19 Satendra Nandan, *Requiem for a Rainbow*, Canberra, 2001.

20 Brij V Lal and Michael Pretes (eds), *Coup: Reflections on the Political Crisis in Fiji*, Pandanus, Canberra, 2001, Introduction.

21 For a contextualisation of the novels by Bedford, 'Rata' and Cox, see Van Ikin, 'Dreams, Visions, Utopias', in *The Penguin New Literary History of Australia*, L T Hergenhan et al. (eds), Penguin, Ringwood, 1988, p 264.

22 David Walker, *Anxious Nation: Australia and the Rise of Asia 1850–1939*, University of Queensland Press, St Lucia, 1999. The quotes which follow are from this source.

23 Annette Hamilton, 'Fear and Desire: Aborigines, Asians and the National Imaginary', *Australian Cultural History*, vol 9, *Australian Perspectives of Asia*, University of New South Wales, Kensington, 1990, pp 14–35.

24 C J Koch, *Crossing the Gap: A Novelist's Essays*, Hogarth, London, 1987.

25 C J Koch, *Across the Sea Wall*, Angus & Robertson, 1965; 1982.

26 Koch, *Crossing the Gap*, p 6.

27 C J Koch, *The Year of Living Dangerously*, Nelson, Melbourne, 1979.

28 C J Koch, *Highways to a War*, Heinemann, Melbourne, 1995.

29 Les A Murray, *Collected Poems*, Collins/Angus & Robertson, Sydney, 1991, pp 50–69.

30 Nicholas Jose, *Avenue of Eternal Peace*, Penguin, Ringwood, 1989.

31 ibid., p 22.

32 ibid., p 24.

33 Nicholas Jose, *The Rose Crossing*, Penguin, Ringwood, 1994.

34 Nicholas Jose, *Chinese Whispers: Cultural Essays*, Wakefield Press, Kent Town, SA, 1995.

35 ibid., p 44.

36 ibid., p 46.

37 *Diaspora: Negotiating Asian-Australia*, in Helen Gilbert, Tseen Khoo and Jacqueline Lo (eds), *Journal of Australian Studies and Australian Cultural History*, Special Joint Issue, 2000.

38 ibid., p 2.

39 Merlinda Bobis, *White Turtle*, Spinifex, North Melbourne, 1999.

40 For example, see Adib Khan, *Seasonal Adjustments*, Allen & Unwin, Sydney, 1994.

41 See Essay 17.

42 Shen Yuanfeng, *Dragon Seed in the Antipodes: Chinese-Australian Autobiographies*, Melbourne University Press, Carlton, 2001.

43 Wenche Ommundsen (ed.), *Bastard Moon: Essays on Chinese-Australian Writing*, Otherland Journal 7, Melbourne, 2001.

44 ibid., p 1.
45 Brian Castro, *Birds of Passage*, Allen & Unwin, Sydney, 1983. Later novels by Castro with an Asian focus include *Pomeroy* (1990), *After China* (1992), *Stepper* (1997) and *Shanghai Dancing* (2003).
46 Brian Castro, *Looking for Estrellita*, University of Queensland Press, St Lucia, 1999.
47 Brian Castro, *Writing Asia and Auto/biography: Two Lectures*, Australian Defence Force Academy, Canberra, 1995.
48 Geoffrey Blainey, *All for Australia*, Methuen Haynes, North Ryde, 1984.
49 Castro, *Writing Asia and Auto/biography*, p 20.

Chapter 19
The Unsettled 1970s—Moorhouse, Wilding, Viidikas

An earlier version of this essay was published in *The Regenerative Spirit*, vol 2, Sue Williams et al. (eds), Lythrum Press, Adelaide, 2004, under the title 'Home and Away: Australian Short Fictionists of the 1970s—Moorhouse, Wilding, Viidikas'.

1 Frank Moorhouse, *Days of Wine and Rage*, Penguin, Ringwood, 1980, p 119.
2 Frank Moorhouse, 'The Bush Against The Laundromat', in *Days of Wine and Rage*, pp 392–3.
3 Moorhouse, ibid., p 398.
4 Frank Moorhouse, *Tales of Mystery and Romance*, Angus & Robertson, London, 1977, pp 134–41.
5 ibid., p 134.
6 ibid., p 137.
7 ibid., p 141.
8 Frank Moorhouse, 'From a Bush Log Book I' in *Forty-Seventeen*, Viking/Penguin Books, Ringwood, Victoria, 1988, first published in *Meanjin* as 'Going into the Bush with the Wrong Person at Christmas'.
9 Moorhouse, *Forty-Seventeen*, p 23.
10 ibid.
11 Candida Baker, *Yacker 3: Australian Writers Talk About Their Work*, Pan/Picador, Sydney, 1989, p 229.
12 ibid., pp 229–30.
13 Moorhouse, *Room Service*, Viking/Penguin, Ringwood Victoria, 1985.
14 Moorhouse, *Grand Days*, Macmillan, Sydney, 1993, and *Dark Palace*, Knopf, Milsons Point NSW, 2000.
15 Michael Wilding, *The West Midland Underground*, University of Queensland Press, St Lucia, 1974, p 13.
16 ibid., p 16.
17 Michael Wilding, 'As Boys to Wanton Flies', *Aspects of the Dying Process*, University of Queensland Press, St Lucia, 1972, pp 80–1.
18 Michael Wilding, 'For Trees' in *This is for You*, Angus & Robertson, Sydney, 1994, pp 117–20.
19 ibid., pp 117–18.
20 ibid., p 118.
21 ibid., p 119.
22 ibid.
23 ibid., pp 119–20.

24 Bruce Clunies Ross, 'A New Version of Pastoral: Developments in Michael Wilding's Fiction', *Australian Literary Studies*, 11, 2, 1983, p 190.
25 ibid.
26 ibid.
27 These published works are supplemented by a collection of manuscripts and correspondence held at the Australian Defence Force Academy Library in Canberra.
28 Vicki Viidikas, *Wrappings*, Wild and Woolley, Sydney, 1974, p 18.
29 ibid., p 7.
30 ibid., pp 8–17.
31 Vicki Viidikas, *India Ink: A Collection of Prose Poems Written in India*, Hale and Iremonger, Sydney, 1984, p 55.
32 Vicki Viidikas, 'The Clothesline in the Himalayas', *Westerly*, no 4, 1973, p 18.
33 ibid., p 27.
34 Viidikas, *Wrappings*, p 121.
35 Susan Chenery, 'Women, Mother and Me: Frank Moorhouse talks to Susan Chenery', *Weekend Australian*, 11–12 November 2000, p 10.

Chapter 20
A West-Side Story

This essay-memoir was first published in the Canberra magazine *Conversations*, 5, 2, Summer 2005.

1 Bruce Bennett and William Grono (eds), *Wide Domain: Western Australian Themes and Images*, Angus and Robertson, Sydney, 1979.
2 Randolph Stow, *The Merry-go-round in the Sea*, Macdonald, London, 1965.
3 Dorothy Hewett (ed.), *Sandgropers: A Western Australian Anthology*, University of Western Australia Press, Nedlands, 1973.
4 Tim Winton, *Land's Edge*, Pan Macmillan, Sydney, 1993.
5 David Malouf, *12 Edmonstone Street*, Chatto & Windus, London, 1985.
6 Robert Drewe, *The Bodysurfers*, James Fraser, Darlinghurst, 1983.
7 William Grono, 'The Way We Live Now', *Westerly* 4, December 1969, p 5.
8 Robert Drewe, 'Seduced Again', *Bulletin*, March 1977, repr. in *Wide Domain*, p 184.
9 John Hepworth, 'Homecoming', Nation Review, 1975, reprinted in *Wide Domain*, p 186.
10 *Land's Edge*, p 10.
11 Matt Price, 'Eagles' hopes get the cold shoulder', *The Australian*, 22 June 2004.

Chapter 21
Some Dynamics of Literary Placemaking

An earlier version of this essay was published in *ISLE: Interdisciplinary Studies in Literature and Environment* (Reno, Nevada), 10, 2, Summer 2003, pp 97–109.

1 J Douglas Porteous, *Landscapes of the Mind: Words of Sense and Metaphor*, University of Toronto Press, Toronto, 1990, p xiv.
2 Barry Lopez, *About This Life: Journeys on the Threshold of Memory*, Vintage/Random House, New York, 1998.

3   ibid., pp 131–2.
4   Barry Lopez, *Arctic Dreams*, Scribner, New York, 1986.
5   Barry Lopez, *River Notes*, Andrews and McMeel, 1979.
6   Mandy Sayer and Louis Nowra (eds), *In the Gutter Looking at the Stars: A Literary Adventure Through Kings Cross*, Random House, Sydney, 2000.
7   ibid., p 125.
8   ibid., pp 210–35.
9   ibid., pp 350–3.
10 Herb Wharton, *Where Ya' Been Mate?*, University of Queensland Press, St Lucia, 1996.
11 Dewi Anggraeni, 'Uncertain Step' in *Stories of Indian Pacific*, Indra Publishing, Eltham North, 1992, pp 97–181. See Essay 17 for discussion of other aspects of this story.
12 ibid., p 107.
13 ibid., p 108.
14 Colin McPhedran, *White Butterflies*, Pandanus Books, Canberra, 2002.
15 Peter Read, *Returning to Nothing: The Meaning of Lost Places*, Cambridge University Press, Cambridge and Melbourne, 1996.
16 Roger McDonald, *The Tree in Changing Light*, Knopf/Random House, Sydney, 2001.
17 ibid., p 14.
18 ibid., p 16.
19 Henry Lawson, 'In a Wet Season', *Short Stories and Sketches 1882–1922* (ed.) Colin Roderick, Angus & Robertson, Sydney, 1970, p 161.
20 Manning Clark, *In Search of Henry Lawson*, Macmillan, Melbourne, 1978, p 55.
21 McDonald, *The Tree in Changing Light*, p 17.
22 ibid., pp 28–9.
23 See Wallace Stegner, *Where the Bluebird Sings to the Lemonade Springs: Living and Writing in the West*, Penguin, New York, 1992.
24 McDonald, *The Tree in Changing Light*, p 22.
25 ibid., p 24.
26 ibid., p 160.
27 ibid., p 169.

Chapter 22
Reconciling the Accounts: Jack Davis, Judith Wright, A D Hope

An earlier version of this essay was produced for the 6th Biennial EASA Conference at the University of Lecce in September 2001 and published in the *Reconciliations* issue of the *Journal of Australian Studies* in 2006.

1   Keith Chesson, *Jack Davis: A Life-Story*, Dent, Melbourne, 1988, pp 5–8.
2   Jack Davis, *The First-Born and Other Poems*, Angus & Robertson, Sydney, 1970.
3   ibid., pp v–xvi.
4   Jack Davis, *Kullark (Home)/The Dreamers*, Currency, Sydney, 1982.
5   Jack Davis, *No Sugar*, Currency, Sydney, 1986.
6   Kim Scott, interviewed by Margaret Throsby, ABC Radio, 16 May 2001.
7   Jack Davis, 'Aboriginal Writing: A Personal View', in Jack Davis and Bob Hodge (eds), *Aboriginal Writing Today*, Australian Institute of Aboriginal Studies, Canberra, 1985, pp 1–19.

8   *The First-born and Other Poems*, pp xi–xii.
9   ibid., p xiii.
10 ibid.
11 Chesson, *Jack Davis: A Life-Story*, p 99.
12 Davis, *The First-Born*, p 17.
13 ibid., p 33.
14 Jack Davis, *John Pat and Other Poems*, Dent, Melbourne, 1988.
15 ibid., p 2.
16 See Betty Meehan and Rhys Jones, 'Jack Leonard Davis', in Bruce Bennett (ed.), *Proceedings 2000*, Australian Academy of the Humanities, Canberra, 2001, pp 64–7.
17 Davis, *The First-Born*, p xvi.
18 Meehan and Jones, p 66.
19 Veronica Brady, *South of My Days: A Biography of Judith Wright*, Angus and Robertson, Sydney, 1998, p 133.
20 Judith Wright, *Collected Poems 1942–1970*, Angus and Robertson, Sydney, 1971, p 20.
21 See Bruce Bennett, 'Judith Wright: An Ecological Vision', in Robert L Ross (ed.), *International Literature in English: Essays on Major Writers*, Garland, New York, 1991, pp 205–21.
22 Judith Wright, *The Coral Battleground*, p 104.
23 See Bob Brown, *The Greens*, with Peter Singer, Text, Melbourne, 1996, p 64.
24 *The Coral Battleground*, op cit., p 3.
25 Judith Wright, *Alive: Poems 1971–72*, Angus and Robertson, Sydney, 1973, p 22.
26 Brady, *South of My Days*, p 308.
27 See Tim Rowse, *Nugget Coombs: A Reforming Life*, Cambridge University Press, Port Melbourne, 2002.
28 Tim Bonyhady, *Places Worth Keeping: Conservationists, Politics and Law*, Allen and Unwin, Sydney, 1993, p 134.
29 Brady, *South of My Days*, pp 396–7.
30 Leonie J Kramer, 'Alec Derwent Hope (1907–2000)', in *Proceedings 2000*, op cit., pp 68–72.
31 See A D Hope, *Selected Poems*, David Brooks (ed.), Angus and Robertson, Sydney, 1992, pp 87–106.
32 David Brooks (ed.), *The Double Looking Glass: New and Classic Essays on the Poetry of A.D. Hope*, University of Queensland Press, St Lucia, 2000, p 9.
33 Hope, *Selected Poems*, op cit., pp 183–4.
34 Kevin Hart, *A.D. Hope*, Oxford University Press, Melbourne, 1992, p 47.
35 See Bruce Bennett, 'Edwin Thumboo and A.D. Hope: Island Men and their Communities', in Tong Chee Kiong et al. (eds), *Ariels: Departures and Returns, Essays for Edwin Thumboo*, Oxford University Press, Singapore, 2001, pp 89–101.
36 Hope, *Selected Poems*, p 177.
37 ibid., p 72.
38 ibid., p 103.
39 ibid., pp 103–04.
40 ibid., p 105.
41 A D Hope, *Collected Poems*, Angus and Robertson, Sydney, 1972, pp 263–78, 222–6.

42 A D Hope, *Dunciad Minor*, Melbourne University Press, Melbourne, 1970.
43 See A D Hope, *Native Companions: Essays and Comments on Australian Literature 1936–1966*, Angus and Robertson, Sydney, 1974, pp 75–9.
44 A D Hope, *The Age of Reason*, Melbourne University Press, Melbourne, 1985, pp 135–6.
45 *Proceedings 2000*, op cit., p 70. See also Ann McCulloch, *Dance of a Nomad: A Study of the Selected Notebooks of A.D. Hope*, Pandanus Books, Canberra, 2005. '[Hope's] attempt to understand female sexuality is recorded throughout the notebooks, as is his awareness of his exclusion from understanding. He felt that an understanding of the differences between men and women was the key to constructing a new metaphysical world view'. (p 245)
46 Fay Zwicky, 'Another Side of Paradise: A.D. Hope and Judith Wright', *The Double Looking Glass*, op cit., p 227.
47 *Proceedings 2000*, op cit., p 70.
48 Judith Wright, Foreword to Jack Davis, *Jagardoo: Poems from Aboriginal Australia*, Methuen, Sydney, 1978, pp viii–ix.
49 *The Double Looking Glass*, op cit., pp 202–5.An earlier version of this essay was produced for the 6th Biennial EASA Conference.

Index